Hooking Up

HOOKING UP

The Psychology of Sex and Dating

Katherine M. Helm

The Psychology of Everyday Life

GREENWOOD™

An Imprint of ABC-CLIO, LLC
Santa Barbara, California • Denver, Colorado

Library of Congress Cataloging-in-Publication Data
Helm, Katherine (Katherine M.) author.
  Hooking up : the psychology of sex and dating / Katherine M. Helm.
    pages cm. — (The psychology of everyday life)
  Includes bibliographical references and index.
    ISBN 978–1–61069–950–1 (hardback) — ISBN 978–1–61069–951–8 (ebook) 1. Sex (Psychology) 2. Sex. 3. Mate selection. 4. Interpersonal attraction. 5. Dating (Social customs) I. Title.
BF692.H4475 2016
155.3—dc23   2015025019

ISBN: 978–1–61069–950–1
EISBN: 978–1–61069–951–8

20 19 18 17 16   3 4 5

This book is also available on the World Wide Web as an eBook.
Visit www.abc-clio.com for details.

Greenwood
An Imprint of ABC-CLIO, LLC

ABC-CLIO, LLC
130 Cremona Drive, P.O. Box 1911
Santa Barbara, California 93116-1911

This book is printed on acid-free paper ∞

Manufactured in the United States of America

This book is dedicated to all of the Lewis University students who have taken my human sexuality course over the years and those students who have participated in my Sex Talks with Dr. Helm series sponsored by the Psychology Club. You have always made these courses and talks fun, interesting, and exciting and truly honed my skills as a teacher and human sexuality educator. I continue to learn from you. Thanks so much for always challenging me to be the best teacher I can be.

Contents

Series Foreword

Psychology is the science of behavior; it is the field that examines how and why people do, feel, and think the things that they do. However, in a very real way, everyone is a psychologist. Each of us observes and tries to understand the thoughts, feelings, and behaviors of people we are around, as well as trying to understand ourselves. Have you ever thought, "I wonder why she did that?" Or perhaps, "Why did I do that; it makes no sense." If you have, then you are asking psychological questions. Most people enjoy being "*students of human behavior*" and observing and thinking about people, human nature, and all of the variants of the human condition. The difference between "most people" and psychologists is that the psychologist has spent many years in school studying and learning about people.

In addition to studying and doing research, psychologists also work directly with people in many settings. For example, clinical and counseling psychologists work with people who are dealing with psychological disorders or are having problems in their lives that require professional assistance, but there are many other branches of psychology as well. Sport psychologists work with athletes and teams to improve performance and team functioning. Industrial/organizational psychologists help workers, managers, and organizations function more effectively and efficiently. Military psychologists deal with military personnel and organizations. Forensic psychologists work with police and other law enforcement organizations to help solve crimes and assist law enforcement personnel. In addition to all of the things that psychologists know about people, for any person, understanding psychology can help take advantage of what psychologists have learned to help all people live better and healthier lives and to deal more effectively with others.

The Psychology of Everyday Life is a series of books that will address many different and important psychological issues and areas, the goal being to provide information and examples of how psychology touches all of our lives on a daily basis. The series will also show ways in which psychological knowledge can help us. These books will address psychological concerns with the most up-to-date and relevant knowledge from the field of psychology. Information from the laboratories, classrooms, clinics, hospitals, and other settings will be brought together to help make sense out of some important and often complex ideas. However, these books will be directed toward readers who are not psychologists, but are interested in learning more about the field and what it has to offer. Thus, the language is not technical but is common language addressing "regular" people. There will be times when professional and technical language may be used, but only if thoroughly explained and related to the issues being discussed.

This series of books will focus on specific facets of our daily lives and show how psychology can help us understand and deal with these issues. A wide range of topics will be covered, from eating to exercising to relaxing to interpersonal conflict. Each book will consist of three distinct parts. Part I will answer the "who/what/where/when/why/how" questions related to the topic. These chapters will examine everything from how the subject manifests in our day-to-day lives and how it impacts our psychological well-being to differences across the life span and cultures to what famous psychologists have to say on the subject.

Part II in each book will focus on "real-life" examples and will address many of the issues that were introduced in each book in Part I, but will do so with examples and explanations that will make the issues even clearer. It is one thing to have knowledge, but it is an entirely different thing to be able to apply and use that knowledge, and this is what will be covered by the scenarios and interpretative analyses in Part II. When people read Part II they will begin to see many of the ways in which our daily lives are touched by psychology, and the many ways that psychology can be used to support and help people.

Part III in each book will address the controversial issues related to the book's subject. Like any academic and professional discipline, psychology has many areas where there are spirited disagreements among academics, practitioners, and researchers about important issues in the field. It will be very instructive for people to understand these issues and to see the careful and systematic ways that scholars think about and conceptualize various topics, and to see how they debate, discuss, and resolve some of their differences of opinion. For non-psychologists, these controversial issues and how they are addressed will lead to a greater understanding of psychological matters, but also a better grasp of how scientists and professionals deal with differences and controversies and how these disagreements are addressed.

Psychology is a broad and diverse field with many different approaches, theories, methods, and ideas, and to capture this field in its breadth and depth would be impossible in a single book. This series of books, however, will serve as an introductory journey through psychology as it relates to the daily lives of ordinary people. I have been teaching, studying, and practicing psychology for many decades and I can hardly wait to read each of the books in this very exciting series, and I welcome readers to take this journey with me.

Rudy Nydegger, PhD, ABPP

Preface

Human sexuality is an interesting topic because it impacts every human being regardless of race, socioeconomic status, gender, religious background, and age. Sexuality affects us our entire lives—literally from birth to death. What makes human sexuality so interesting? Why is sexuality education sometimes controversial? The answers to these questions are complicated but a probable explanation is that teaching human sexuality is not simply about teaching the facts. What makes these topics so controversial is that individuals' values regarding sex and sexual behavior tend to significantly influence which facts get taught, how they are received, and even how they are perceived. Some people come from households where discussing sexual issues is completely taboo while other individuals were encouraged to ask their parents questions. It may not surprise you to know that in every human sexuality class I have taught, I survey my students and the large majority of them report either never having conversations about sex with their parents or having only one or two conversations. Most students report that these conversations were awkward and the information they received from their parents was not always factual.

Society and the media have a significant role in shaping our perceptions about appropriate sexual behavior, as do our families, religious background, cultural heritage, and age. Our attitudes about sex are constantly evolving. One thing that can be counted on is that individual behavior is not predictable. For example, in the 1940s, much of American society supported the belief that people should wait to have sex until marriage. However, as you will read about in this book, the majority of Americans have had sex prior to marriage. This was also true in the 1940s! This is just one example of how individuals may state a particular value regarding sexual behavior (i.e., no sex prior to marriage) but behave in ways contrary to that particular value.

Although the Internet is now a solid source of information for human sexuality topics, students really need adults to talk to who can hear them honestly and without judgment. Students need a reliable source of factual data but also a consistent source of sexual values. Sexual behavior always has consequences—sometimes, these consequences are positive and sometimes they are negative.

This book covers current topics in human sexuality in a (hopefully) non-judgmental way. It provides a historical, theoretical, cultural, and factual overview. It is my hope that students reading this book come away with a broader understanding of human sexuality topics as well as a solid idea of how sexuality impacts their identity and behavior.

The book is divided into three parts, each speaking to a different aspect of human sexuality. The first part reviews factual data, the second part provides hypothetical scenarios/case studies in human sexuality along with an analysis of each scenario, and the third part presents several debate topics in which scholars take different sides of a current dilemma in the human sexuality literature. The book's format is designed so that students can skip around and read things in the order that makes the most sense for them, given their specific questions. I hope you find this book a quick, easy, and educational read. Enjoy!

Acknowledgments

This book would not be possible without the support of my husband, Anton Lewis. Thanks as well to Jamie Kontos, Matt Caston, Donna Lordi, and Lisa Brown for their help in the production of this book as well as their critical thinking skills and their willingness to help me remain current in the field through valuable conversations and sharing of references.

Part I

Sex in Everyday Life

1

❖

What: The Many Forms of Sex

What types of things influence the ways we view sex? Do some things influence us more than others? This chapter will explore many of the things that influence our ideas about sex as well as our sexual behavior. *Human sexuality* can be thought of as part of one's total personality and it involves the interrelationship of biological, psychological, and sociocultural dimensions (Greenberg et al., 2011). Our views on human sexuality are shaped by many things, including our values, religious/spiritual beliefs, familial upbringing (parents), peer influences, our experiences, the media, and our own individual worldview. Each of these factors contributes to our views on human sexuality as well as what is considered "normal" sexual behavior. Children in the United States often receive mixed messages regarding sex. For example, our movies, television shows, magazines, and the Internet are full of examples of permissive sexual behavior. However, children tend to get more restrictive messages regarding sexual behavior from their parents and education. In one *Time* magazine/CNN survey, 74 percent of teenagers said that friends and television were their major sources of information about sex, compared with only 10 percent who listed parents or sex education (Stodghill, 1998; see also Nonoyama et al., 2005, as cited in King, 2009, p. 2) as primary informational sources. We are exposed to significant sexual content in the media on a daily basis, which greatly shapes our views on sexuality, but the majority of parents still do not regularly talk to their children about sex. Many families consider this a taboo and embarrassing topic. This chapter will explore the many reasons why many of us still find it difficult to talk about sex.

FAMILY, RELIGIOUS, CULTURAL, AND PEER INFLUENCES

Family

Our families have a significant influence in our lives. They shape our values, morals, behavior, sense of self, identity, self-worth, and who we eventually become as individuals. *Values* are important and lasting beliefs and/or ideals shared by the members of a culture about what is good, bad, and/or desirable or undesirable. Values have a major influence on an individual's behaviors and attitudes and serve as broad guidelines in particular situations. *Morals* relate to what is right and wrong in human behavior and are typically considered right and good by most people. They often serve as an agreed-upon standard of correct behavior. We are taught values and morals by our families. They are also shaped by our culture, peer group, religious practices, and society in general. Sexual values are socially modeled to us by our parents as well as directly taught (e.g., "In this family we do not believe in sex before marriage" or "We don't think that teenagers should be sexually active. Wait until you are older."). We could say that sexual values and morals are socialized into us by the environment in which we exist. *Socialization* refers to the manner in which a society shapes individual behaviors and expectations of behaviors (norms) (King, 2009). Peers, family, parents, school, religion, and the media are often referred to as *socializing agents*. Sexual socialization is a life-long process beginning in childhood, increasing in adolescence, and continuing into adulthood (Gagnon, 1990; Longmore, 1998, as cited in L'Engle & Jackson, 2008).

Very young children are exposed to messages about modesty, nudity, privacy, and the ways in which their parents refer to their genitalia (e.g., using proper names vs. nicknames) (Shtarkshall et al., 2007). The ways in which parents respond to their children's masturbating, sexual curiosity, displays of physical affection, and observation of parents' physical affection/interactions with one another shape children's sexual values and their understanding of sexuality (Shtarkshall et al., 2007). Parents shape their children's use of sexual language as well as their ideas about sexuality in implicit and explicit ways.

Research highlights that socializing agents differentially impact adolescents' sexual behavior. For example, parents and schools tend to promote sexual health while peers and mass media provide information often encouraging teens to engage in sexual behavior (L'Engle et al., 2006). L'Engle and Jackson (2008) find that families have an early and consistent role in socializing children's sexual values. For example, their research demonstrates that children and teens who have positive connections to their families and schools tend to have less advanced sexual behavior. Additionally, they state that adolescents who report high levels of connectedness to parents/family, parental monitoring of activities, and frequent communication about sex with their parents have intercourse later than peers who report lower levels of connectedness to their parents/families. This may be because these adolescents have internalized their parents' values about delaying sexual intercourse. Additionally, adolescents who are connected to their school communities and have positive feelings about school (and high expectations for further education in college) also report having sexual intercourse later than teens with poor school connections and performance. L'Engle and Jackson (2008) surmise that parents and schools may delay the onset of sexual intercourse in their adolescent children by instilling disapproving attitudes about early sexual intercourse and consistent expectations for delaying sexual intercourse.

It is well known that teens' focus shifts to their peer group during adolescence. Most teens seek independence and begin developing romantic relationships. L'Engle and Jackson (2008) note that peers may become a more powerful socializing influence than parents during the adolescent years. Adolescent peers often encourage teens to have sex. If this is the case, teens are more likely to engage in intercourse due to peer influences.

Additional research demonstrates that female adolescents aged 15–19 from very conservative Christian backgrounds, who attend religious services regularly, were less likely to engage in premarital sex than their non-conservative peers; however, 40 percent of the girls in one study from the same conservative background had engaged in premarital sex. Interestingly, religious beliefs seemed to have very little effect on whether or not birth control was used (King, 2009). Thus, although the individuals in the study may consider religion to be an important part of their lives, other socializing influences also play a major role in shaping their sexual attitudes and behaviors (King, 2009). Dr. Bruce King, a college professor and human sexuality instructor, found in surveying his students that fewer than 33 percent of students had ever had a meaningful discussion with their parents about sex. He found that when students did talk to their parents about sex, it consisted of one birds-and-the-bees talk and nothing else. I have surveyed my own students and found that my results closely resemble his. When students are asked where they learn about sex, most state that they get their sexual information from the Internet, peer group, and movies (sometimes pornography). Most report being dissatisfied with their formal school-based sexual education. This is problematic for many reasons. One, the Internet, peer group, and movies are not always reliable sources of information. Two, children and adolescents do not always get their questions completely answered by these sources. Three, although there is nothing wrong with going to these sources for some information, going *only* to these sources often creates a distance and distrust of learning about sexual information from one's parents. Parents often tell their children, "You can talk to me about anything"; however, many children and teens learn (sometimes just by their parents' silence surrounding sexual issues) that sex is not something a parent wants to talk or hear about. Thus, children and teens get mixed messages about parents' openness to sexual discussions and often simply give up the idea of talking about sex to their parents. This represents a missed opportunity for closeness between parents and their children/teens. Many parents themselves were not talked to about sex by their own parents and therefore may not have a model for talking about these issues to their children.

Regardless of whether parents directly talk to their children about sex, children and teens develop a high level of awareness regarding their parents' sexual values. How is this possible? Socialization to parental values happens in several ways. Here are a few examples: children observe their parents' behavior (e.g., Does the parent behave in honest ways?), parents may comment on a TV show (e.g., "She is too young to be having sex."), parents comment on their children's friend's behavior (e.g., that may be OK to do in their household but you are not allowed to behave that way in this household), and sometimes the parent may give a specific values-based directive (e.g., "We don't believe in that."). Parents socialize particular values in their children in multiple ways (both directly and indirectly) and children quickly learn parents' messages. Parents should be aware, however, that children will behave as their parents behave regardless of the parent's verbal message. For example, if a parent tells a child not to lie but the parent lies consistently, the child will learn that it is okay to tell a lie. It is easy to see why the majority of children do not have discussions with their parents about sex. In this way, we are passing down our own discomfort with sexual issues over multiple generations. Students whose parents do consistently talk to their children about sex and those who take human sexuality courses often break the silence surrounding discussions of sexual issues.

One study examining parents' socializing influences on their teen's sexual behavior found that stronger connections to parents and schools and less exposure to permissive sexual norms from peers and media were associated with less susceptibility and sexual behavior, especially among white adolescents (L'Engle & Jackson, 2008). The study looked at adolescents aged 12–14 who had never had sexual intercourse. The study found that encouraging the postponement of sexual intercourse is important because teens who initiate first coitus before they are 16 years old engage in riskier sexual behavior and experience more adverse sexual health outcomes than those who delay the onset of sexual intercourse until age 16 (Alexander & Hickner, 1997; Kirby, 2001; O'Donnell et al., 2001, as cited in L'Engle & Jackson, 2008).

Religion

Religion is another significant socializing agent in our sexual values and behaviors. Many religions emphasize the value that sexuality is a divine gift only to be used within the confines of marriage. Many traditional Christian, Islamic, and Orthodox Jewish religious faiths teach their followers that premarital sex is sinful and forbidden. Even religious traditions that are more liberal (e.g., Reform Judaism and some nondenominational, liberal-leaning Christian faiths) encourage their followers to consider sexual intercourse a spiritual act that should be carefully considered prior to sexual engagement and primarily done within a monogamous, committed relationship. Religion provides followers with moral codes about sex to help guide decision making regarding sexual behavior. We can think of these as standards of sexual conduct. Religions significantly differ in their teaching of sexual moral codes. Some view sex as a negative, sinful act while others view sex as the ultimate divine act of love between two people. In U.S. society, religious influences on sexuality and the expression of sexual behavior are powerful, even in those who may not consider themselves religious. This is because U.S. society has been shaped in large part by Judeo-Christian religious traditions; thus whether or not individuals uphold the religious values of these particular faiths, U.S. society, both past and present, continues to be largely influenced by these religious ideals. In Chapter 4, we discuss religious influences on sexual behavior more comprehensively as well as look at religious influences from a historical basis.

Culture

Culture can be defined as the beliefs, customs, arts, and so forth of a particular society, group, place, or time; a particular society that has its own beliefs, ways of life, art, and so forth; and/or a way of thinking, behaving, or working that exists in a place or organization (such as a business). For example, in the United States there is a *southern culture* just as there is an *American* culture. In the United States, "culture" is sometimes confused with *ethnicity*, which relates to or is characteristic of a human group having racial, religious, linguistic, and certain other traits in common, or relates to the classification of mankind into groups, especially on the basis of racial group membership. An example of an ethnic group might be Mexican American or Native American. For the purposes of this book we will consider culture and ethnicity similarly because each ethnic group also has a culture. Both culture and ethnicity serve as socializing agents for our sexual behavior and attitudes. *Attitudes* generally refer to whether or not we evaluate a topic positively or negatively. As we are learning in this chapter, sexual beliefs, values, and attitudes are multi-determined, in that several influences shape what we believe and how we evaluate and respond to certain topics. Cultural influences are broad because most of us belong to several different cultural groups. For example, a 16-year-old, African American, Christian female from the south belongs to the following cultural groups: African American, teenage culture, Christian, female, and southern. We all belong to a geographic culture (e.g., north vs. south), gender (male vs. female), religious group (some but not all belong to a specific religious faith), a specific age cohort/group, and a cultural or ethnic background (e.g., African American). Thus, all of the various cultural groups we belong to exert influences on our views about sexuality and sexual behavior. Different groups support different viewpoints (e.g., an Islamic religious tradition may promote a different belief system than an atheist tradition) and there is significant variation of beliefs within the same group (e.g., not all Italian Americans have the same belief system about sexuality). As you can see, there are many different cultural influences on our views about sex. According to Lawrence B. Finer, author of *Trends in Premarital Sex in the United States, 1954–2003*, the majority of Americans (95 percent), regardless of the cultural groups they belong to, have had sex prior to marriage. Additionally, notions that the majority of Americans, especially women, did not have sex prior to marriage in previous decades (e.g., 1940s and 1950s) are also not true. Finer's research demonstrates that even among women who were born in the 1940s, nearly 9 in 10 had sex before marriage. We will return to this finding later; however, we might hypothesize the meaning of this finding. It could potentially mean that although we all belong to different cultural groups within the United States, *American culture* clearly socializes or accepts sex before marriage, because the large majority of adults have had sex prior to marriage. This may have significant implications for sexual education as well as parents' understanding of their children's sexual behavior. Chapter 6 will look more specifically at cultural viewpoints on sex and sexuality outside the United States.

Peer Influences

As reviewed earlier in this chapter, one's peer group, especially in adolescence, has a strong influence on one's sexual views and behavior. One factor correlated with the age at which adolescents begin having intercourse is *cognitive susceptibility*, which is the state of mind that could predispose them to initiating sexual activity (Kelly, 2011). Research finds that the younger adolescents are when they have sex, the more likely they are to engage in riskier sexual behavior, such as not using contraceptives and engaging in sex with multiple partners. Adolescents who are more cognitively susceptible to initiating intercourse tend to be more physically mature, have more feelings of sexual desire than their peers, report higher levels of social confidence, and a greater perception that their peers are sexually active (L'Engle & Jackson, 2008). They also are more likely to have fewer positive connections with parents, schools, and religious institutions (L'Engle & Jackson, 2008). Very young adolescents are more susceptible to peer influences. For example, if very young adolescents are surrounded by sexually active peers, they are much more likely to engage in intercourse whether they actually want to or not. If they are surrounded by peers who believe in sexual abstinence, they too are more likely to remain abstinent (Kelly, 2011).

As previously stated, for most teens, the peer group becomes more influential in early adolescence, even more than teens' parents. This is why it's especially important for parents to socialize sexual values to their children very early. It is also important for parents to monitor their child's peer group, as the peer group has significant influence over their children's sexual behavior. Peers can be both positively and negatively influential. Psychologist Neil Bernstein (2005) finds that the more comfortable a teen is with his or her identity (sense of self), the less likely he or she will be swayed by negative peer influences. Peer pressure is so powerful because an adolescent looks to peers for positive reinforcement (i.e., validation for who he or she is). Teens sometimes value the peer groups' emotional and psychological support over that of their families. Adolescence is usually the time where teens try on more independent, adult-like roles (e.g., driving a car). Additionally, adolescence is also a time when a teen can make a mistake that seriously impacts his or her future (e.g., drug use, teen pregnancy, dropping out of high school). It is often true that some mistakes in adolescence have significant consequences in adulthood. This is why the peers a teen chooses as friends are highly important to his or her development, sense of self, decision making, and overall well-being. This is especially true when it comes to decisions about sex.

Media Influences

Multiple long-term studies link exposure to sexy content in TV, movies, music, magazines, and other forms of social media with earlier onset of sexual intercourse for teens. Since the majority of teens have private access to the Internet, cell phones, text messaging, and social media (e.g., Facebook, Snapchat, and Twitter), they frequently use these means to engage in sexual chats, ideas, and behaviors. Today's media influences may greatly impact teens' cognitive susceptibility to engage in intercourse and other sexual behaviors. L'Engle and Jackson (2008) find that the mass media also provide models for sexual behavior. Adolescents use media frequently and there is a large amount of sexual content in the media they use. As discussed earlier, the more sexually explicit content teens are exposed to, the greater the likelihood they will become sexually active earlier. Adolescents frequently rely upon the media for information about sex and sexual norms, especially if they find the character depicted to be similar to themselves, attractive, and socially desirable (L'Engle & Jackson, 2008). Exposure to sexual content across a variety of media (i.e., television, movies, music, magazines) is associated with greater intentions to initiate sexual intercourse and more advanced sexual behavior among adolescents (Brown et al., 2006; Collins et al., 2004; L'Engle et al., 2006; Ward & Friedman, 2006, as cited in L'Engle & Jackson, 2008). The media may act as a "super peer," in that adolescents exposed to sexier, more explicit media are socialized by these mediums, similar to the sexual socialization they receive from peers (L'Engle & Jackson, 2008).

SEX EDUCATION IN THE UNITED STATES

Sex education in the United States is still a hotly debated topic. Although the majority of parents strongly support schools teaching about sex in schools, there is still significant disagreement on how it should be done. Sex education in the United States is taught in two forms: abstinence and comprehensive sexual education, also known as abstinence-only and abstinence-plus education. Comprehensive sex education promotes abstinence as a choice, often a preferred one, but also gives adolescents information about contraception, sexually transmitted diseases, sexual health issues, pregnancy, and other sexual topics. Abstinence-only education emphasizes ways to avoid having sex until marriage and does not teach about or provide information about contraception and safe sex practices. Abstinence-only sex education emphasizes abstinence from sex to the exclusion of all other types of sexual and reproductive health education. Adolescents are encouraged to be sexually abstinent until marriage.

Earlier in this chapter it was noted that approximately 95 percent of Americans have had sex prior to marriage. Remember the study conducted by Finer (2007) that found that the majority of Americans have been sexually active prior to marriage for decades? He states: "The data clearly show that the majority of older teens and adults have already had sex before marriage, which calls into question the federal government's funding of abstinence-only-until-marriage programs for 12–29-year-olds. It would be more effective to provide young people with the skills and information they need to be safe once they become sexually active—which nearly everyone eventually will." Although there is significant variability from state to state and school to school, many schools start with a basic introduction to puberty and changes the body will go through around fifth grade (10 years old). Typically, students are separated into same-sex groups and then a same-sex teacher will tell the students about changes they can expect in puberty. In junior high school (sixth to eighth grades), students may be taught about sexual health issues such as sexually transmitted diseases, sexual abuse, factual, ethical, and moral issues having to do with abortion, and sexual orientation. Parents are allowed to opt out if they do not want their children to learn about these issues. Many parents are conflicted about schools teaching their children about birth control and other safe sex practices. Some parents are highly supportive of comprehensive sex education while others feel that when information about contraceptives is taught and contraceptive use encouraged, the abstinence/wait-to-have-sex message is lost. In high school, some school districts get into more detail about sexual issues and provide specifics about contraceptives, sexual orientation, and sexual health issues while others may once again provide abstinence-only education.

Until 2010, the federal government only funded abstinence-only sex education. Since the majority of public schools received federal funding for their sex education programs, most taught abstinence-only sex education. The federal government remains divided on this issue. There are some federally funded evidenced-based sex education programs that are comprehensive but schools remain divided. Some continue to teach abstinence-only sex education while others have switched over to comprehensive sex education. Research does show that comprehensive sex education programs *do not* increase teens' sexual behavior. This was a fear parents had about comprehensive sex education but it has not been supported by research. Finer's earlier reviewed study of premarital sex in the United States emphasizes that adult sexual behavior in regards to premarital sex has not significantly changed in over 75 years. Instead, people now wait longer to get married, so they are sexually active and unmarried for much longer than in the past. Finer concludes that, during this period, young adults have an especially great need for accurate information about how to protect themselves against unintended pregnancies and sexually transmitted infections. He states his support for comprehensive sex education based on his findings that approximately 95 percent of Americans have sex prior to marriage. Additionally, marriage rates in the United States are down. Some individuals and couples are choosing not to get married; therefore, it is probably unrealistic to expect these individuals and couples to maintain lifelong abstinence. This may be another argument in favor of comprehensive sex education.

SEXUAL ORIENTATION

Although *sexual orientation* describes our sexual, affectional, and emotional attachment to particular sexual partners, it is a great deal more than that. Sexual orientation informs who we are, specific ways in which we choose to identify ourselves, whom we are attracted to and choose to form romantic relationships with, and the way society treats us and our romantic relationships. Sexual orientation will be discussed at length in Chapter 2, but here I will introduce how sexual orientation impacts us on an everyday basis. It is often true that either a numerical majority or those in power in society set the rules, norms, and expectations for appropriate human behavior. This becomes the standard by which we are all judged. Heterosexuals (opposite sex sexual attraction) make up a numerical majority in terms of sexual orientation. Most of the couples depicted on TV programs, in movies, and in songs on the radio are heterosexual couples. Heterosexuality is considered the norm. Although societal attitudes toward other sexual orientations such as homosexuality (same sex sexual attraction) and bisexuality (being sexually attracted to opposite and same sexual partners) appear to be in the process of changing in a positive direction, heterosexuality is still considered the norm.

Our sexual orientation impacts how we see and identify ourselves. This has implications for how we behave and how our behaviors are perceived by society. If a male and female are walking down the street holding hands, they probably will not attract much attention and may even receive encouraging glances from onlookers who might think the behavior "romantic" and/or "cute." If two women walk down the street holding hands, onlookers may assume they are good friends or romantically linked, and might even have a more pronounced reaction to the couple. If two men walk down the street holding hands, many onlookers may react negatively for several reasons. One, society continues to have a difficult time accepting and witnessing physical affection between two romantically linked men. Two, in many places, this behavior is still considered abnormal. Three, our society tends to interpret male-on-male romantic affection as feminine and not "manly." This is a damaging perspective because it does not allow gay male couples to be openly affectionate with one another. Lesbian couples experience this kind of discrimination as well; however, society tends to be most rejecting of gay male couples' public physical affection toward one another. This is known as *heterosexual privilege*. The North Dakota State University (2010) Ally Training Program describes heterosexual privilege as follows: "Living without ever having to think, face, confront, engage or cope with discrimination based on one's sexual orientation; being able to kiss, hug, and be affectionate in public without threat, punishment, or being stared at in negative ways; being able to talk about, display pictures, travel with, and openly live with one's romantic partner without fear of being harmed or discriminated against. It also includes not having the normalcy of one's romantic relationships being questioned, receiving social support and acceptance from neighbors, colleagues, one's spiritual community, and society as a whole and being able to freely marry one's romantic partner" (p. 18). Recently, on June 6, 2015, in *Obergefell v. Hodges*, the U.S. Supreme Court ruled in favor of marriage equality, effectively allowing all consenting adults the right to marry. Same-sex couples can now marry in every state in the United States and receive all the legal benefits of marriage. Marriage includes the following privileges (Mongan-Rallis, 2005):

- Public recognition and support for an intimate relationship (receiving cards or phone calls celebrating your commitments to a person; supporting activities and social expectations of longevity and stability for your committed relationships)
- Paid leave from your employment and condolences on grieving the death of your partner/lover and other members of your "family"
- Inheriting from your spouse automatically under probate laws
- Sharing health, auto, and homeowners' insurance policies at reduced rates

- Immediate access to your loved ones in case of accident or emergency
- Automatically owning property and other assets jointly
- Joint taxes filing, rates, tax laws that favor married people

In American society, marriage is the social, cultural, and spiritual (some-times religious) recognition of a relationship. Although marriage rates in the United States are significantly declining, marriage continues to re-present a highly valued, socially sanctioned and supported declaration of a permanently binding long-term committed relationship.

As you can see, sexual orientation shapes our views of ourselves, our relationships, and sometimes how we are treated in society. It is a cultural identity (e.g., gay culture or heterosexual culture) with emotional, social, psychological, and legal implications for our everyday lives.

LOVE AND RELATIONSHIPS: TYPES OF RELATIONSHIPS

Love and relationships are a fundamental part of the human experience. If one peruses popular magazines, one would find numerous articles about how to get into relationships, how to get out of relationships, how to have fabulous sex with one's romantic partner, how to know if he or she is "the one," as well as how to deal with the break-up of a romantic relationship. So many of our books, movies, and songs on the radio talk about and explore love and relationships. Our relationship expectations are shaped by multiple factors, including family influences (parents), peer group, the media, religious/spiritual, and cultural forces. Many individuals have the expectation of *intimacy*, both emotional and sexual, in their relationship. Sternberg (1986) views intimacy as a constitutive element of love that encompasses feelings of closeness, connectedness, and bondedness. Components include emotional closeness, psychological relatedness, sex-ual intimacy, empathy, understanding between couples, interdependency, and trust, which is the most important component of intimacy. Our ability to give and receive intimacy can be reflective of our past relationship expe-riences (e.g., Have we been hurt before? Have we experienced infidelity? Have we witnessed divorce or domestic violence?). Trust is a fundamental part of healthy intimacy between two people. Without trust there can be no intimacy. If trust is broken in our romantic relationships, this can shape our behavior in future relationships going forward. In other words, if we had trust issues in one or two previous relationships, we often bring these issues with us to our future relationships unless these trust issues are worked through. Our relationship expectations speak to our needs and wants in relationships. For example, some individuals have the expectation that their romantic partners should be their "soul mates," their best friend, or someone who "fits them perfectly."

We all have different expectations of our romantic partners. Many people neglect to talk to their partners about their specific expectations, which can lead to confusion, communication issues, disappointment, and hurt. In many ways, our relationship expectations are a deep part of who we are and shape our behavior and satisfaction in our romantic relationships. Sometimes, we expect our partners to predict what we are thinking or feeling without our telling them. This is usually an unfair expectation as no one can predict what is inside someone else's head and heart. Yet, some individuals believe that if their partners truly understood them, they would be able to know what they are thinking and feeling. This tends to place an unfair burden on the other person in the relationship as well as burdening the relationship itself.

Why are romantic relationships so important to us? Romantic relationships often contribute to our sense of self, self-esteem, identity, and sense of meaning. Human beings are social creatures by nature. We are born with an innate desire to connect and build social and interpersonal relationships with others. We must form deep attachments with others to survive. Typically, our first attachment relationships are with our parents or caregivers. We later form interpersonal attachments with other family members, our peer groups, colleagues, and in our romantic relationships. It is considered a healthy need to want to connect with others. In Chapter 3, we will review both healthy and unhealthy relationship styles as well as signs of a dysfunctional relationship.

There are many types of romantic relationship styles and/or patterns. We will explore these styles below. First, however, we will explore how individuals become involved in romantic relationships in the first place.

Dating and Sexual Scripts

Dating scripts are the cognitive models that guide individuals' dating interactions. We are socialized into particular scripts by societal, familial, peer, media, and religious/spiritual influences and also they shape our expectations and behavior in the dating realm. Dating scripts are often also strongly influenced by gender. For example, a societal expectation is that in heterosexual romantic scripts the man asks the woman out and/or pays for the first date. Many individuals do not follow this script or change the script to meet their own situation (which can be a very healthy thing to do); however, scripts often shape our behavior around dating issues as well as put forth a common set of expectations. Our dating and sexual scripts have been shaped since childhood. Information we receive about how members of the same and opposite sex interact in romantic situations tends to form the foundation of the scripts.

A traditional gendered heterosexual dating script might look something like this. A man and woman are sitting at a bar. They strike up a conversation and the man asks the woman if he can buy her a drink. She accepts or rejects his offer. His offer to buy her a drink initiates further contact with her and might suggest his interest in her romantically. If she accepts, this might mean that she is interested in him romantically (or that she was interested in a free drink). Once the drink offer is accepted, there is an implied obligation for further conversation, at least based on a traditional dating script. Gendered dating scripts are influenced by gender roles and expectations of behavior based on one's gender (e.g., the man initiates a date). If the pair appear to have a mutual interest in one another, they may exchange numbers. In traditional dating scripts, the man asks for the woman's phone number (although in today's world, women ask for the phone numbers of men and invite men out for a date). There is typically a mutual expectation that the pair will talk on the phone or exchange texts prior to their first date in attempts to get to know one another. During their first date, the couple may engage in conversation and sometimes light physical touching (a pat on the back, a hug, kissing, etc.). At the end of the date, they may decide on a future date or decide that one or the other does not have future interest in the individual. When the date concludes, either person may initiate physical contact (e.g., a kiss). In traditional dating scripts, women are often socialized to resist sexual intimacy on a first date; however, many couples have early sexual contact (e.g., on a first date) and many do not. Some men are socialized to initiate sexual contact early in the relationship. *Sexual scripts* are the cognitive models that guide individuals' sexual interactions. Sexual scripts also shape our sexual behavior, expectations, and perceptions of what normal sexual behavior is.

Social psychology literature finds that dating scripts allow for the participants to know what to expect and help a couple to move further along into getting to know one another without causing a sequence of misinterpretations and accidental or intentional manipulations and miscommunication that result in unnecessary feelings and awkward situations. Scripts become less influential once two people get to know and allow each other in one's intimate space; they then understand each other's intents and actions with a different perspective than making presumptions as acquaintances, avoiding much of the problems of first contact. Dating and sexual scripts can be healthy or unhealthy. We will explore both healthy and dysfunctional scripts in Chapter 3.

Flirting

Flirting is another important part of dating and sexual scripts. Flirting usually consists of physical, verbal, and emotional communication suggesting romantic interest in another individual. It may involve giving the person of interest direct eye contact and then looking away, standing or sitting close to the person of interest (proxemics), touching the other person (in ways that are socially acceptable but push the boundaries of social acceptability; for example, putting your arm around a person you just met or laying one's hand on the back or thigh of the person of interest). Flirting is typically conveyed through body language, tone of voice, intermittent eye contact, as well as using language that might convey a sexual or romantic interest in the other person.

Flirting is significantly shaped by culture, gender, social, and societal expectations. Its goal is to convey romantic or sexual interest as well as to receive reinforcement from the other person that the initiator (person flirting) is attractive and receptive to further contact. Flirting usually involves speaking and behaving in a way that suggests a mildly greater intimacy than the actual relationship between the parties would justify, though within the rules of social etiquette, which generally disapproves of a direct expression of sexual interest. Flirting can involve playful gestures, verbal challenges, feigned disinterest, sexually suggestive behavior, and/or physical movements (e.g., touching) (Mead, 2004, pp. 145–149).

Hooking Up

"Hooking up" is a more recent term that typically implies having casual sex outside the confines of a committed romantic relationship. Although there seems to be little consensus on the definition of "hooking up," at minimum it implies some form of sexual contact and at maximum it implies full sexual intercourse. Hooking up has typically been studied in college students although high school students and young adults also report hooking up. College students who have participated in research exploring hook up culture often state that they are too busy for long-term romantic relationships and that hooking up fulfills both physical and emotional needs for closeness on a temporary basis. Drugs and alcohol are sometimes involved in hook ups, which can influence one's judgment and make it more likely to hook up with someone an individual not under the influence of drugs and alcohol would not. Many college students report that they regret hooking up; sometimes hooking up can lead to unintended consequences, such as sexually transmitted infections, unwanted pregnancies, hurt feelings, relationship disappointment, and/or date rape. Research clearly shows that college students overestimate just how many of their classmates are actually hooking up. For example, surveyed college students reported that they believed that over 85 percent of their classmates regularly engaged in hook ups. Approximately 60–80 percent of college students report having had some experience with casual sexual behavior. Research finds that the actual number is far lower. Approximately 20 percent of college students report having regular hook ups. The more an individual hooks up, the more likely he or she is to continue casual hook ups. College students who regularly hook up tend to have less experience in dating and long-term romantic relationships. Although college students may talk about hooking up, the majority of college students still engage in serial monogamy (see definition below). Social psychologists and relationship experts fear that if the hook up culture persists, the security of long-term romantic relationships will be at risk as hooking up does not develop the necessary relationship skills one needs to initiate, maintain, and be satisfied in a committed monogamous relationship. The positive and negative consequences of hooking up will be reviewed in Chapter 3.

Catfishing

A catfish "is someone who pretends to be someone they're not using Facebook or other social media to create false identities, particularly to pursue deceptive online romances," according to UrbanDictionary.com. The catfish phenomenon was first popularized by the film documentary *Catfish*, in which the main character, Nev, falls in love with a woman over the Internet. Most millennials (those born between the years 1982 and 2000) view technology and social media as a valued form of communicating with others (e.g., text messaging, Twitter, Facebook, and Snapchat). In *Catfish*, Nev and his love interest, Angela, communicate via Facebook. They become each others' "friends" and begin to share a mutual online community (i.e., Nev's and Angela's friends begin interacting with one another as well). Nev begins to suspect that Angela is not who she presents herself to be when he finds that several songs she said she wrote and sang for him were actually copied from another artist off of the Internet. The documentary shows Nev and two friends (the film's producer and cameraman) going to visit Angela in Michigan (Nev is from

New York) for an unannounced surprised visit. Nev finds that Angela is not at all who she says she is and that she posted a false profile (including her age and physical appearance) on her Facebook page.

The catfish phenomenon has received a great deal of media attention through the TV show *Catfish* as well as the Manti Te'o scandal. Manti Te'o was a famous Notre Dame football player who helped lead his team to an undefeated season. His story was considered both tragic and heroic, as he reported that the deaths of his grandmother and his girlfriend, Lennay Kekua, happened in the same year but only helped him play harder. It was later discovered that Manti Te'o had lied about his girlfriend dying from leukemia. As reporters dug into the story and explored his inconsistencies, Manti Te'o stated that he never actually met her (a contradiction from an earlier version of his story) but that they consistently communicated online and by phone. The truth is that Manti Te'o lied about having a girlfriend in the first place, although he showed pictures of her that turned out to be lifted from the Internet and was a woman he never met.

Why would someone deceive another individual with a phony online profile? There are many answers to this question. Some experts have proposed the idea that since so many more people communicate through the Internet, individuals' online identities have become crucial to who they are. On the Internet one can be who one wants to be. If an individual does not like the way he or she looks, he or she can simply lift a picture from the Internet and post it to his or her social media Web site; the individual can therefore present his or her ideal physical appearance to others. Other experts suggest that those most vulnerable to being catfished are individuals with low self-esteem or those who are confused about who they are. Still others feel that the catfish may enjoy manipulating and using others (i.e., getting someone else to fall in love with you or getting validating attention from someone else) to feel good about themselves. The answers are not clear but given our extensive use of social media, the catfish phenomenon is probably here to stay.

Serial Monogamy

As we grow up, most of us are taught the importance and expectation of faithfulness in our romantic relationships: the value of *fidelity*, which is defined as loyalty to an allegiance or person, vow, promise, or sexual faithfulness to a sexual partner. Most marriage vows include the stated expectation of sexual fidelity and faithfulness. These strongly held societal values influence our relationship styles and behavior. Research demonstrates that most Americans engage in *serial monogamy*, which is the practice of having a number of long-term romantic or sexual partners in succession. For many individuals, their first serious romantic relationships occur in high school. This is often when many adolescents begin dating. Most adolescents articulate values of faithfulness to one's romantic partner. The expectation, then, is that while being romantically involved with one person, both partners in the relationships are sexually faithful to one another. If or when the relationship ends, the expectation of sexual fidelity ends as well. However, if one or both of the individuals get involved in another romantic relationship, they are expected to be sexually faithful to the new relationship. This is the essence of serial monogamy. Although many people assume that sexual faithfulness is the implied expectation within a relationship, individuals should always discuss this expectation with one's romantic partner because not everyone prizes sexual faithfulness in their relationships.

Cohabitation

Cohabitation is a relationship style popularized in the 1970s, in which two unmarried romantically involved adults live together and have a serially monogamous relationship. Today, more than 66 percent of married adults report living together prior to marriage. Early research on cohabitation found that those couples who cohabitated were less likely to get married and more likely to divorce when they did marry. Recent research finds that the age of the couple cohabitating is far more predicative of marital success than the fact that the couple cohabitated prior to marriage. For example, very young couples (aged 18–22) who cohabitate are less likely to get married and more likely to divorce when they do marry. Older cohabitating couples are more likely to get married than those couples who did not live together prior to marriage and not likely to divorce when they do marry. Earlier research neglected to explore how the couple's maturity influenced the long-term strength of their relationship.

Cohabitation continues to be a growing trend. Currently, couples of all ages are cohabitating. Typically, cohabitating couples remain monogamous and committed to one another without being married. Some have children and raise them together as well. Research suggests that cohabitating couples report living together as a way of testing their mutual compatibility prior to getting married. The United States is currently experiencing a decline in marriage rates and an increase in cohabitation rates. This will be discussed next in this chapter.

Marriage

Marriage is a social and culturally prescribed ritual that formally recognizes a couples' relationship in legal, (sometimes) religious, social, psychological, and emotional terms. Marriage typically implies sexual and emotional intimacy shared between spouses. Marriage in the United States has changed significantly over the last 100 years. For example, well over 100 years ago, individuals got married because just about everyone in society did. Couples married to combine assets (e.g., property, wealth), legitimize the birth of children (i.e., produce an heir), and solidify connections between families. Today, most people state that falling in love with another person and the need for emotional intimacy are the most important reasons to get married. Other changes to marriage during the latter half of the twentieth century include couples marrying later (e.g., mid-to-late twenties and thirties), fewer people marrying at all, and couples choosing to cohabitate instead of marrying. A few hundred years ago, married women were considered the property of their husbands. Married women typically had few rights. Because the twentieth century brought about significant changes regarding the roles of women, the institution of marriage changed as well. The women's movement in the 1960s brought about women's sexual freedom and marked their en mass entry into the workforce. This changed the institution of marriage in several ways. One, women were no longer expected to be sexually inexperienced upon entering marriage. Two, women were no longer automatically expected to stay home and raise children. In fact, most families struggled to survive on one income, so for many families, a woman's ability to work outside the home became a necessity, not a luxury. Three, men's roles changed as the result of the changes to women's roles. Men were now expected to take an active role in raising children (as opposed to just being the primary breadwinner) as well as do more housework then generations of men in the past.

At the turn of the millennium, the gay marriage movement picked up significant momentum. As stated previously, federal law now supports marriage equality for all couples. Same-sex couple marriage is changing the institution of traditional heterosexual marriage as the roles gay individuals take on within their romantic relationship do not follow traditional gender lines. For example, in heterosexual couples, the roles each takes on within one's relationship may be shaped by gender (e.g., he takes out the trash, she cooks the food). Although this is not always the case, heterosexual couples have frequently been socialized to take on prescribed roles shaped by gender. Gay couples often have more flexibility in negotiating particular roles (e.g., who does what in terms of household tasks) because they can write their own scripts not based on traditional gender roles. It will be interesting to see how gay marriage will shape society's idea of the institution of marriage.

Declining Marriage Rates

Since the 1990s there has been a decline in marriage rates in the United States. Current survey data collected by the Pew Research Center suggests that only 51 percent of adults aged 18 and older were married in 2010 compared with 72 percent in 1960. This represents an all-time low for married adults in the United States. Marriage rates continue to drop drastically. Between 2009 and 2010, the number of marriages dropped by 5 percent. Young adults (between 18 and 29) experienced the most significant drop in marriage rates. Just 20 percent of them were married in 2014. In 1960, 72 percent of all adults under the age group of 18 and older were married. Additionally, the age at first marriage now is much higher than in the 1960s. Currently, the median age for first marriage is 26.5 for women and 28.7 for men. Experts suggest that the decline in marriage rates in the United States is due to increases in cohabiting couples, single person households, and single parenthood. Each of these factors is far more acceptable in today's society than it was in the 1960s. It may be that marriage is no longer the preferred romantic relationship style. It appears as if society is embracing more flexible romantic relationship patterns than in previous years.

Swingers

Swinging, or partner swapping, describes a romantic relationship style in which long-term committed couples (often married) will open their relationship (sometimes referred to as an "open marriage") to allow for or include sexual relationships with other people. Swinging is viewed as a way to increase sexual variety and satisfaction within the primary couple's relationship. Swinging couples typically meet other swinging couples through swingers clubs, Internet chat sites, or other swinging social networks.

Swinging has probably always existed in some form or fashion; however, it appears to have increased during the sexual revolution in the 1960s, which represented the relaxing of stricter sexual standards. For the first time, birth control became more widely available to women, which made swinging free from the burden of pregnancy. Swinging is considered a romantic relationship lifestyle often referred to as "the lifestyle" or "the alternative lifestyle." Research estimates that 2–4 percent of couples regularly engage in the swinging lifestyle. As many as 15 percent of other couples may have tried swinging but are not considered swingers because they may have tried it once or twice and then decided against this lifestyle.

CONCLUSION

As you can see from this chapter, there are many ways sex impacts our everyday lives. From the relationships we form with others to our expected norms of those relationships, sex and our ideas about sexual norms influence our thoughts, values, and sexual behaviors. In this chapter, we have covered sexual socialization and cultural, familial, peer, and religious influences on sexual behavior; taken a brief look at sexual orientation; explored the influence of dating and sexual scripts; and explored the types of sexual relationships that exist in society. Future chapters will investigate these topics in greater detail.

REFERENCES

Alexander, E., & Hickner, J. (1997). First coitus for adolescents: Understanding why and when. *Journal of the American Board of Family Practice, 10,* 96–103.

Bernstein, N. (2005). Sex and peer pressure. Retrieved from http://www .nbcnews.com/id/6867362/t/sex-peer-pressure/#.UxeSn02YZdg.

Brown, J. D., L'Engle, K. L., Pardun, C. J., Guo, G., Kenneavy, K., & Jackson, C. (2006). Sexy media matter: Exposure to sexual content in music, movies, television and magazines predicts Black and White adolescents' sexual behavior. *Pediatrics, 117,* 1018–1027.

Collins, R. L., Elliott, M. N., Berry, S. H., Kanouse, D. E., Kunkel, D., & Hunter, S. B. (2004). Watching sex on television predicts adolescent initiation of sexual behavior. *Pediatrics, 114,* e280–e289.

Finer, L.B. (2007 January/February). Trends in premarital sex in the United States, 1954–2003. *Public Health Reports,* 73–78. Retrieved from http://www.publichealthreports.org/issueopen.cfm?articleID=1784

Gagnon, J. (1990). The explicit and implicit use of the scripting perspective. *Annual Review of Sex Research, 1,* 1–44.

Greenberg, J.S., Bruess, C.E., & Conklin, S.C. (2011). *Exploring the dimensions of human sexuality* (4th ed.). Sudbury, MA: Jones and Bartlett Publishers.

Kelly, G.F. (2011). *Sexuality today* (10th ed.). New York: McGraw-Hill Higher Education.

King, B.R. (2009). *Human sexuality today* (6th ed.). Upper Saddle River, NJ: Pearson Education.

Kirby, D. (2001). *Emerging answers: Research findings on programs to reduce teen pregnancy.* Washington, DC: The National Campaign to Prevent Teen Pregnancy.

L'Engle, K.L., Brown, J.D., & Kenneavy, K. (2006). The mass media are an important context for adolescents' sexual behavior. *Journal of Adolescent Health, 38,* 186–192.

L'Engle, K.L., & Jackson, C. (2008). Socialization influences on early adolescents' cognitive susceptibility and transition into sexual intercourse. *Journal of Research on Adolescence, 18*(2), 353–378.

Longmore, M.A. (1998). Symbolic interactionism and the study of sexuality. *Journal of Sex Research, 35,* 44–57.

Mead, M. (2004). A case history in cross-national communication. In W.O. Beeman (Ed.), *Studying contemporary Western society: Method and theory* (pp. 144–161). New York: Berghahn Books.

Mongan-Rallis, H. (2005). Understanding GLBT issues. Retrieved from http://www.d.umn.edu/~hrallis/professional/presentations/ally_training/het_privilege.htm.

Nonoyama, M., et al. (2005). Influences of sex-related information for STD prevention. *Journal of Adolescent Health, 36,* 442–445.

North Dakota State University (2010). *Safe Zone Training* [PDF document]. Retrieved from http://www.fs.fed.us/cr/Safe_Zone_Training_PacketUpdated.pdf.

O'Donnell, B. L., O'Donnell, C. R., & Stueve, A. (2001). Early sexual initiation and subsequent sex-related risks among urban minority youth: The reach for health study. *Family Planning Perspectives, 33,* 268–275.

Shtarkshall, R.A., Santelli, J.S., & Hirsch, J.S. (2007, June 11). Sex education and sexual socialization: Roles for educators and parents. *Perspectives on Sexual and Reproductive Health, 39*(2), 116–119.

Sternberg, R.J. (1986). A triangular theory of love. *Psychological Review, 93,* 119–135.

Stodghill II, R. (1998, June 15). Where'd you learn that? *Time,* 52–59.

Ward, L.M., & Friedman, K. (2006). Using TV as a guide: Associations between television viewing and adolescents' sexual attitudes and behavior. *Journal of Research on Adolescence, 16,* 133–156.

2

❖

Why: The Importance of Sex in Our Lives

Why is sex so important? Why do people have so many different ideas and values about sexual behavior? How does sex impact our everyday lives? These are important questions we will explore throughout this chapter. Sexuality is important for many reasons. First, it helps to shape who we are. Our sexual identities incorporate our understanding of gender and gender roles, our sexual orientation, our sense of masculinity and femininity, the way we interpret the behaviors of others, and our understanding of our environment. In other words, sex and sexuality impacts our entire *worldview*. Our worldview encapsulates our understanding of the way our worlds work. For example, when we make sense of our environments (our behavior, others' behavior, events that happen around us, etc.) we do so based on our previous experiences, our individual values and morals, our societal social norms, the way we were raised, peer and media influences, our cultural background, our gender identity and age, as well as many other factors. We have a cognitive representation of our worlds, which helps us make sense of the things going on around us. Our thoughts, ideas, and beliefs about sex are incorporated into our worldview. Our worldview is shaped from the time we enter the world until the time we leave it and it is constantly being shaped and added to over time. The more knowledge we have about something, the broader our worldview. One example of how we use our worldview to understand our environment is through the use of schemas. *Schemas* are cognitive frameworks or concepts that help us organize and interpret information. They allow us to make shortcuts in interpreting information in our environments. They are highly influenced by our past experiences, values, and belief systems. They can be thought of as shortcuts in thinking. These are the mental frameworks that strongly influence our worldview. Schemas can cause us problems, however, when we solely rely on them (some of the information in our schemas is based on stereotypes) because they can lead to cognitive processing errors (errors in thinking) and a lack of critical thinking. For example, if you went for a job interview and the first person you encountered was a female sitting behind a desk, you might assume that she is a secretary as this might fit your gendered notion that most secretaries are females. You might be correct in your assumption; however, she might also be the chief executive officer of the company waiting to interview you. If you mistake her for the secretary, you might not even get an interview! As you can see, our worldview is specific to each of us. It is not necessarily correct or incorrect. Our worldview is simply our understanding of the world based on our own experiences. This chapter will explore the importance of sex in our lives as well as how it influences our worldview.

SEX SELLS: THE IMPACT OF SEX IN ADVERTISING

Sex impacts our everyday lives on several levels. We are impacted on a daily basis by advertisers using sex to sell their products. We see beautiful, shapely women laid across a new car with a man smiling in the background. Possibly, the message here is that if he buys that car, he can have a beautiful shapely woman too. This is problematic for several reasons. One, it implies that women can be bought as easily as one can buy any object. Two, it implies that a woman's body is for sale. Three, it positions men as the individual's whose job it is to acquire women. Four, it suggests that a woman's value is only as good as she looks physically. Five, it suggests that men are only motivated by beautiful women. Six, this form of advertising seems to imply that men can only get women interested in them through their material possessions. Perhaps this advertisement says none, some, or all of those things. The point here is that we are bombarded by sexual messages all day long both consciously and unconsciously. We see them in commercials, in print ads, on the Internet, in movies, TV shows, and hear about them on the radio. As you can see, sex continues to sell!

The above example of a car commercial illustrates that on a daily basis, our stereotypes about gender are reinforced and uncritically evaluated, even if we do not believe in some of the stereotypes. The use of sex in advertising can be damaging for the reasons stated above (e.g., the reinforcement of gender stereotypes). Advertisements typically utilize visual imagery (a picture of a muscular man with his shirt off, a beautiful woman in a bikini) that has nothing to do with the product being sold. Advertisers use sex because it works. On some level most of us respond to this use of sexual images. It is possible that we have some unconscious biological response (e.g., lust) to the image. Use of sex in advertising is either direct (overt) or indirect (subtle). For example, some makers of perfume make the bottle in the shape of the female form, which tends to appeal to both men and women. Possibly, the message here might be the following: use this perfume if you want to look like this or to draw someone's romantic interest. As successful marketers of products already understand, most individuals are inherently interested in sex, whether they admit it or not. Although each of us has very specific notions about sex and sexuality, most of us respond in significant ways to sex when it is used to market products. Within each of us is a biological drive (controlled by hormones and certain brain structures, including the *hypothalamus*, which is responsible for the four primary drives: feeding, fight-or-flight response, sexual reproduction as well as controlling body temperature, and parental attachment behaviors). In reviewing recent findings about how sex impacts our everyday lives, Campbell (2014) found that often has a reward focus. He quotes recent research in which a team of researchers lead by Anouk Festjens of the University of Leuven, Belgium, found that when participants in their experiments touched sexual content (e.g., underwear), it activated monetary craving and reduced the general feeling of loss aversion (people strongly prefer avoiding losses than acquiring gains) that most humans have. Because advertising is such a powerful media, we are frequently unaware of the significant impact it is having. Problems arise when unconscious messages about sex and gender are reinforced and then we treat individuals according to our stereotypical beliefs, which does not allow for much variation in behavior and often leads to automatic judgments about others solely on the basis of gender or other characteristics (e.g., race).

THE IMPACT OF GENDER

As you will see by the conclusion of this section, the impact of gender, gender socialization, and gender roles is notable in our everyday lives. Not all psychologists agree on the definition of gender. For our purposes *gender* is defined as the physical, mental, psychological, and social expression of masculinity and femininity. *Sex* refers to one's biologic expression of being male or female, often based on chromosomal makeup (females have XX chromosomes and males have XY chromosomes) and/or basis of female appearing (vagina) or male appearing (penis) genitalia. Why all the controversy regarding a simple definition? It depends on one's view of gender. For most individuals, their *gender identity* (biological, social, and cultural norms shaping who we are based on our maleness or femaleness) and biologic sex matches. In other words, for one individual her gender would be woman and her biologic sex would be female. Therefore, to most people, there is little distinction between gender and sex. However, individuals who are *transgender, transsexual,* or *intersexed*— these terms will be defined later in this chapter but they refer to individuals whose gender/gender identity and biologic sex do not match or have sexual characteristics of males as well as females—may feel as if they are in the wrong body and were always meant to be born the opposite sex of what their physical body is currently.

This may all seem confusing but that is because in our society we are taught to view things in a binary way. We view sexual orientation as gay or "straight." We view gender as male or female. We view race as black or white. This black-and-white way of thinking does not allow us to understand that not everyone fits into discrete categories, especially in regards to gender. This view also does not allow us the freedom to critically evaluate some of the accepted stereotypes about gender that do not fit everyone. It will be important to understand that gender, sex, gender roles, and sexual orientation are not nearly as clear as the categories most people know them by imply.

When a woman becomes visibly pregnant one of the first questions she is asked is, "Is it a boy or a girl?" Clearly, *gender role socialization* starts prior to birth. *Socialization* is the process of guiding people into socially acceptable behavior by providing information, rewards, and punishment. Gender socialization is specific to familial and societal expected norms, behaviors, roles, styles of dress, communication, and emotional expression based on gender. Research has demonstrated that boy and girl babies are socialized very differently early on in their existence. When people are told that the baby they are holding is male, they hold him more roughly, play more roughly with him, describe him differently, and project different career paths onto him than they would if they assumed he was female (e.g., "This one is going to play football."). Girl babies are held more gently, cuddled more, described in more feminine terms, assumed to have higher emotional needs, and are projected to follow more traditional female career paths. Other research also shows that fathers may be more concerned with gender role socialization than mothers. For example, there were studies done where fathers and sons (and separately mothers and sons) were left in a room to play with toys. In the room, there were gender-typed (e.g., dolls for girls, trucks for boys) and gender-neutral toys (a teddy bear). Most mothers were unconcerned when their boys played with dolls. Fathers, on the other hand, often physically got on the floor with their sons, removed the doll from the son, and placed a male gender-typed toy (e.g., truck) in the child's hands. Gender role socialization sends children powerful messages about gender appropriate behavior. Families and peers both subtlety and directly punish non-gender-conforming behavior and reward gender-appropriate behavior. Families are often unaware that they are doing this or of the double standard of behavior they prescribe in their sons and daughters.

Troy Campbell, a social science researcher at Duke University and journalist at the *Huffington Post* wrote an article entitled *It's Adam then Eve, Not Adam and Eve*, in which he describes gender assumptions. His girlfriend is set to finish her PhD 1 year before he finishes his. Many of his colleagues made the assumption that she will wait for him to finish and then follow him wherever he goes (as opposed to him following her). He discusses the implications of this assumption, which is that it is the woman's job to follow the man, not vice versa. This is frequently an automatic assumption in academic couples—she follows him and not the opposite. He makes the point that when it matters, the man comes first and this seems to be an unquestionable truth. He discusses that automatic assumptions about gender are damaging because they do not allow for individuality and that society judges non-gender-conforming behavior harshly.

Below is a list of common gender-socialized messages that impact the way men and women view and treat one another.

Men are competitive, are not supposed to show emotional vulnerability, are to be strong and knowledgeable at all times, are rarely to ask for help, are never to lose to a girl/woman, are supposed to protect and take care of women, are never supposed to cry, are not supposed to talk about emotionally painful things with anyone (or rarely), are not supposed to hurt, are supposed to want sex all the time, are not supposed to be overly involved with child care and household chores, are supposed to be the primary breadwinners, are supposed to have money, prestige, and power, are supposed to be driven.

Women are supposed to be soft, are competitive only with other women (not men), are not supposed to be driven, are allowed by societal norms to show vulnerability, are not supposed to show anger, are supposed to be nurturers, are good with children, are supposed to be automatically good at child care, are supposed to be primarily responsible for household chores, are not supposed to want money, power, and prestige on their own without getting in from a man, are always supposed to take care of others, are to suppress their own needs, and so forth.

These messages have extreme implications for how we see ourselves. If we match up to these gender messages, we may feel good about ourselves but if we diverge significantly from them, we may feel like we do not belong or that something is wrong with us. Another example of unquestioned gender roles came up during the 2008 presidential campaign. For the first time in United States history, we had a woman running for president (Hillary Clinton) and a woman running for vice president (Sarah Palin). The press paid special attention to Hillary Clinton's attire. There was countless speculation about the pants and suits she wore. Sarah Palin was asked how she would handle being president (if something happened to the president) and also take care of her children. Interestingly enough, no one had ever asked a male presidential candidate how he would take care of his children as well as be the president and no male candidate for president had ever received such attention for his attire as did Hillary Clinton. Both women were competing for roles (i.e., president and vice president) that women had not held previously. Many people struggled to see women in these roles because the roles were contrary to the gender stereotypes people had about women. Therefore, both Clinton and Palin were subjected to gender stereotypic questioning regarding their ability to perform these roles. The difference here is that the female candidates were subjected to gender stereotypes and the male candidates were not. The male candidates were questioned about their ability to perform the job well based on who they were. The female candidates were subjected to a different line of questioning as well as questioning regarding their ability to do the job solely on the basis of their being female.

Gender roles change depending on the society in which one grows up. They are taught throughout the life span but have the most impact in early childhood. Gender roles are the overt expression of attitudes that indicate to others the degree of one's maleness or femaleness. They include the public expression of one's gender identity (e.g., masculine or feminine traits). We take on different roles that are often prescribed or influenced by gender. For example, there are few male cheerleaders in junior high or high school (only college). There are few girls on football teams (male or female). Based on their lack of existence, most individuals get the idea that boys are not supposed to be cheerleaders and girls are not supposed to be football players. These are roles strongly influenced by gender.

Therefore, few girls grow up wanting to join the NFL and few boys express a desire to join the cheerleading squad. *Gender-role stereotyping* is the expectation that individuals will behave in certain ways because they are male or female. Again, this is typically an automatic assumption deriving from our *gender schemas*. When individuals behave contrary to these stereotypes, they are often overtly discouraged, punished, or ostracized from the peer group (e.g., a boy wearing a dress). Most children achieve *gender constancy* (the idea that they are a boy or girl and that this will not change) around the age of 5. Children also have internalized gender-appropriate behavior and inform their peers if they are not supposed to do something because "that's for boys" or "that's for girls." Peers end up being another powerful socializing influence on gender norms as the peer group rarely tolerates gender-discrepant behavior. *Sexism* is a damaging form of discrimination that typically affects women. Sexism is prejudice, stereotyping, or discrimination, typically against women, on the basis of sex. It includes the prejudgment that because of gender (usually female) a person will possess negative or weak traits/behaviors. Sexism is often based on *male privilege*, which is perpetuated by both men and women; however, men are the beneficiaries of this type of privilege. Male privilege refers to the social theory that argues that men have unearned social, economic, and political advantages or rights that are granted to them solely on the basis of their sex, and which are usually denied to women. This is a controversial concept; however, if male privilege does exist, it restricts both men and women as it locks both into predetermined gender roles that allow for little individuality and expression of one's gender free from these gender-typed restrictions. This is not to say that differences between men and women are negative or bad, because they are not. What is negative is the determination of who someone can or cannot be, or roles they can or cannot take on, simply on the basis of one's gender.

SEXUAL ORIENTATION

Sexual orientation describes our sexual, affectional, and emotional attachment to particular sexual partners. *Heterosexual* orientation is an individual with a sexual orientation primarily toward members of the opposite sex. *Homosexual* orientation is an individual with sexual orientation primarily toward members of the same sex. *Bisexual* orientation is an individual with a sexual orientation toward both men and women. Kinsey (1948) forever changed the way we view sexual orientation because his research demonstrated that sexual orientation does not typically exist in discrete categories. Instead, sexual orientation should be viewed on a continuum where heterosexuality and homosexuality are at either end and bisexuality is in the middle. He found that most people tended toward one end or the other but there were few absolutes. He also found that for some women, sexual orientation is more fluid than for most men. This might explain how some women who define themselves as heterosexual can fall in love with and have a sexually intimate relationship with another woman. Kinsey also found that a percentage of the population fit more into a bisexual orientation than heterosexual or homosexual. Kinsey also discovered that many men and women had engaged in same-sex sexual experimentation and this was far more common than once believed.

Asexuality is a less well-known sexual orientation and another sexual minority group. Being asexual is frequently defined as an individual having a very low or absent interest in sexual activity or sexual connection with another individual. There is little scientific research on the asexual population but asexual individuals may comprise around 1 percent of the population. Asexuality is thought to be a sexual orientation because it is enduring and consistent over time.

We must remember when looking at sexual orientation that it—sexual orientation—is more than just sexual behavior (i.e., who someone has intercourse with). It includes how one chooses to identify one's self socially, psychologically (identity), culturally, and relationally. One example of this is men in prison. Some men who go to prison have same-sex intercourse while incarcerated; however, before entering prison and after getting out, they exclusively engaged in heterosexual intercourse and relationships. Are these men gay? Most would not identify themselves that way. Thus, someone can engage in a sexual behavior that does not match their sexual identity or sexual orientation. Additionally, because the heterosexual orientation is privileged in our society (e.g., received preferred status and advantages based on being heterosexual) many individuals who are not heterosexual often engage in heterosexual behaviors prior to "coming out" or stating that they are gay or bisexual. Heterosexuals have many advantages in our society that gays and lesbians do not. For example, all the songs on the radio are assumed to be about heterosexual relationships. Most of the commercials on TV depict heterosexual couples and families lead by heterosexual parents. This representation of heterosexuality preferentially places it above all other sexual orientations. Most gay and bisexual relationships are absent from media coverage, TV commercials, and movies, though there are some rare exceptions (e.g., the popular TV show *Will and Grace*). The word *gay* is often used to describe a homosexual orientation because the word *homosexual* has a negative connotation. This may be because until 1973, the word *homosexual* was used to describe a mental disorder in the *Diagnostic and Statistical Manual* (DSM) for diagnosing mental health disorders. Until 1973, homosexuality was considered a mental illness that required treatment. It is no longer considered a mental illness but the negative connotation for the word *homosexual* remains. Additionally, the term *gay* generally refers to both male and female homosexuals, though many lesbians (homosexual orientation specific to female same-sex relationships) prefer the term *lesbian* to *gay*. In this book the word *gay* will be used in place of *homosexual* or *homosexuality* and the word *lesbian* will be used when referring specifically to female same-sex romantic relationships.

It is difficult to ascertain the percentage of the population that identifies as gay as statistics vary widely. Some national surveys of Americans indicate that 1.6 percent of the sexually active population has had a same-sex partner in the last year (Cochran & Mays, 2000, as cited in King, 2009) while other figures suggest that as much as 10 percent of the population is gay. It does appear that the number of women engaging in same-sex relationships has increased fourfold over the last few decades (Turner et al., 2005, as cited in King, 2009). Bisexuality seems to be the most confusing sexual orientation for society to accept and understand. This is probably because we tend to view sexual orientation as dichotomous (gay or straight) leaving no room for understanding sexual attraction to both sexes. Several studies indicate that self-identification of gay, lesbian, or bisexual can change over time, especially for women (Diamond, 2005; Kinnish et al., 2005, as cited in King, 2009). For example, some women get married, have children, and remain in heterosexual relationships until middle age and then have a long-term, same-sex relationship. Bisexuality may be more common in women than in men and research shows that bisexuality for most is not a transitional phase but consistent over time (Diamond, 2008, as cited in King, 2009). However, most people who demonstrate bisexual behavior still tend to self-identify as either heterosexual or homosexual (gay), which emphasizes societal discomfort with the bisexual identity. It has been suggested that sexual orientation has at least three separate components: affective (sexual attraction, feelings of desire and love), behavioral, and self-identity (Garnets & Peplau, 2001, as cited in King, 2009). Bisexuality is a legitimate sexual orientation; however, it is probably the most misunderstood sexual orientation.

Sometimes, individuals confuse sexual orientation with sexual identity. For example, some mistakenly assume that gay men want to be women. This is not true and a harmful stereotype. The majority of gay individuals have a gender identity consistent with his or her anatomic sex. Being gay, bisexual, or straight (heterosexual) has nothing to do with reversing or confusing gender roles. The media often portrays gay men as effeminate and lesbians as masculine; however, this is a stereotype and an oversimplification of sexual orientation and gender identity. Remember our discussion earlier about how harshly many families and peer groups punish or ostracize gender non-conforming behavior. Whenever someone does not fit the societal idea of masculinity or femininity based on his or her biologic sex, we tend to question that person's sexual orientation but gender non-conforming behavior is not always predictive of sexual orientation. Thus, assuming that a more masculine female is a lesbian is a negative and harmful stereotype that may simply not be true. Most individuals, regardless of sexual orientation, have both masculine and feminine traits.

In the 1970s, Sandra Bem researched masculine and feminine traits using her instrument, the Bem Sex Role Inventory. This scale measured which kinds of sex roles an individual fulfills. Her work did a great deal to dispel the idea that gender is strictly defined in terms of masculine and feminine traits. She measured gender identity with the guiding principle that individuals can have both masculine and feminine traits and this is psychologically healthy. She found that many of her subjects fell into a range of categories based on her questions about masculine and feminine traits. Subjects fell into four categories: masculine (these individuals endorsed the questions measuring masculine traits highly and feminine traits in very low numbers), feminine (these individuals endorsed the questions measuring feminine traits highly and masculine traits in very low numbers), undifferentiated (these individuals had low identification on both masculine and feminine traits), and androgyny (a person who had high identification with both masculine and feminine traits). Through her work on gender traits and gender identity, she identified *gender schema theory*, which speaks to our earlier discussion about how we tend to rely upon schemas to understand gender without critically evaluating gender differences. Bem studied gender, gender identity, and gender schemas independent of sexual orientation.

Though our society still privileges the heterosexual orientation, given the recent Supreme Court decision that now allows gays to become married, attitudes about sexual orientation seem to be changing. Many gays and lesbians, however, are still discriminated against in personal and professional realms due to society's bias toward heterosexuality. How does sexual orientation develop? Are people born gay, straight, or bisexual? We will explore some of the psychological theories and existing research around sexual orientation.

NATURE OR NURTURE?

Sexual orientation tends to be a controversial topic and there is no defini-tive answer to the nature-versus-nurture question about sexual orientation. As long as people have existed, so have differences in sexual orientation. One interesting point of note is that historically and currently, there was little interest in discovering how a heterosexual orientation came to exist, which clearly demonstrates society's preference for heterosexuality. Today, when scientists explore sexual orientation, they frequently attempt to look at sexual orientation's origins as a whole and not just homosexuality. Because historically, homosexuality was considered an aberrant sexual behavior, much of the early hypotheses regarding the origins of sexual ori-entation was biased by the view that homosexuals (gays and lesbians) were mentally ill. One of the most infamous psychological explanations regard-ing the existence of homosexuality came from Freud. Freud assumed that sexual orientation was determined by the environment (i.e., one is not born with a sexual orientation). He explained the existence of homo-sexuality by a man's unresolved Oedipal complex. The Oedipal complex will be explained in Chapter 4. He believed that cold, domineering, rejecting mothers set their sons up to be homosexual because the boy was unable to turn to his mother for comfort. The son instead turns to his father and then to men later in life for sexual and emotional comfort. He hypothesized that women's homosexuality was due to a girl's unre-solved issues with her father. Freud further believed that when a girl loves her mother and identifies with her father (instead of her mother) at the Oedipal stage, she becomes fixated (stuck) and same-sex attraction to girls as the result. As a whole, the field of psychology seemed to accept Freud's views on sexual orientation without much question until the 1960s, during the sexual revolution. Kinsey's research on sexual orientation and sexual behavior in the 1940s and 1950s may have been key to society's beginning to openly question the origins of sexual orientation. This became a more accepted truth as opposed to an area to be studied further. Freud's explan-ations of poor relationships with opposite-sex parents really did not explain the existence of homosexuality in most individuals.

Social learning theory was next used to understand differences in sexual orientation in the psychological literature. Social learning theory, discov-ered by Albert Bandura, states that we learn things by observing others. There are three important components to social learning theory: Individuals can learn through observation; internalization of what was learned is an important part of the process; just because something was learned does not mean that it will be repeated or that a change in behavior was made. Thus, we can learn things by watching others. If we remember their behavior we can choose to do that behavior at a later time or choose to not perform the behavior. With regards to sexual orientation, social learning theory would state that we learn a heterosexual, homosexual, or bisexual orientation from our environments—through observing the behavior of others. For example, gay individuals would initially have pleasurable experiences with members of the same sex (reinforcing same-sex relationships as being rewarding) and negative experiences with the opposite sex (reinforcing the idea that opposite-sex relationships are punishing/not rewarding). This might lead to initiating or being receptive to same-sex sexual acts, which would be perceived as pleasurable. Then, a person might become gay by having positively reinforcing experiences both socially and sexually, with members of the same sex. The problems with this theory are as follows: (1) Most gay individuals are raised by heterosexual parents, which means they did not observe homosexual behavior at home, and (2) many gays and lesbians report positive sexual and interpersonal relationships with members of the opposite sex but report simply preferring same-sex sexual/romantic relationships. Research has also not supported the idea that the majority of children who do not strongly conform to gender-specific behavior (i.e., boys who wear a dress instead of pants) do not eventually report being gay—some do and most do not. Therefore, social learning theory does not truly explain the existence of homosexual sexual orientation.

Biological and genetic factors have also been explored in explaining sexual orientation differences. For example, identical-twin studies have been closely examined (because identical/monozygotic twins share 100 percent of their DNA). A study of 167 pairs of identical twin brothers found that 52 percent of the identical twin brothers of gay men were also gay compared with 22 percent of nonidentical twins and 11 percent of adoptive brothers (Bailey & Pillard, 1991). Another study of 143 pairs of twin sisters found that 48 percent of identical twins of lesbians were also lesbian compared to 16 percent of nonidentical twins and 6 percent of adoptive sisters (Bailey et al., 1993). Other researchers have found that male homosexuality, in part, may be determined by a gene in a specific region of the X chromosome, although this is not true of female homosexuality. These studies suggest that sexual orientation does have a significant biological factor; however, how much is genetic and how much is due to environmental factors is undetermined. Bailey, author of multiple twin studies, suggests that sexual orientation is anywhere between 30 percent and 70 percent. Other biological studies have explored brain differences, specifically the hypothalamus, between homosexuals and heterosexuals. Although some differences were found, the number of participants in these studies was very small. Birth order effects were also explored. The idea was that the uterine (womb) environment changes with each successive pregnancy, which may impact the eventual sexual orientation of the child. For example, some studies have found that on average, gay men have more older brothers than heterosexual men and that each additional older biological brother (but not sister) increases the probability that the younger brother will be homosexual by 33 percent (Blanchard, 2001; Cantor et al, 2002, as cited in King, 2009). Blanchard and Bogaert (1996) have suggested that "the birth order effect for sexual orientation for men may be due to a reaction of the mother's immune system (to the Y chromosome chemicals) triggered by the previous male fetuses. This affects sexual differentiation of the brain as well as birth weight" (King, 2009, p. 231). Although this may give us more ideas about the biologic origins of sexual orientation, there are many gay men who are firstborns and/or have no older brothers. Thus, this explanation is certainly not definitive and does not explain the majority of those with same-sex sexual orientations. Blanchard and Bogaert's (1996) findings may explain sexual orientation in some but certainly not all individuals who are gay. Additionally, much of the research on sexual orientation has looked at men only, which is problematic when trying to explain homosexuality in general because women were mostly left out of the research.

Another biologic explanation explores the role of hormones. There is some evidence to suggest that in vivo (in the womb) girls who are exposed to large amounts of masculinizing hormones during prenatal development and boys who are exposed to large amounts of feminizing hormones during prenatal development are more likely to develop a homosexual or bisexual sexual orientation as adults. This is known as the *prenatal androgen theory* and is discussed later in this chapter, in the discussion of biological research on the transgender population. There is also a hypothesized relationship between handedness and sexual orientation. Homosexuals are more likely to be left-handed. Again, although this may be true for some gays and lesbians, it is not true for many, so we cannot conclude that we have definitively found the cause/reason for a homosexual (gay) orientation. Many researchers believe that sexual orientation, in part, is determined prenatally between the second and fifth month of pregnancy. There is not a clear explanation for why there are several sexual orientations. Most experts agree that sexual orientation, whether homo, hetero, or bisexual, is a combination of biological and environmental factors. It does appear to be that male sexual orientation tends to be more clearly defined than female; however, there are still many aspects to the sexual orientation puzzle that are unknown.

HISTORICAL AND CURRENT ATTITUDES ABOUT HOMOSEXUALITY

As discussed in Chapter 4, in ancient Greek times same-sex sexual relationships between boys and men was considered a normal part of male adolescent's developmental experience and was not considered aberrant sexual behavior. In ancient Rome, marriage between two same-sex individuals was legal among the upper class, during the time of the Roman Empire. Same-sex sexual activities were practiced in ancient Hebrew times as part of religious rites; however, during the Reformation, male homosexuality was condemned. During this same time period, lesbian behavior was dealt with less punitively because it did not involve the spillage of seed. St. Thomas Aquinas (A.D. 1225–1274) began teaching the later predominating view that sexual intercourse was for the purpose of procreation only. He emphasized that sex outside of this purpose was a sinful act and therefore concluded that homosexuality—since gays cannot procreate— is a sin against God and nature. Throughout the middle ages, though homosexuality was considered a sin, homosexuals were not overtly discriminated against as vehemently as they came to be in later times. The rise of the Victorian era (1800s) brought about the extreme discrimination of gays and lesbians. Freud referred to homosexuals as sexual perverts and Westernized medicine reinforced the view that homosexuality was a mental illness and that gays were a dangerous threat to society. As a result, gay men were subjected to horrific "treatments" to "cure" them of their homosexuality, including electric shocks to the genitals, brain frontal lobe injuries, castrations (men) or hysterectomies (women), hormone injections, and forced psychotherapy. These torturous treatments were mostly ineffective.

As discussed previously in this chapter, Kinsey's research was critical in contributing to the science on sexual orientation, as was the work of Evelyn Hooker in 1957. Previous research on gay men used subjects in prisons and psychiatric (mental) institutions. Hooker researched gay men outside of prison and mental institutionalized settings, demonstrating that the majority of gay men in her sample could not be distinguished by psychological tests from heterosexual men. In other words, her work demonstrated that gay men were just as well psychologically and emotionally adjusted as heterosexual men. Additionally, in 1973 homosexuality was no longer considered a mental disorder by the American Psychiatric Association and taken out of the DSM. In 2003, the U.S. Supreme Court removed all of the sodomy laws (laws specifically used to target male homosexual sexual behavior and arrest such males), declaring them unconstitutional. Sodomy generally refers to anal sex and was considered illegal in some states prior to 2003; although anti-sodomy laws were primarily used to discriminate against and persecute gay men, many heterosexual couples regularly engaged in sodomy (anal sex) and did so without fear of prosecution by the law. At the time of the June 2015 Supreme Court ruling supporting marriage equality for all couples, only 17 states had legalized gay marriage. Some of the 33 states that banned gay marriage also banned civil unions, which meant that same-sex relationships in these states had no legal standings and these couples had no legal rights (e.g., rights to make financial and health decisions on the part of one's spouse or romantic partner). So although some attitudes in our country are changing toward fully accepting same-sex relationships as equal to heterosexual relationships, there is still a significant amount of discrimination, harassment, and physical and psychological abuse faced by the gay community and gay couples.

Many people cite the Bible's objections to homosexuality. This is another hotly debated topic. Biblical scholars frequently debate what they believe the Bible says about homosexuality. One of the most commonly cited Biblical tales against homosexuality is the story about Sodom and Gomorrah—two ancient cities. The general story is that God found out that the citizens of Sodom and Gomorrah were engaging in sinful behaviors and evil, wicked practices. They were defying God's wishes. These behaviors included sinful sexual practices (e.g., homosexuality, adultery, sodomy). As the story goes, God was so disturbed by the widespread evil that he destroyed both cities and all the people in them. The word *sodomy* means anal or oral intercourse between human beings or humans and animals and the word *sodomy* was taken from the Biblical city of Sodom. Sodomy was also considered unnatural and a form of bestiality (sex with animals). Today, we most commonly think of sodomy as anal sex and this type of sexual activity is far more common today among gay and heterosexual couples than in previous years. The story of Sodom and Gomorrah is synonymous with sin and God's wrath and continues to be used to emphasize the idea that same-sex sexual behavior is sinful. There are other Biblical passages that scholars debate that suggest the sinful nature of homosexuality. Many individuals who are highly religious believe that homosexuality is a sin. Other highly religious individuals do not believe it is a sin. Others still struggle with conflicting feelings about whether it is a sin or not. Some gay individuals are themselves religious and frequently struggle with the idea that their behavior and identity is sinful. This will be explored further in the section of this chapter reviewing the coming out process.

THE PERCEPTION OF HOMOSEXUALITY
AROUND THE WORLD

On December 20, 2013, Uganda's Parliament passed an anti-homo-sexuality bill, requiring people to turn in suspected homosexuals: a 14-year mandatory prison sentence for a single "offense" of homosexuality and life in prison for repeated "offenses." Uganda's constitution allows the president to reject a bill from Parliament and send it back for amendment. Uganda's president Museveni recently told representatives from the Kennedy Center for Human Rights that he would not sign it if scientific evidence convinced him that gays do not have a choice in their attractions. A letter was written by psychiatrist Jack Drescher and Warren Throckmorton, a mental health professional, summarizing the scientific evidence for sexual orientation and dispelling some of the myths in biased research. Drescher and Throckmorton state:

> From a scientific perspective, the causes of homosexuality are unknown. What is known is that it is unlikely that there is one biological or genetic cause for homosexuality in all people. Some data suggest that genetic and hormonal factors during prenatal development have some impact on sexual orientation. For example, homosexuality can be found at a significantly higher rate among identical twins when compared to non-identical twins or non-twin siblings. However, the rate is not 100% among identical twins and the reasons for these differences remain unknown. We do know that faulty parenting does not play a role, nor is homosexuality a mental illness. There is little support for the idea that the majority of individuals who were sexually abused as children become gay. We also know that homosexuality is difficult if not impossible to change. The American Psychological Association (2009) issued a report that studied the peer-reviewed scientific literature to date and discovered that no study found scientific evidence that therapies designed to change sexual orientation are effective. While some individuals reported that their sexual orientation changed, the majority of individuals reported that it did not. Homosexuality is also not the same thing as pedophilia which involves sexual feelings towards, sexual fantasies about, and sexual behavior with children. In fact the significant majority of pedophiles are heterosexual, though historically, the idea that homosexuals sexually abuse children was spread around helping to heighten the discrimination against gays. (Drescher & Throckmorton, 2014)

The Pew Research Center explored attitudes about homosexuality across several countries in the spring of 2013. They found broad acceptance of homosexuality and gay rights in North America, the European Union, and much of Latin America but equally widespread rejection in predominantly Muslim nations, African, parts of Asia, and Russia. Opinions are divided in Israel, Poland, and Bolivia. The survey was conducted in 39 countries and had about 38,000 participants. Specific findings include that acceptance of homosexuality is especially widespread in countries where religion is less central to peoples' lives. In poorer countries with high levels of religiosity, few believe homosexuality should be accepted (Pew Research Center, 2013). In July 2013, Russian president Vladimir Putin signed into law a ban preventing any gay rights "propaganda" that could be accessible to minors, less than a year from the winter Olympics being hosted in Sochi, Russia (Fierstein, 2013). Although several athletes protested the ban and there was international outcry from all over the world asking for the law to be repealed, the president did not give in to the international demands. Many human rights and gay rights groups actively protested the law at the Russian Olympics. As you can see, feelings about gay marriage and individuals expressing a homosexual orientation are still mixed and controversial. While the gay community has achieved significant gains in some areas (gay marriage), they still face discrimination and hatred in others.

THE COMING OUT PROCESS

Coming out is defined as disclosing to others one's homosexual orientation, from the expression "coming out of the closet." This definition refers to the idea that given society's often negative views of homosexuality, gay individuals may try to hide the fact that they are gay, while working to accept themselves as gay. The coming out process is individual to the person going through it. For example, some individuals really struggle with what it means to be gay and how to express his or her gay identity. Others embrace their gay identity very early and do not seem to have an issue acknowledging that they are gay. There are several factors influencing the coming out process. They include the following: how supportive the individual's peer group and family is; one's own perceptions, ideas about and experiences being gay; one's religious beliefs, and how an individual believes he/she will be perceived. The coming out process is in many ways a lifelong process because not everyone a gay individual comes into contact with will know he or she is gay. Individuals have to make decisions such as the following: Do I put a picture of my same-sex partner/spouse on my desk at work? Do I bring my same-sex partner/spouse to a holiday party? Should I tell my parents/grandparents/peer group that I am gay? These are all decisions that have to be made. Such questions make the coming out process a lifelong process. There have been several stage models proposed for the coming out process that describe it as a developmental experience (similar to Erikson's psychosocial developmental model). For example, Cass (1979) came up with one of the first developmental models to describe the coming out process, underscoring the idea that gays and lesbians have to "come out" against a backdrop of heterosexism (strong societal preference toward heterosexual orientation leading to the automatic assumption that everyone is heterosexual and that the heterosexual orientation is the only "normal" orientation). Her model includes the following stages: identity confusion, identity comparison, identity tolerance, identity acceptance, identity pride, and identity synthesis. Each stage describes how a person learns to understand and accept oneself as being gay. An individual understands that sexual orientation is an important (but not only) part of who he/she is and that sexual orientation goes beyond sexual behavior. For some it describes their affiliation with others (e.g., gay culture) and their understanding of themselves. Not everyone gets through all of the stages. Individuals stuck in the earlier stages may not accept themselves as gay and may only see their sexual orientation as a problematic behavior ("I am attracted to men but I am not gay"). This model has implications for one's self-confidence and self-esteem in that those who embrace themselves and accept their identity may be considered more psychologically healthy than others who do not.

TRANSGENDER, TRANSSEXUAL, INTERSEXUAL, TRANSVESTIC FETISHISM, AND DRAG QUEENS

The above terms are only grouped together because they are frequently confused with one another—not because they all bear similarity to one another. This section will clarify these terms and describe how our society views individuals who fall into these categories. As stated earlier, society tends to view gender in a dichotomous way. Male and female genders are viewed as discrete categories with little to no room for variation. For some individuals, however, their gender identity does not match their biologic sex. One example of this would be if a female was born with normal, female genitalia, yet overwhelmingly felt that she was male. For an individual who is *transgender*, he or she strongly believes that he/she was born into the wrong body. Thus, although a biologic female may have female genitalia, she may from early childhood always believed (and sometimes behaved in stereotypic male ways) that she was a male. Many transgender individuals believe that they are *assigned* a gender at birth (based on the appearance of that individual's genitalia) that is inconsistent with who he/she actually is. There is a significant body of research that points to biological reasons someone might be transgender. During pregnancy, the brain and genitalia are masculinized or feminized. In other words, the brain and genitalia are subjected to large amounts of male or female hormones so that the developing fetus becomes biologically and psychologically male (masculinizing) or female (feminizing). At the start of pregnancy, the only difference between a male and a female embryo is that the male embryo contains XY chromosomes and female embryos contain XX chromosomes. This is the beginning of gender determination but the process takes months to complete. During the first two trimesters the fetus has the potential for both male and female genitalia. Fetuses contain Mullerian and Wolffian duct systems. In some ways, nature preprograms all fetuses to be female. For example, if the fetus will be female, development will proceed without any activation of sex hormones. During the third trimester of pregnancy, sex hormones are activated. If the fetus has a Y chromosome, male hormones (androgens) will turn the fetus into a male with fully developed male genitalia. The Y chromosome contains a gene called testis determining factor, which contributes to the construction of the testes. The testes secrete testosterone, which masculinizes the Wolffian (male) duct system to continue the development of male genitalia. In conjunction with the release of testosterone, a hormone is released to inhibit or destroy the Mullerian (female) duct system. If the fetus is female (has an X chromosome), however, the Mullerian duct system develops into female genitalia, without the assistance of sex hormones. Without the Y chromosome and androgens, the fetus will develop as a female, which also results in the feminization of the developing brain. The Y chromosome and androgens result in the masculinization of the male brain (Wilson & Rahman, 2005). This is known as the prenatal androgen theory. There is significant research that points to an incomplete masculinization or feminization of the brain as one of the causes of a transgender identity. In other words, the genitalia is expressed as male (or female) but the brain may be gender discrepant (e.g., the genitalia is male but the brain has been feminized or exposed to female hormones). This might result in a person feeling gender incongruent or gender dysphoric. A person may feel he or she were born with the wrong genitalia and that genitalia does not match his or her gender identity.

While *transgender* refers to an individual who feels as if he/she was born into the wrong body or his or her brain and physical body (genitalia) do not match, the term *transsexual* frequently refers to a person who strongly identifies with the opposite sex and may seek to *live* as a member of this sex, especially by undergoing surgery and hormone therapy to obtain the necessary physical appearance (as by changing the external sex organs). Thus, it might be viewed that an individual may start as transgender but eventually become transsexual if he/she wishes to and seeks out means to (e.g., dressing as a member of the sex in which they believe they are, having surgery) fully become gender congruent (their genitalia, physical body, and psychological identification of being male or female all match).

The prenatal androgen theory explores some of the potential determinants of transgender and sexual orientation. It hypothesizes that the androgen receptor protein plays a significant role in determining male sexual development, especially in the brain. The androgen receptor dictates the actions of sex hormones. The prenatal androgen theory suggests that different levels of testosterone exposure influence "the structure and function of brain regions that control the direction of sexual attraction" (Wilson & Rahman, 2005, p. 70). This theory proposes that homosexual males are exposed to less testosterone than heterosexual males and female homosexuals are exposed to more testosterone than heterosexual females. This theory is an incomplete explanation, however, because it does not explain why some traits in homosexual males appear "hyper-masculine" instead of feminized. Wilson and Rahman (2005) believe that one explanation of this is if testosterone fails to bind with the enzyme 5-alpha-reductase or aromatase, hyper-masculine traits may result from a residue of testosterone in other parts of the brain and/or body.

According to the *Diagnostic and Statistical Manual*, version 5 (DSM-5), which is the document mental health professionals use to diagnose mental health, being transgender is based on having *gender dysphoria*, a condition in which an individual is very unhappy about his or her biologic sex. The American Psychiatric Association makes it clear that gender nonconformity is not in itself a mental disorder. The critical element of gender dysphoria is the presence of clinically significant distress associated with the condition. In DSM-IV-TR, the earlier version of the DSM, being transgender meant that a person was diagnosed with *gender identity disorder*; however, as the science and our understanding of transgender evolved to include more biological explanations for why transgender exists, gender identity disorder was taken out of DSM-5 and renamed gender dysphoria. This is to acknowledge that gender incongruence is not necessarily a mental disorder: an individual who is gender incongruent is frequently distressed or dysphoric (profound state of unease/dissatisfaction) about it. This dysphoria often comes from society's strong views that gender is dichotomous and society's lack of understanding and acceptance of gender diversity as well as the experience of sexual minorities. The American Psychiatric Association explains gender dysphoria in these terms. For a person to be diagnosed with gender dysphoria, there must be a marked difference between the individual's expressed/experienced gender and the gender others would assign him or her, and it must continue for at least 6 months. In children, the desire to be of the other gender must be present and verbalized. This condition causes clinically significant distress or impairment in social, occupational, or other important areas of functioning. Gender dysphoria is manifested in a variety of ways, including strong desires to be treated as the other gender or to be rid of one's sex characteristics, or a strong conviction that one has feelings and reactions typical of the other gender. The DSM-5 diagnosis adds a post-transition specifier for people who are living full time as the desired gender (with or without legal sanction of the gender change). This ensures treatment access for individuals who continue to undergo hormone therapy, related surgery, or psychotherapy or counseling to support their gender transition (American Psychiatric Association, 2013).

Intersexual is a term that refers to those individuals whose variation in gonads, chromosomes, and/or genitals do not allow for distinct identification as male or female. One explanation is that the gender differentiation process (that identifies one's psychological gender and genitalia as male or female) is incomplete. Unlike with a person who is transgender, an individual who is intersexed may have ambiguous genitalia. Research shows that gender identification as male or female is completely independent of sexual orientation. In 2013, Germany became the first European nation to allow babies with characteristics of both males and females to be labeled as *indeterminent gender* on their birth certificates. There is a movement in the medical community to view intersexed traits as normal biological (although rare) variation instead of an abnormality.

Transvestite or its full name *transvestic fetishism* is frequently confused with the above terms (*transgender, transsexual,* and *intersexual*) as well as *drag queen*; however, these terms have very different meanings. In the DSM-5, transvestic fetishism is described as an individual (most typically a heterosexual male), over a period of at least 6 months, has recurrent and intense sexual fantasies, sexual urges, or sexual behaviors involving cross-dressing (dressing in stereotypically female clothing). The fantasies, sexual urges, or behaviors cause clinically significant distress or impairment in social, occupational, or other important areas of functioning.

Thus, transvestic fetishism or being a transvestite is classified as a mental disorder. The term *drag queen* typically refers to gay men who dress up in stereotypical female clothing for the purposes of entertainment. The term *drag queen* does not denote a mental disorder. Gay or heterosexual men who dress up as women for the purposes of entertainment or fun (e.g., Halloween) would not be labeled with a disorder. A man (usually heterosexual) who dresses up in female clothing for the purposes of sexual arousal might be labeled as a transvestite (transvestic fetishism). These terms were discussed together in this section because people often confuse them and get their meanings mixed up. As you can see, however, these terms are highly distinct and have very different meanings.

COMMUNICATION ABOUT SEX

Thus far in this chapter, we have covered several topics that have illustrated many aspects of sex, sexual issues, and sexual identities that are relevant to our everyday lives. The final section of this chapter will cover topics that more directly explore how sex, sexual behavior, and sexual morals and values impacts who we are as sexual beings. As we explored in Chapter 1, most individuals' parents did not consistently nor comprehensively talk to them about sex. Additionally, most people felt that their formal education (in a school setting) about sexual issues and sexual health was also lacking. This may be one of the reasons most people find it difficult to communicate with romantic partners about sex. For many people, open communication about sex brings about embarrassment and anxiety. We communicate with our partners about sex both verbally and nonverbally, and directly and indirectly. We will now explore some ways communication about sex occurs in relationships.

Most experts agree that the majority of communication (approximately 93 percent) is nonverbal. We communicate through our tone of voice, emphasis on particular words, facial expression, physical touch, as well as the amount of physical space between ourselves and the individual with whom we are communicating. Communication also takes place in overt (direct) and covert (indirect) ways. With these multiple ways of communicating, sometimes the receiver of the message misinterprets the message. Sometimes conflict can occur due to misunderstandings. Most communication about sex between romantic or potential romantic partners is nonverbal. Nonverbal communication is at an especially high risk for being misunderstood; however, many people are simply too uncomfortable about direct verbal sexual communication. Research demonstrates that women tend to be more competent at reading nonverbal communication.

Nonverbal communication is reliant upon physical cues (e.g., touch), smiling, facial expression, raising of eyebrows, and so forth. The three most important forms of nonverbal communication are proximity, eye contact, and touching. In Chapter 1, we explored dating and sexual scripts (schemas or cognitive frameworks that help us organize information). Much of communication and the assumptions we make about the specific sexual messages we are sending as well as what we expect from the receiver is shaped by our sexual and dating scripts. These scripts are shaped by past experiences, messages we have received about sex from the media, peers, and our families, as well as our feelings about sexual selves. Also, these scripts are based on heterosexual relationship models. Gay couples may develop different scripts. For example, if a man approaches a woman sitting at a bar and offers to buy her a drink, what might we predict would happen? If she accepts his offer, what message does this send him? In a typical heterosexual dating script, a man approaches a woman, and offers to buy her a drink. If she says yes, this may denote her interest in him. If she says no then she is probably not interested in him. All of this has happened without directly verbally communicating interest. If she accepts his drink, they begin a conversation and she touches his arm, which also sends a message. Finally, if he asks for her phone number and she gives it to him, this sends yet another message. The problem with relying upon unspoken messages is the high potential for miscommunication. At the end of a date, if a couple is kissing and touching, this may signal that the couple may be headed toward sexual intercourse. On the other hand, maybe one member of the couple only wants to kiss and touch but not go any further. Again, most communication around sexual issues is nonverbal.

This is potentially problematic because women are frequently socialized to turn down sex early in a relationship and men are often socialized to try to convince a woman to have sex. Both are usually aware of this gendered expectation. If a couple follow this script without discussing what they individually want, it could (in rare cases) lead to one person pushing for sex against the other's will. This would be known as *date rape*, which sometimes happens when couples get their signals crossed or when sex is not mutually desired. It can also happen when one person disregards the other's wishes *not* to have sex and forces the other person into intercourse. This is a crime and can be devastating for the individual who was forced into having sex against his or her will. This topic will be covered more extensively in Chapter 3.

There are several barriers to effective sexual communication. They include *bypassing* (all of us attach different meaning to words), *frame of reference* (one's frame of reference is dependent upon one's own unique experiences), *lack of language skills* (not knowing or having the words to communicate about sex directly), *lack of listening skills* (we often selectively listen and interpret messages to our own advantage), and *mind-altering drugs* (the use of drugs or alcohol are powerful barriers to communication and frequently skew the message being sent and received) (Guffey, 1999, as cited in Greenberg, Bruess, & Conklin, 2011). Other things shaping our communication about sex include our understanding and expectation of gender roles, gender expectations, and our attitudes about sexuality. For example, some people are prevented from communicating openly about sexuality because of attitudes they learned growing up. If parents and families did not talk to their children and teens about sex, it is projected as a taboo topic and as the children grow up, they may not have the language or confidence to talk to their romantic partners about sex. As individuals develop sexual relationships·with romantic partners, they may make assumptions (as opposed to directly communicating) about what pleases the other person and what the sexual values and agreed-upon rules are for their relationship, as well as when the couple experiences sexual problems. When children are encouraged to ask questions about sex in the home and parents engage in open age-appropriate dialogues about sex with their children, the children grow up with more confidence about sexual issues and sexual communication, and they have a language for communicating about sex. Chapter 5 discusses direct suggestions on how to talk to children about sex in age-appropriate ways.

THE IMPORTANCE OF SEXUAL AND NONSEXUAL TOUCHING IN ROMANTIC RELATIONSHIPS

Touching in a romantic partnership usually conveys our sense of love, connectedness, and caring with our partners. Nonsexual touches are as—if not more—important than sexual touches. Nonsexual touches can sometimes indicate how close a couple feels to one another, though this is not always the case. Some people are raised in households where touching and cuddling are the norm, while others are not. Both are normal and acceptable. Touching and cuddling behavior is often shaped by cultural norms and by the stage of a romantic relationship. For example, it is not uncommon for couples newly dating or newly in love to touch more than couples who have been together for longer periods of time. This is not necessarily indicative of problems in the older couple. It just may indicate that the couple is at a different stage in their relationship than the couple who have not been together as long. In Chapter 3, relationship stages will be discussed in more detail. Nonsexual touching can include things like holding hands, a gentle back or foot rub, hugs, cuddling with one another in bed or on the couch, as well as other types of touching. Nonsexual touching conveys a sense of caring for one's partner and they tend to be meant and received as acts of affection.

Although nonsexual touching can lead to sexual touching, it does not have to. Sexual touching is usually directed toward increasing desire. It may include the touching of breasts, genitalia, kissing, massage, oral sex, finger stimulation of genitals, and other types of sexual touching. Sexual touching is usually meant to end in sexual intercourse. It may be known as *foreplay* or sexual stimulation preceding sexual intercourse.

OXYTOCIN: THE BONDING HORMONE

People enjoy having sex because it feels good and it allows us to feel emotionally and physically closer to our romantic partners. Recent research has discovered a biological basis for this, called *oxytocin*, also known as the bonding hormone. Oxytocin is involved in the neuroanatomy of intimacy, specifically in sexual reproduction during and after childbirth and also helps to stimulate lactation (breast feeding). Oxytocin is released in large amounts during and after labor for maternal bonding directly after the baby is born. Oxytocin is also implicated in orgasm, social recognition, and romantic pair bonding during and directly after sex. Physical effects of oxytocin include increased sensitivity of nerve endings, stimulated muscle contractions, increased heart rate plus an urge to touch and cuddle. The emotional feelings it produces are associated with affection, bonding, caring, love, peace, nurturing, security, attachment, and even the afterglow of sex. It is true that both men and women feel the effects of oxytocin but do so to varying degrees. It is believed that men's levels of oxytocin rise about three to five times during orgasm, but women's levels rise even more dramatically and continue to rise during subsequent orgasms. Women's brains also have more oxytocin neural receptors, and pregnancy may increase the number of receptors. Women's special connection with oxytocin may have wide-ranging influences. Some research suggests that the regret many women often feel after casual sex may be tied to increased oxytocin levels and a need for physical touch after sexual intercourse that goes unfulfilled because there is no continued physical contact after a brief sexual encounter. Additional studies imply that some women may have more addictive relationship patterns because they feel love and loss in relationships more intensely (Kalafut, 2008). Clearly, we know that strong feelings often strongly impact sexual intimacy. These are some hypotheses about how oxytocin affects feelings of emotional closeness and intimacy. Researchers are still exploring this powerful hormone's impact on human sexual and relational behavior.

CONCLUSION

In this chapter we have explored the many ways in which sex and sexual issues impact us on a daily basis, including our worldviews, gender roles, sexual orientation, sexual identity, the role of oxytocin in bonding, and sexual and nonsexual touching. Sexuality is also a powerful influence on our dating and romantic lives. We will continue to explore how sex impacts us in both positive and negative ways in Chapter 3.

REFERENCES

American Psychiatric Association. (2013). *Gender dysphoria*. Retrieved from http://www.dsm5.org/Documents/Gender%20Dysphoria%20Fact%20Sheet.pdf.

Bailey, J. M., et al. (1993). Heritable factors influence sexual orientation in women. *Archives of General Psychiatry, 50,* 217–223.

Bailey, J. M., & Pillard, R. C. (1991). A genetic study of male sexual orientation. *Archives of General Psychiatry, 48,* 1089–1096.

Blanchard, R. (2001). Fraternal birth order and the maternal immune hypothesis of male homosexuality. *Hormones and Behavior, 40,* 105–114.

Blanchard, R., & Bogaert, A. F. (1996). Homosexuality in men and number of older brothers. *American Journal of Psychiatry, 153,* 27–31.

Campbell, T. (2014, March 6). Touching men's sexy boxer shorts activates brain's reward system in women, study suggest. *The Huffington Post.* Retrieved from http://www.huffingtonpost.com/2014/03/06/touching-boxer-women-think-differently_n_4906315.html.

Cantor, J. M., et al. (2002). How many gay men owe their sexual orientation to fraternal birth order? *Archives of Sexual Behavior, 31,* 67–71.

Cass, V. C. (1979). Homosexual identity formation: A theoretical model. *Journal of Homosexuality, 4,* 219–235.

Cochran, S. D., & Mays, V. M. (2000). Relation between psychiatric syndromes and behaviorally defined sexual orientation in a sample of the U.S. population. *American Journal of Epidemiology, 151,* 516–523.

Diamond, L. M. (2005). A new view of lesbian subtypes: Stable versus fluid identity trajectories over an 8-year period. *Psychology of Women Quarterly, 29,* 119–128.

Diamond, L. M. (2008). Female bisexuality from adolescence to adulthood: Results from a 10-year longitudinal study. *Developmental Psychology, 44,* 5–14.

Drescher, J., & Throckmorton, W. (2014, February). Letter to the president of Uganda. Message posted to cesnet-1@listserv.kent.edu. Listserve for Counselor Education and Supervision.

Fierstein, H. (2013, July 21). Russia's anti-gay crackdown. *The New York Times.* Retrieved from http://www.nytimes.com/2013/07/22/opinion/russias-anti-gay-crackdown.html?_r=0.

Garnets, L. D., & Peplau, L. A. (2001). A new paradigm for women's sexual orientation: Implications for therapy. *Women and Therapy, 24,* 111–121.

Greenberg, J. S., Bruess, C. E., & Conklin, S. C. (2011). *Exploring the dimensions of human sexuality* (4th ed.). Sudbury, MA: Jones and Bartlett.

Guffey, M. E. (1999). *Business communication: Process and product* (3rd ed.). Belmont, CA: Wadsworth.

Kalafut, M. (2008). *Oxytocin: 'The cuddle & love hormone'.* Retrieved from http://molly.kalafut.org/misc/oxytocin.html. Weblog comment.

King, B. R. (2009). *Human sexuality today* (6th ed.). Upper Saddle River, NJ: Pearson Education.

Kinnish, K. K., Strassberg, D. S., & Turner, C. W. (2005). Sex differences in the flexibility of sexual orientation: A multidimensional retrospective assessment. *Archives of Sexual Behavior, 34,* 173–183.

Kinsey, A. C. (1948). *Sexual behavior in the human male.* Philadelphia, PA: W.B. Saunders.

Pew Research Center (2013, June 4). The global divide on homosexuality: Greater acceptance in more secular and affluent countries. *Global Attitudes & Trends.* Retrieved from http://www.pewglobal.org/2013/06/04/the-global-divide-on-homosexuality/.

Turner, C. F., et al. (2005). Same-gender sex among U.S. adults: Trends across the twentieth century and during the 1990s. *Public Opinion Quarterly, 69,* 439–462.

Wilson, G., & Rahman, Q. (2005). *Born gay: The psychobiology of sex orientation.* London: Peter Owen.

3

---❖---

How: The Positive and Negative Effects of Sex

This chapter will explore ways in which sex impacts our mental, psychological, and emotional health for better or worse. Specifically, the chapter will provide an overview of the biological basis for sexual motivation, how love and lust can sometimes get mixed up, and how sexual behavior can impact us emotionally. Additionally, other positive and negative consequences of sex will be explored.

THE BIOLOGICAL BASIS OF SEX

From the first two chapters, we know that sex has social, emotional, and psychological consequences; however, these consequences begin within a biological framework. Sexual arousal is in part based in a small but important brain structure called the *hypothalamus*. This part of the brain regulates the release of hormones from the pituitary gland. The *pituitary gland* is located at the base of the brain and secretes several important hormones relevant to reproduction, sexual arousal, and the development of secondary sexual characteristics during puberty (e.g., pubic hair, breast development). The brain is known as the most sexual organ in the human body because sexual desire, arousal, and pleasure have its basis in the brain. "The brain translates nerve impulses from the skin into pleasurable sensations, controls the nerves and muscles used in sexual behavior, regulates the release of hormones necessary for reproduction and is the origin of our sexual desires" (King, 2009, p. 55). Although several areas of the brain are involved in sexual functioning, the hypothalamus is the most important part. The hypothalamus is a small structure located at the base of the brain consisting of several nerve cell bodies. It receives information from the *limbic system* (which is known as the emotional system of the brain). The limbic system forms a border between the central part of the brain and the outer part (cerebral cortex), which includes structures such as the amygdala, hippocampus, cingulate gyrus, the fornix, and the septum. A group of studies with monkeys found that when an electrode was inserted in certain areas of the brain to deliver electrical stimulation, this stimulation produced erections (MacLean, 1962; Van Dis & Larsson, 1971, as cited in Shibley Hyde & DeLamater, 2003). Three erection centers were found in the limbic system. Similar results have been found with humans. Other studies have found that when a particular anterior portion of the hypothalamus is stimulated in males, their sexual behavior increases significantly. If this region is destroyed, they lose all sexual interest in copulation. Research also demonstrates that when men are shown erotic films, several limbic structures became active by the erotic films. These are known as the brain's "pleasure centers." Clearly, this research shows that sex is located in the brain first and the physical body second.

One classic study discovering the brain's pleasure centers (Olds & Milner, 1954) found that when electrodes were implanted in the brains of rats and were wired so that a rat could stimulate its own brain by pressing a lever (specifically the septal region and hypothalamus), the rats would press the lever thousands of time per hour and would forgo food and sleep to stimulate these regions (Shibley Hyde & DeLamater, 2003). These researchers found that the location of these pleasure centers are very close to the sex centers, which may explain why sexual experiences are so intensely pleasurable (Shibley Hyde & DeLamater, 2003). Other research has found that there are "rage" or "aggression" centers of the brain (i.e., when stimulated animals go into a rage and attack anything in their cages). These centers are close to the sex and pleasure centers, which might explain the association of sex and aggression in rape and competition over mates (MacLean, 1962, as cited in Shibley Hyde & DeLamater, 2003).

Hormones also play a crucial role in sexual behavior, desire, reproduction, and sexual growth and development. *Hormones* are chemical substances that are released into our bloodstream by ductless glands and carried to other parts of the body to exact certain effects. For example, the beginning of the menstrual cycle is in large part based on the release of certain hormones. The hormonal network of ductless glands is known as the *endocrine system.* Male and female hypothalamus's differ because of the amount of testosterone males have versus females. Testosterone changes the hypothalamus. Sex hormones impact the anatomy of the brain.

Sexual responses are controlled by many factors, including spinal reflexes, psychological forces (e.g., fantasy), and environmental (being raised in a household where sex is considered dirty) and physiological (e.g., hormonal) factors. The multiple influences of these factors demonstrate the complexity of the brain's control of human's sexual responses. In Chapter 5 we will discuss the sexual response cycle, which includes the stages desire (lust), excitement (arousal), plateau, orgasm, and resolution (in men). The sexual response cycle is controlled by and its basis in the brain.

GENDER DIFFERENCES IN EMOTIONAL EXPRESSION

Gender stereotypes enhance commonly held societal beliefs that women are more emotional than men. There has been a great deal of research on emotional differences between men and women. Research shows that when measured with an affect (emotional) intensity measure, women report greater intensity of both positive and negative emotion than men. Women also reported experiencing a wider range of, greater intensity of, and more frequent emotions, both positive and negative than men. For example, women in one study reported experiencing more intense and frequent joy, embarrassment, guilt, shame, sadness, anger, fear, and distress. Men, however, reported experiencing more pride than women. It would be difficult to determine *why* women reported experiencing more intense emotions than men because the reasons are probably numerous. For example, it may be that there is little biologic difference (i.e., in the brain) between men and women when it comes to the experience of emotion but society is clearly more accepting of women's greater range of emotional expression than men's. When interpreting these data, it is important to remember that society sanctions women's emotional expression much more than men's. Societally, women are "allowed" to and expected to experience fear, shame, guilt, vulnerability, and a wider range of emotions than are men. In this way, society consistently reinforces the idea that women are more emotional than men. When boys are young, they are socialized to believe that "big boys" and/or men don't cry. To do so means that the boy is not manly, is effeminate, or is weak, which is a significant taboo against masculinity. Boys and men are socialized to appear competent, knowledgeable, rational, and nonemotional most of the time. Thus, in interpreting the data that women report experiencing more emotions and more intense emotions than men, one really needs to consider the strongly gendered emotional socialization process when exploring the differences between male and female emotional expression. It may be that men and women experience similar emotions in similar circumstances but society does not allow men to express these emotions as much as it does women. Therefore, this may influence the way male subjects in experiments on emotional experiencing report their actual emotions.

There may, however, be some brain differences in the ways that men and women process emotions. For example, women show greater activity in the amygdala when storing and remembering emotionally arousing pictures (e.g., a bloody murder scene). Men and women also may use different neural pathways when storing information in memory. Women are more likely to use the left cerebral hemisphere than men when shown emotionally arousing pictures and men were more likely to use the right hemisphere. Research also demonstrates that there are sex differences in pain responses: women are more likely to use the limbic system (the emotional centers of the brain) when responding to pain and men are more likely to use the cognitive areas of the brain. Thus, for women, there may be more of a connection between pain responsiveness and emotions than men.

It has been demonstrated that women are also more likely to take on the problems and emotions of those around them, which may be one of the many reasons women report higher levels of depression than men. There is a great deal of literature exploring the gender differences between men and women and the ways they express emotions. These explanations explore social, cognitive, cultural, psychological, and physiological realms; however, so far, there is no clear-cut explanation for why men and women express emotions differently.

SEXUAL INTERCOURSE AND EMOTION

Because men and women may express and even interpret emotional data differently, this may explain why each may have different emotional reactions when sexual intercourse is introduced into relationships. Men are more likely in some circumstances to be able to separate sex from love. Social scientist Russell Vannoy (1980, as cited in King, 2009) argues that love is unnecessary and sex can and should be enjoyed for its own sake; however, the predominating value in the United States is that sexual relations should be reserved for emotionally close romantic relationships. Many women report that they find sex un-enjoyable outside the confines of a loving relationship. Men are more likely than women to enjoy sex without emotional involvement. The hook up culture may change the societal view that sex and relationships go together, but this is still the predominant view. There may be many reasons for this. Some experts point to evolutionary explanations to explain why women tend to prefer to have sex within emotionally attached relationships. In evolutionary psychology, the two most important goals are survival and the reproduction of one's offspring (which in many ways ensures one's survival over multiple generations). From an evolutionary perspective, men may be driven to propagate their genes with different, women thereby ensuring that their genes live on. Women, on the other hand, have to ensure that they pick the best mate possible because they have to carry the offspring, which takes a great deal of time and effort—therefore, they had better make the best choice possible in terms of mate. Men, since they cannot ever really know (remember DNA testing did not exist in ancient times) if the offspring is 100 percent theirs, may feel the need to have as many children as possible to propagate their genes. These evolutionary explanations have been used to explain why men are more likely to cheat than women as well as why men are more likely to rape than are women. Although evolutionary explanations may provide some interesting theoretical explanations to ponder, they do not explain everything. For example, how would these theories explain the fact that many men are faithful to their partners? What would be the explanation for women who cheat?

Other explanations for why men and women may interpret emotions around sexual behavior may include the societal expectation that men are more inherently sexual then women (e.g., want sex more often), women release a bonding hormone during and after sex (oxytocin), and women are more desirous of romantic relationships than are men.

When two people have different expectations regarding a relationship, hurt feelings can happen. Let's say that two college students, both ages 20, decide to have a FWB (friends with benefits) relationship in which they have casual sex without an emotional commitment or the expectation of mutual monogamy. If one person begins to have strong feelings for the other, this not only impacts their relationship but can cause hurt feelings if romantic intentions for more than just a FWB is desired. Sex often changes a relationship that was previously nonsexual because it can change expectations surrounding the relationship as well as enhance the individuals' feelings toward one another.

As stated above, there often are emotional consequences when sex is introduced into a relationship. Having sex too young may not prepare us to deal with these issues. When a relationship turns sexual, some individuals may experience feelings of lust, love, jealousy, attraction, confusion, hurt, shame, and insecurity as well as many other emotional reactions. These emotions can be frustrating and scary because they are powerful and have a distinct impact on our behavior. These can be the negative consequences to having sex. Many people find it difficult to cope with these feelings because they make them feel vulnerable and open to getting hurt. When our feelings of attraction, like love and lust, are returned in equal measure by our partners, we feel good about ourselves and the relationship. When these feelings are not returned, we can feel angry, hurt, rejected, and ashamed. People can deal with these feelings in a variety of ways. When one feels wronged by a sexual partner one can put up an emotional wall to deal with hurt by telling one's self that he/she does not really care (even though he/she does).

Obviously, there are benefits to having sex. It can be a deep expression of love and caring between two people. It can increase bonding in the relationship and it can be a special expression of affection unique to a committed romantic relationship. It is also a physical and emotional expression of lust and attraction. Sex is a great exercise that can be fun and relaxing and increase one's sense of well being (orgasms have health benefits). It is also an expression of one's self. Consensual sex can be a wonderful way two people connect to one another. Sexuality is a healthy part of life. This chapter will continue to explore the positive and negative consequences of sex.

ATTRACTION

Interpersonal attraction is the desire to approach someone. It is at the fundamental basis of attraction (Miller, 2012). Attraction is based on a direct and indirect reward system. For example, direct rewards are based on the pleasure we as individuals receive when someone shows interest in us. This interest makes us feel good about ourselves. We get a self-esteem boost from others' complimentary behavior toward us and may even feel a sense of power because someone wants us/is attracted to us. Indirect rewards are more subtle. They include things like passing on potential advantages to our offspring (e.g., finding a partner who is smart so that you will have smart offspring). Indirect rewards, although equally important as direct ones, are frequently unconscious. Attraction is complicated and influenced by many things, including proximity (how nearby someone is), perceived familiarity and similarity, beauty/handsomeness, reciprocity (liking those who like us), as well as many other factors.

PROXIMITY

Multiple studies show that we are more likely to make friends and have romantic relationships with individuals who are physically close to us. College students are more likely to make friends with other students who sit by them in class versus sitting across the room. One hypothesis for why physical proximity makes such a difference is that when an individual is near to us, it makes it easier for us to access the rewards he/she has to offer. Distant relationships are less rewarding. Research does not support the assertion that "absence makes the heart grow fonder." Physical proximity also increases our exposure to the person, which in turn makes us feel a sense of *similarity* and *familiarity*. Research demonstrates the *mere exposure effect*, which states that mere exposure increases our liking for another individual (Zajonc, 2001, as cited in Miller, 2012). Repeated contact then makes a person seem more attractive to us.

Proximity does have its limits. Overexposure to another individual can decrease feelings of liking and attraction. Proximity to a dislikable or obnoxious person will not increase feelings of liking or attraction toward another. If a physically close individual is problematic (dislikable), it will increase our feelings of dislike toward that person. Thus, it seems that physical proximity can enhance feelings of attraction as well as feelings of dislike (Miller, 2012).

One of the first things we notice about someone is how he or she looks. Physical attraction has a significant impact on one's first impression of another person. Research demonstrates that "we tend to assume that good-looking people are more likeable and better people than those who are unattractive" (Brewer & Archer, 2007, as cited in Miller, 2012, p. 74). Society tends to have a *beauty bias*, which is the assumption that what is beautiful is good. Studies show that when subjects view photos of attractive and non-attractive people, they judge the attractive people to be more intelligent, be more engaging, and have more positive personality traits versus the non-attractive individuals. Attractive people may be presumed to be more interesting and sociable and professionally successful than non-attractive individuals (Miller, 2012). We tend to make these judgments without conscious awareness or thought. This is one of the reasons the beauty bias is so powerful. More attractive people tend to make more money than average or non-attractive people. Although intelligence influences one's future earnings more than one's physical attractiveness, physical attractiveness is obviously still an influential variable. From an evolutionary psychology point of view, this bias lies in the brain. As human beings were evolving, attractiveness was seen as a sign of health and fertility. Symmetry of features (e.g., width of eyes, nose, and mouth in one's face) is a universal feature of attractiveness. Although beauty is no longer considered a health variable, it is possible that our brains continue to be hardwired to gravitate toward attractive people. The beauty bias is culturally universal, as in what we consider physically attractive in the first place. Although there is some cultural variation in what is considered beautiful, there is far more consensus across cultures than disagreement about what makes an individual attractive (Miller, 2012). Even babies tend to look at attractive faces longer than unattractive ones long before they have a chance to be socially influenced by social/cultural determinants of attraction.

Women with large eyes, a small nose and chin, and full lips tend to be considered universally attractive all over the world. Men with strong jaws, broad foreheads—those who look "strong and dominant"—are assumed to be more attractive than men with more feminized faces. For example, George Clooney and Brad Pitt are thought to be universally attractive. Men with slightly more feminine faces are thought to be attractive too, as their faces are considered "warm and friendly" (Miller, 2012). Research demonstrates that when heterosexual women are ovulating (fertile), they prefer "ruggedly handsome" men. The rest of the month they report being more attracted to boyish good looks.

Certain body types also tend to be rated as more or less physically attractive. For example, heterosexual men tend to rate women's body shape as highly attractive when they are of normal weight (not too heavy or slender) and their waists are noticeably slimmer than their hips (Furnham, Swami, & Shah, 2006, as cited in Miller, 2012). This is known as a *waist-to-hip ratio* (WHR) and the most attractive WHR is the "hourglass figure" (0.7 where the waist is 30 percent smaller than the hips). The preferred male body type tends to be when men's waists are only slightly narrower than their hips (WHR of 0.9) combined with broad shoulders and muscles. Heterosexual men with this body type actually have sex with more women at earlier ages than those with lower shoulder-to-hip ratios (Frederick et al., 2007)! This is true around the world. Men's attractiveness to women, however, is also considered with their resources. Heterosexual men with more financial resources tend to do better in the dating pool than those with fewer resources regardless of their shoulder-to-hip ratios. Finally, universally, heterosexual men and women tend to prefer that the male partner be taller than his female counterpart. In the United States, height is considered an attractiveness variable for men. Taller men earn more money on average than do shorter men.

The way a person smells can also influence how attractive we find that person. Women tend to be more influenced by the smell of male partners. Research has found that study participants apparently find the smell of attractive (symmetrical faced) individuals more attractive than nonattractive or average people. Other universal attractiveness features include the length of a women's hair (longer is considered more attractive by most men), male chest hair (women prefer smoother, less hairy chests), intelligence (women tend to prefer smarter partners), and the color red (is considered attractive on both men and women).

Although the above features of attractiveness have been researched, there is still a great deal about attraction and attractiveness that we do not understand. Individual differences in what each person finds attractive is less well studied. Also, attractiveness studies contain an inherent hetero-sexual bias in that participants are usually assumed to be heterosexual and thus attracted to the opposite sex. There is little literature on what same-sex couples or bisexual individuals find attractive.

BODY IMAGE

Most people are very much aware of what society considers attractive. The majority of the population may not meet the beauty ideal. For some, this can cause feelings of low self-worth, insecurity, and confidence issues. This is especially true for women given that society tends to be harsher in its evaluation of women's bodies than it is for men. This may be because men are often judged (in addition to their physical attractiveness) on their financial resources and/or physical height. Thus, some men without finan-cial resources may struggle with some self-image issues similar to some women who do not meet society's body ideal. It is well known that young girls who regularly read fashion magazines are more likely to have body image issues and express negative feelings about their own bodies versus young girls who do not read these magazines. It is important to remember that there is inherent beauty in all body types. Not everyone can or should meet the "ideal body type." Individuals who are accepting of their bodies, regardless of specific body type, tend to feel good about themselves.

SEXISM

In earlier chapters we explored gender stereotypes and the influence of sex-ism on these stereotypes. One of the ways sexism can influence sexual rela-tionships is the double standard society tends to hold for men's and women's sexual behavior. For example, women with "too many" (this number is influenced by culture and age as to what is considered "too many") sexual partners may be considered "sluts" or "loose." In the age of social media, pre-teen and adolescent girls are often bullied by having their sexual reputation called into question. Pre-teen and adolescent boys, how-ever, are often considered "cool" and desirous if they have had multiple sexual partners. In our society, masculinity is often evaluated by the perceived number of sexual partners a boy/man has had. Girls and women are more likely to be persecuted for having had multiple sexual partners (even if it is not true) than are boys/men.

Research highlights that early maturing girls are objectified (viewed in terms of their body parts) and are more likely to socialize with older peers. They are also more likely to have sexual intercourse earlier, do drugs, and have more peer conflict than their later maturing female counterparts. This is because when a girl develops breasts and hips, she is often treated looked at (objectified) as if she was an adult woman regardless of her actual age. This can be scary for young girls as the attention their developing bodies receive is often unwanted. For some later maturing girls, this provokes feelings of jealousy because early maturing girls may get increased attention. This is often a recipe for bullying the early maturing girl by spreading rumors about her perceived sexual encounters, which leads her to be more vulnerable to social isolation from peers and to feelings of depression. This can also lead to her engaging in sexual relationships to connect socially and to decrease these negative feelings. The opposite appears to be true for early maturing boys, which tends to be popular and more likely to be involved with athletics. Early maturing boys attain a more masculine body type quicker than their later maturing counterparts, which is perceived by the peer group more positively.

SEXUAL ORIENTATION AND DISCRIMINATION

In previous chapters, we reviewed the definition of sexual orientation and explored research on sexual orientation. What has not yet been discussed is the extreme discrimination faced by the GLBT (gay, lesbian, bisexual, and transgendered) community. This influences our views of sex in many ways. Most individuals (and society) have a *heterosexual bias*, in which heterosexuality is automatically considered the norm. This is influenced by *heterosexual privilege*, which includes things like being able to express physical affection to one's partner in public without fear of public ridicule, assuming that love songs on the radio apply to your romantic relationship, not having to justify/explain your relationship to others, receiving validation and support from your religious community, and not having to fear being fired because of your sexual orientation. Even when we review the sexuality research integrated throughout this book, there is an assumption that the participants are heterosexual and that all of the information applies to heterosexual relationships. This is a systemic and institutionalized bias that acts to discriminate against the GLBT community simply by not including them or their experiences in research or in society's view of relationship. Although this is changing in some spheres, it is not changing in others. Additionally, sex between same-sex partners (especially two men) is still viewed negatively and as a "special exception" to "normal sexual behavior." When a love scene is depicted in a movie, it is almost always with a heterosexual couple. Part of heterosexism is that gay or bisexual individuals' sex lives/behavior is still considered outside the norm. It remains difficult for the GLBT community to find positive sexual images of same-sex (or bisexuality) relationships within popular media. When we look at the negative consequences of sex, the author of this volume would be remiss in not including the inherent heterosexual bias of this book as a negative consequence.

HEALTHY AND DYSFUNCTIONAL RELATIONSHIPS

Other positive and negative effects of sex tend to be the relationships we do or do not form around sexual partnerships. In Chapter 5 we discuss types of attachment (the type of connection an infant will have with his or her caregiver). We also discuss the notion that the types of attachment relationships we have with our caregivers are often predictive of the types of romantic attachments we form in adulthood. Romantic relationship expectations have evolved significantly over the last 100 years in that couples now expect romantic emotional intimacy as well as friendship with one another. This was not true 100 years ago. Marriage was often viewed as a contract between two families and a way to increase a family's financial and land resources. What is considered "healthy" or "dysfunctional" in terms of relationships is significantly influenced by culture (and even the time period in which the relationship exists). In mainstream American society today, healthy romantic relationships have characteristics of mutual emotional support, open and respectful communication, sexual and emotional intimacy, appropriate interpersonal boundaries, healthy conflict resolution strategies, honesty and integrity, shared power and responsibility, individual and joint accountability, equality, and negotiation and fairness and acceptance of one another. Partners are expected to relate to one another and to be good (if not best) friends. Individuals typically get into romantic relationships in search of emotional support, physical and emotional intimacy, and friendship. Monogamy is also usually an agreed-upon relationship norm.

Characteristics of dysfunctional relationships include issues with power and control; using intimidation, coercion, and threats; destroying property; jealousy; possessiveness and isolation; emotional, physical, sexual, or economic abuse; minimizing, denying, and/or blaming; substance abuse;

and domestic violence. These characteristics can lead one or both partners to be unhappy at the least and physically and/or emotionally damaging at the most. Remember that all romantic relationships have functional and dysfunctional characteristics from time to time; however, the evaluation of the health of a relationship has more to do with its overall quality and level of satisfaction between partners.

You might ask yourself how or why someone could get into or remain in an abusive relationship. There are many reasons for this. The relationships we have with our family of origin (parents, siblings, grandparents, etc.) significantly influence our view of relationships, relationship expectations and behaviors, and type of relationship we seek with a romantic partner. Thus, the types of relationships we see growing up influence us in some significant ways. If one grew up in a family in which one parent was an alcoholic, one may unknowingly be attracted to a romantic partner who has an addition. This is not because the individual liked growing up with an alcoholic parent but it may feel "normal" to be in a relationship with someone who has addictive behaviors. We often gravitate toward the familiar even if we do not like it. This is sometimes a non-conscious process. It is not until an individual looks deep within and examines his or her relationship patterns that some of these issues—if they exist—may come to light or he/she gains insight into his or her dysfunctional relationship choices. This introspective process can allow an individual to break this pattern and make healthier relationship choices. Sometimes, going to counseling to explore one's family and romantic relationship patterns can be helpful in this regard. This is not to say that everyone who grew up in a dysfunctional household will get into dysfunctional romantic relationships; however, it is true that those who grew up in dysfunctional households may be at greater risk for doing so. The section below will highlight some serious dysfunctional relationship behaviors that have negative consequences. These behaviors are sometimes passed down through the family line. They include cheating, domestic violence, and sexual abuse.

Cheating

If you read any popular women's magazine, there are usually plenty of articles on how to keep your man happy and why men cheat. The definition of cheating today has broadened, given the Internet and social media, but emotional betrayal and a violation of trust is always involved. Romantic cheating typically involves breaking the emotional and/or physical agreed-upon relationship contract between two people. As discussed in previous chapters, the current American norm for romantic relationships includes *serial monogamy*, which is sexual fidelity within the committed relationship until that relationship ends. Many individuals consider emotional "cheating" to be another type of violation of trust. Emotional cheating involves one person in the relationship turning to another individual (in heterosexual relationships, it is typically someone of the opposite sex) for emotional support (or providing the other person support) without their romantic partner's awareness. A consequence of this is that the individual no longer turns to his or her romantic partner anymore. Emotional cheating is harmful to a relationship because it tends to be a precursor to a physical relationship. Also, the primary relationship is devalued because one partner is looking to get his or her emotional/ romantic needs met outside the romantic relationship.

Physical cheating typically involves sexual touching or intercourse with an individual who is not his or her romantic partner. Within most romantic relationships, this is considered the ultimate form of cheating— the most serious type of betrayal as sexual intimacy (through the serial monogamy expectation) is supposed to be within that committed relationship only. Individuals cheat on their partners for many different reasons. Some want to end the committed relationship and do not know how to tell the other person. Some feel that they are not getting their physical/ emotional needs met within the primary relationship so they look outside of it to get these needs met. For others, it may be that they use other romantic encounters to enhance their sense of self and self-esteem. Finally, some may be scared to commit to one person for fear of getting hurt, so they may sabotage their primary relationship as a way of not really connecting with their romantic partner. The reasons are varied; however, it is clear that cheating has negative consequences on the relationship. Once trust is broken, it is very difficult to repair it. Cheating—regardless of the type—significantly compromises trust. Without trust, there can be no emotional intimacy and no healthy relationship.

Domestic Violence and Stalking

Domestic Violence

Domestic violence is another extremely harmful relationship behavior. Domestic violence is about power and control. It cuts across racial, gender, and socioeconomic lines. Batterers and those who are battered may have grown up in households where they witnessed acts of physical violence. This is true for some batterers/battered individuals but not all. Domestic violence typically involves emotional, physical, economic, and verbal abuse. When an abuser feels out of control, he or she is likely to gain control by abusing his or her partner. Battering is a pattern of force and terror. It often begins with minor battering incidents (smacking) and escalates over time (punching, choking). Once it begins, it gets worse and more frequent over time. It includes intimidation, threats, economic deprivation, psychological warfare, emotional abuse, verbal insults, and public humiliation. The victim often internalizes this negativity and has low feelings of self-worth validated by the abuser. Victims are often "brainwashed" by abusers to think that no one else will want them but the abuser himself or herself. Women are far more likely to be abused than are men, although men too can be victims of domestic violence. It occurs in heterosexual and same-sex relationships.

When there is an increase in stressful events for the abuser/abused, there is likely to be an increase in domestic battering incidents. Things such as pregnancy, economic hardship, work issues, having very young children or adolescents in the home, or large sporting events (e.g., Super Bowl) can contribute to battering incident. Frequently, these incidents may also be fueled by intoxication. Characteristics and/or behaviors of abusers include an individual who

- keeps track of what you are doing all the time and criticizes you for little things;
- constantly accuses you of being unfaithful;
- isolates you from family and friends;
- prevents or discourages you from seeing friends or family, or going to work or school;
- gets angry when drinking alcohol or using drugs;
- expresses feelings of insecurity;
- shows superficial remorse after the battering incident and then justifies the incident by saying it was your fault or that he/she loves you so much that you "push" his or her buttons;
- controls all the money you spend;
- humiliates you in front of others;
- states that "no one will ever love you like I will";
- destroys your property or things that you care about;
- threatens to hurt you or the children or pets, or does cause hurt (by hitting, punching, slapping, kicking, or biting);
- uses or threatens to use a weapon against you;
- forces you to have sex against your will;
- blames you for his or her violent outbursts;
- shows excessive jealous;

- shows unrealistic relationship expectation ("If you love me, you will do everything I ask");
- may hold rigid gender stereotypes (e.g., women are inferior to men);
- thinks it is okay to solve conflicts through violence;
- uses verbal threats;
- refuses to take responsibility for his or her actions;
- has feelings of low self-worth/insecurity, not knowing what true love is;
- has a previous history of being in abusive relationships (or of growing up in a household with domestic violence).

Characteristics and/or behaviors of those who are victimized by domestic violence include

- feelings of low self-worth/insecurity;
- denial/minimization of abuse;
- lack of knowledge of what domestic violence is or its signs;
- ignoring warning signs of abusive behavior;
- difficulty trusting others;
- acceptance of responsibility for abuse;
- feelings of guilt, shame, hopelessness;
- utilizing a passive coping style;
- not knowing what true love is;
- a previous history of being in abusive relationships (or of growing up in a household with domestic violence).

Domestic violence is often captured through the *cycle of violence* proposed by Lenore Walker (1979) in her work with battered women. The three phases are tension (which builds over time), violence (battering incident), honeymoon period (calm period where abuser may be remorseful). This cycle is described below.

A battering incident occurs. It can be physical, emotional, sexual, or verbal. There is tension building where the abuser gets angry and lashes out against his or her partner. There is a breakdown of communication and the victim typically engages in behaviors designed to calm/appease the abuser. The victim may feel as if he/she is "walking on egg shells" and his or her attempts to appease the abuser are not effective (which the victim typically blames himself/herself for). After the abusive incident (and it is usually multiple incidents) occurs, the abuser may apologize for the abuse and promise it will not happen again. The abuser may also blame the victim for causing the abuse, deny the abuse, or minimize the damage sustained by the victim (e.g., "it's not that bad."). The abuser typically only shows superficial remorse (if he/she shows any at all) and it does not last very long. Sometimes, the abuser may give the victim gifts as an apology. Then the cycle starts all over again and lasts differing periods of time. This is predominating pattern in the relationship. Often, as time goes by, the clam periods and honeymoon phases may disappear altogether. All relationships are different; thus this cycle may not apply to all relationships in which there is domestic abuse. For example, there are some relationships in which both partners abuse one another. Domestic violence is a serious issue. The time when an individual is most vulnerable is when he/she decides to leave the relationship. This is when the abuser feels the most threatened and is most likely to seriously harm or even kill the victim.

The question is often asked: "why doesn't he/she leave?" The answer is quite complicated and can include many factors including religious belief, love of the other person, having children, financial/economic dependence, fear of being alone, loyalty, the belief that "no one else will want me," pity, duty to partner, wanting to help the abuser, feelings of worthlessness, denial ("it's not really that bad"), guilt, shame, fear, depression, learned helplessness/hopelessness that the situation can improve, and/or lack of support from others. There is a significant amount of shame the victim usually feels about being abused. These factors make it extremely difficult and scary to leave the relation.

For some, domestic violence begins as teen dating violence/abuse at adolescence. Adolescents and adults are often unaware that teens experience dating violence and the degree to and frequency with which it happens. In a nationwide survey, 9.4 percent of high school students reported being hit, slapped, or physically hurt on purpose by their boyfriend or girlfriend in the 12 months prior to the survey (Centers for Disease Control and Prevention, 2011). About one in five women and nearly one in seven men who ever experienced rape, physical violence, and/or stalking by an intimate partner first experienced some form of partner violence between 11 and 17 years of age (Centers for Disease Control and Prevention, 2010). This is alarming on many fronts. Teen dating violence frequently turns into adult domestic violence. Also, many teen victims feel that they cannot tell their parents or friends because of the shame or fear they feel. Remember that abuse often begets more abuse; thus abusive patterns of behavior often escalate over time. These abusive patterns do not change on their own without some outside intervention.

Stalking

Stalking and domestic violence often go hand in hand. Stalking involves unwanted or obsessive attention by an individual or group toward another person. Batterers may stalk their partners. Stalking is illegal and consists of the following behaviors: physical following (physical pursuit), surveillance, telephone or social media harassment, sending unwanted gifts, and so forth. One study of stalkers (Mullen et al., 2000) identified five types of stalkers:

- *Rejected stalkers* pursue their victims in order to reverse, correct, or avenge a rejection (e.g., divorce, separation, termination).
- *Resentful stalkers* pursue a vendetta because of a sense of grievance against the victims—motivated mainly by the desire to frighten and distress the victim.
- *Intimacy seekers* seek to establish an intimate, loving relationship with their victim. Such stalkers often believe that the victim is a long-sought-after soul mate, and they were "meant" to be together.
- *Incompetent suitors*, despite poor social or courting skills, have a fixation/obsession, or in some cases, a sense of entitlement to an intimate relationship with those who have attracted their amorous interest. Their victims are most often already in a dating relationship with someone else.
- *Predatory stalkers* spy on the victim in order to prepare and plan an attack, often sexual, on the victim.

Some stalkers are mentally ill and may have delusions (irrational belief systems) that the person he/she is stalking wants a romantic relationship with him or her. Other stalkers are more interested in using physical intimidation to scare the victim or to get the other person to comply with certain wishes (e.g., be in a relationship). Stalking makes victims feel threatened, insecure, paranoid, and scared. It is a form of intimidation. There are laws designed to protect victims of stalking. Unfortunately, these laws are not always effective because victims are reluctant to come forward, especially if the stalker is someone they know or they feel as if they do not have enough evidence that they are being stalked.

Sexual Abuse, Sexual Assault, and Date Rape

Sexual abuse of children is more common than we may realize. According to the 1992 National Health and Social Life Survey, 17 percent of women and 12 percent of men had sexual contact (as a child) with an older adolescent or adult (Laumann et al., 1994, as cited in Shibley Hyde & DeLamater, 2003). Only 22 percent of victims told anyone. For girls, nearly all cases involved inappropriate sexual contact with males, whereas for boys inappropriate sexual contact was with men and women, but mostly with adolescent/adult men. Sexual coercion often involved contact with the genitals, forced oral or anal sex, as well as intercourse (although full intercourse tends to be more rare). Sexual abuse may occur at very young ages (before 7). Sometimes, it consists of one incident but often it consists of multiple ongoing incidents by someone the victim knows. Sexual abuse by strangers is not common. Most abuse is perpetuated by family friends and relatives.

Sexual abuse can be very damaging to its victims. Victims are often threatened with physical (harm) or psychological consequences. Victims are often made to believe that no one will believe them if they tell. Many keep the "secret" for years and it is reinforced by the shame victims often feel. It becomes more complicated and psychologically damaging when victims do tell an adult and they are not believed. Finally, when abusers live with the victim (e.g., father, brother, grandparent) it is even more psychologically damaging as the victim has little means of escaping the abuse. *Incest* is defined as sexual contact between blood relatives (although it can occur between a stepparent and stepchild). The majority of cases go unreported and if reported, unprosecuted. Incest is perpetuated by parents, grandparents, stepparents, and siblings.

The effects of both sexual abuse and incest are long lasting and serious. It can cause its victims to experience posttraumatic stress disorder, depression, anxiety, feelings of shame and isolation, relationship problems (romantic and friendship), extreme feelings of mistrust, sexual issues, body image issues, low self-esteem, health complaints, aggressive and/or antisocial behavior, inappropriate sexual behavior, social/behavior problems in school, and so forth. Most research finds that victims experience more severe symptoms when (1) the perpetrator was a member of the family, (2) the sexual contact was frequent or occurred over a long period of time, and (3) the sexual activity involved penetration (vaginal, oral, or anal). Brother-sister incest appears to be the least damaging type of sexual contact provided they are close in age and it is consensual. Coercion seems to be the key factor influencing psychological damage.

Counseling and psychotherapy, as well as emotional and psychological support from others, can be key to the healing process for victims of sexual abuse. Critical to the healing process is victims' understanding that the abuse was not their fault and decrease in feelings of shame surrounding their abuse. Counseling can be very effective in helping individuals explore how their abuse has impacted their lives. Unfortunately, counseling is not nearly as effective in the treatment of sexual abusers. Many abusers show chronic patterns of abuse as lack of insight/denial into how their abusive behavior has harmed their victims.

PARAPHILIAS

Paraphilia is the experience of intense sexual arousal to atypical objects, situations, or individuals. The *Diagnostic and Statistical Manual*, 5th version, used for diagnosing psychiatric disorders, distinguishes between paraphilias and paraphilic disorders. Paraphilic disorders involve an individual's disruption in social, relational, and occupational functioning. *Psychology Today* defines a paraphilia as a condition in which a person's sexual arousal and gratification depend on fantasizing about and engaging in sexual behavior that is atypical and extreme. A paraphilia can revolve around a particular object (children, animals, underwear) or around a particular act (inflicting pain, exposing oneself). The majority of paraphilias are far more common in men than in women. The focus of a paraphilia is usually very specific and unchanging and has an almost obsessive quality about it. The person may find it difficult to achieve sexual gratification if the paraphilic object is not present. Paraphilias are long standing and treatment resistant. Paraphilias include sexual behaviors that society may view as distasteful, unusual, or abnormal as most individuals do not find these things sexually stimulating. Common paraphilias include exhibitionism (exposing one's nude body parts/genitals to unsuspecting others), fetishism (sexual arousal to an inanimate object), frotteurism (rubbing one's genitals against an unsuspecting other to attain sexual arousal), pedophilia (sexual arousal is achieved primarily and repeatedly through sexual activity with prepubescent children), transvestism/transvestic fetishism (sexual arousal is achieved primarily through dressing as a member of the opposite sex), sexual sadism (individuals repeatedly and intentionally inflict pain on others in order to achieve sexual arousal), sexual masochism (individuals obtain sexual pleasure primarily from having pain and/or humiliation inflicted upon them), urophilia (sexual arousal caused by the act of urination), corprophilia (sexual arousal caused by the act of defecation), bestiality (the act of having sexual contact with an animal), and mysophilia (sexual arousal caused primarily by filth or filthy surroundings). There are many other paraphilias—some literature estimates the number may be well over 500. The key feature of a paraphilia is that individuals need their sexual needs met apart from an emotional connection within a human relationship. As in the case of pedophilia, the child is objectified. Additionally, the object of the paraphilia must be present more often than not for the person to be sexually gratified.

SEXUALLY TRANSMITTED DISEASES/INFECTIONS

Each year over 19 million Americans contract a sexually transmitted infection (STI) although the number may be higher than this, given the number of unreported cases. One in four teenage girls have an STI (Centers for Disease Control and Prevention, 2007, as cited in King, 2009). STIs are not punishment for having sexual intercourse or other types of sexual behavior, although we are often socialized to believe this. "STIs are not caused by sexual behavior itself. The behavior is merely the mode of transmission for bacteria, viruses, or parasites that must be present for the infections to be transmitted" (King, 2009, p. 100). STIs are generally spread through sexual contact with someone who has bacteria, viruses, or parasites that have caused infections and are highly contagious. STIs can be classified as *bacterial, viral,* or *parasitic. Bacteria* are small, single-celled organisms that lack a nuclear membrane but have all the genetic material (RNA or DNA) to reproduce themselves. A *virus* is a protein shell around a nucleic acid core. Viruses have either RNA or DNA, not both, and thus cannot reproduce themselves (King, 2009). They invade host cells that provide the material to manufacture new virus particles. While STIs are infections usually transmitted by sexual contact, STDs (sexually transmitted diseases) are diseases of the reproductive system or genitals that are not contracted through sexual activity often involving overgrowths of bacterial, yeasts, viruses, or fungal organisms that are found naturally in sexual and reproductive organs. King (2009) provides a comprehensive list of STIs, their symptoms, and their treatments. A thorough review of STIs and their treatments is beyond the purview of this chapter; however, a list of each type of STI will be provided. General recommendations for treatments will be included. STIs and STDs are typically broken down into three categories: bacterial, viral, and parasitic. Many STIs have been around as long as humans have been sexually active! Consistent and proper condom use significantly decreases STI transmission.

Bacterial STIs

Treatment for bacterial STIs usually involves a course of antibiotics. Unlike viral STIs bacterial STIs are usually more "curable." They include gonorrhea, chlamydia, syphilis, and pelvic inflammatory disease (PID) and are spread through sexual, oral, and/or anal contact. These STIs are typically diagnosed with medical intervention (i.e., a swab tested under a microscope). Women may be completely asymptomatic while men may have a burning sensation upon urinating or a strange-colored discharge from the penis. If untreated, these infections can cause sterility. In women this may include the development of PID and/or a blockage of the Fallopian tubes, which can negatively impact fertility. PID involves the development of scar tissue and/or inflammation in the female reproductive tract.

These bacterial STIs can be passed to infants born through the birth canal; therefore, mothers are regularly tested for them (and treated if found) and drops are routinely placed in the eyes of newborns preventing transmission and STI-induced blindness.

Viral Infections

Unlike bacterial STIs, viral STIs are treatable but not curable. Most viral STIs stay in the body and are not eradicated by antibiotics; thus an individual contracting a viral STI must live with that STI forever; however, there are many treatments available to help reduce the symptoms. Symptom reduction does not prevent transmission of the STI. Herpes is a highly contagious STI and nearly one in six Americans have the disease, with women and African Americans being at the highest risk for contracting it. There are different types of herpes and they are caused by herpes simplex virus type 1 or type 2. Oral herpes infections occur in or around the mouth. Genital herpes appears in the genital region and is also caused by herpes simplex virus 1 or 2. The infection is spread by direct skin-to-skin contact from an infected person to a noninfected person. Herpes during pregnancy can contribute to the baby being born premature, spontaneous abortion or still birth, brain damage, and/or mental retardation.

Human papillomavirus (HPV) is the most common type of STI. According to the Centers for Disease Control, nearly all sexually active men and women will get it at some time during their lives. Over 20 million Americans are infected with it and there are approximately 6.2 million new cases each year. There are several different types of HPV. The large majority of HPV infections (80 percent) will go away on their own within several months. However, for others, serious conditions can result. There are well over 100 different types of HPV. Some cause visible symptoms, such as genital warts (warts on the genitals or anus caused by HPV) and others cause no visible symptoms to the naked eye. Having HPV can increase a woman's risk for developing cervical cancer. This is why it is recommended that girls and boys get the HPV vaccine in preadolescence.

Human immunodeficiency virus (HIV) is one of the most well-known STIs. It was discovered in the early 1980s when men started dying in rapid numbers who appeared to be infected with severe pneumonia-like symptoms. HIV is a virus that kills CD4+ cells and eventually results in AIDS (the acquired immunodeficiency syndrome). There are two types of HIV: HIV-1 and HIV-2. Once HIV becomes AIDS, the immune system is so depressed (weak) that it leaves an infected individual prone to opportunistic diseases (diseases that take advantage of a weak immune system). HIV belongs to a special class of viruses called *retroviruses*. Retroviruses consist of a protein shell surrounding the genetic material ribonucleic acid (RNA). HIV attacks human cells by first attaching itself to special receptors on the cell's surface, and then it attaches to the T4 lymphocytes, which is a type of white blood cells that aid the immune system in fighting diseases. Once attached to the T4 cell, HIV enters the cell and releases its RNA, eventually enabling HIV to reproduce itself. HIV continues to infect other T4 cells, which seriously compromises the body's ability to fight off diseases. HIV tends to disproportionately affect African Americans, young gay and bisexual men, and women and IV drug users. It is most commonly spread through vaginal and/or anal intercourse as well as using infected (used) needles.

There are three stages: acute infection, clinical latency, and symptomatic infection (AIDS). Because of the scientific advancements in medication, HIV is now considered a treatable disease; thus it is no longer the death sentence it once was. Due to the stigma of having HIV, many individuals do not get tested, which is the only reliable way to treat HIV and prevent its spreading to others. If HIV progresses to the final stage of AIDS, there is little effective treatment at that point. This is why individuals who are sexually active, especially those with multiple partners, should consistently test so that they are aware of their HIV status.

A blood test still remains the most reliable source of HIV infection, though a test of one's saliva can also reveal if there are existing HIV antibodies. Individuals can get tested at their doctor's offices and clinics, do a home test and mail in the results, or use the many "mobile" HIV testing units that come to communities and test community members. Testing can be confidential (where for example the patient and person testing him or her know the result) or anonymous (where the patient is only identified by a number and not a name). Tests taken 12 weeks after exposure are the most accurate; however, antibodies may develop (and can be detected) in the blood stream in as few as 2–4 weeks after exposure to HIV. Early detection is critical to the effective treatment and management of HIV. The earlier a person begins HIV medication, the longer his or her survival rate. Pregnant women can pass the infection onto their newborns in utero (as well as through breast milk); however, if infected pregnant women are administered anti-HIV medication, the likelihood of transmission of HIV from mother to newborn drops from 26 percent to 8 percent. Without early treatment, most HIV infected infants will die prior to their second birthday. Proper condom use greatly reduces the transmission of HIV.

Hepatitis is another viral infection. There are three types: A, B, and C. Hepatitis involves the inflammation of the liver and is spread through sexual contact, direct or indirect contact with feces (e.g., anal sex, poor hand-washing habits), and contact with other bodily fluids (e.g., blood, vaginal secretions). Needle sharing is a common way for some types of hepatitis to be transmitted. It can cause liver conditions such as cancer and cirrhosis.

Parasitic Infections

Parasitic infections consist of parasites that house themselves in the pubic hair, under the skin, or inside the anus or vagina. They include pubic lice, scabies, and pinworms. Symptoms for these infections include intense itching, bumps under the skin, and skin scaling. These can be sexually transmitted or transmitted through other means (e.g., children having hand-to-mouth contact with other children, contaminated sheets).

Vaginitis refers to any inflammation of the vagina and can be caused by any numbers of STIs. There are three common types: trichomoniasis, moniliasis (candidiasis or yeast infection), and bacterial vaginosis. Various symptoms for these STIs include odiferous and/or vaginal discharge, genital itching/dryness, and urethral irritation in men. If left untreated, these conditions can lead to fertility issues. Some men are asymptomatic. These conditions are typically diagnosed by examination of the infected swab under a microscope.

SOME OTHER STIS: MONILIASIS, BACTERIAL VAGINOSIS, CYSTITIS, AND PROSTATITIS

Moniliasis is caused by an overgrowth of the microorganism *Candida albicans*, which is normally found in the vagina. It is considered a fungal infection and most commonly known as a yeast infection. Most women will get a yeast infection at some point in their lives because of how common they are. They are not specifically sexually transmitted and may be caused when the body's hormonal balance is thrown off and the body reacts by producing an overgrowth of yeast killing off the normal bacteria that keep the yeast in check in the body's moist areas. Sometimes, pregnancy, hormonal forms of birth control, or taking antibiotics can cause yeast infections. This infection can cause vaginal dryness and intense itching, making sexual intercourse painful. Yeast infections can be passed between partners during intercourse. They are treated through over-the-counter or prescription antifungal creams or suppositories. There are oral forms available too.

Bacterial vaginosis is the most common type of vaginitis. It is caused by several types of vaginal bacteria. It is not always caused by sexual intercourse, though having multiple sexual partners is considered a risk factor. The most common symptom is a foul-smelling odor and lumpy gray discharge. Without treatment, this can lead to an infection in the upper reproductive tract. The treatment usually consists of a course of antibiotics. Cystitis is a bacterial infection of the bladder. It can be caused by bacteria exchanged during sexual intercourse or by other things such as wiping from back (anus) to front (vagina), which can pass bacteria from the anus to the urethra. The most common symptom is painful urination and lower pelvic and abdominal pains. It can often result in a urinary tract infection. Cystitis is treated with a course of antibiotics. For men, *E. coli* bacteria can be transmitted to a man's prostate during sexual activity, which can result in *prostatis*. Symptoms include lower back and groin pain, fever, and burning during ejaculation. It is commonly treated through a course of antibiotics.

SAFE SEX

The above discussed risk for transmission of STIs is significantly cut for couples who use condoms every time they have sex. The term *safer sex* is typically used to describe consistent condom use during sexual intercourse (including oral and anal sex) in addition to monogamous sex within the confines of a trusted relationship. The only true way to erase any chance of contracting an STI is to abstain from sex. It is true to a certain extent that when we have sexual intercourse with one partner, we are essentially having sex with the partners he/she has had in the past because of the highly contagious nature of STIs. This is why it is so important that sexually active individuals not only regularly communicate with new and existing partners about their sexual history in honest ways but also consistently get themselves tested for STIs. As we have learned, many individuals with an STI do not show symptoms and thus easily pass it onto an unsuspecting partner. Embarrassment, shame, fear of judgment, and ignorance frequently prevent partners from communicating honestly about their sexual histories; however, as we have read in the earlier parts of this chapter, this can have extremely negative consequences for our individual sexual health. Part of having sex should be honest communication with our partners but this frequently does not happen.

CONTRACEPTION/BIRTH CONTROL

Contraception is the prevention of conception. Since the 1960s, when the birth control pill became available in the United States, most sexually active individuals have engaged in some type of pregnancy prevention until they are ready to have children. When individuals have children before they are ready, a series of negative consequences may result for both parents and children. For example, teenage moms are far less likely to finish high school, which significantly limits their ability to make a solid living. Additionally, raising a child is a large emotional, financial, and psychological undertaking. If this happens before an individual or couple is ready, it can lead to negative feelings and resentment toward the child.

Contraceptive methods can primarily be divided into several categories: barrier, non-prescription, and hormonal methods. Barrier methods place a barrier between the woman's cervix and man's ejaculate (semen). Hormonal methods use a combination of hormones to prevent contraception. Non-prescription methods often involve things such as ovulation monitoring, douching, and withdrawal. When research explores the effectiveness of contraceptive methods, it does so looking at the *typical use* rates versus the *perfect use* rates. The typical use explores the ability of a method of contraception to prevent pregnancy as actually used at home by individuals when they are not monitored in a research lab. For example, most sexually active couples may not use the birth control pill perfectly each time. She may forget to take the pill once or twice during a cycle or may not take it at the same time every day. This would be the "typical use" of an individual utilizing the birth control pill as a contraceptive method. The perfect use rate explores the ability of a method of contraception to prevent pregnancy as measured by consistent and correct use each time. Abstinence can refer to the absence of sexual contact of any kind or no penetrative behaviors (e.g., vaginal, oral, or anal intercourse). This section of the chapter will review several of the most common types of contraceptive methods as well as their effectiveness rates.

Abstinence is the only 100 percent effective way to prevent pregnancy and most STIs. Abstinence typically refers to avoiding sexual intercourse and individuals who are abstinent may choose to engage in other types of sexual activity. Obviously, one can catch an STI from oral sex. Ninety-five percent of Americans have engaged in premarital sex, although some individuals may practice abstinence after a sexual relationship ends. This is why abstinence-only sexual education programs, where the primary educational thrust is to teach individuals to abstain from sexual activity, are not nearly as effective as abstinence-plus programs. Abstinence-plus programs teach and emphasize sexual abstinence as a valid form of contraception but also teach more comprehensively about other forms of birth control and sexual health issues. A full description of each birth control method is beyond the purview of this chapter; however, a list of each method and type will be provided.

Barrier forms of contraception include condoms, both male and female types. When used consistently and properly, this is a highly effective form of contraception and provides significant protection against STIs.

Non-prescription methods of birth control include the withdrawal method, where the man removes his penis from the vagina prior to ejaculation. This method has limited effectiveness because prior to a male ejaculating semen, the penis has clear pre-ejaculate fluid on its surface, which could contain a few stray sperm. Douching, which has been used as a form of birth control historically, is not at all effective and can actually push sperm up into the cervix.

Douching involves a woman washing her vagina with liquid. Douching, even when not used for contraception, is problematic and can actually increase the risk of infections and other health complications. Some women douche after their menstrual cycle to "clean out" the vagina and reduce unpleasant odors. The vagina is a self-cleaning organ and does not need douching. Douching can upset the vagina's natural chemical balance, which can contribute to increasing yeast infections. Pelvic inflammatory disease, cervical cancer, and preterm birth rates are all higher in women who regularly douche. The vagina's normal acidity will clean the vagina and control bacteria. Washing with soap and water through bathing is really enough.

Lactational amenorrhea and fertility awareness methods are often known as *fertility awareness* or natural-family-planning type of contraception because they involve women monitoring the phase of their menstrual cycle, especially ovulation. Women learn their bodies and become aware of their most "fertile days" (i.e., when they are ovulating) and avoid intercourse on those days. The lactational amenorrhea method is used when women are breast feeding. When women breast feed, the newborn's sucking the nipple inhibits the release of FSH and LH from the pituitary gland, which prevents ovulation temporarily. It tends to be effective only when a woman consistently breast feeds and is mostly effective for about 6 months.

Women can only get pregnant within the first 24 hours after the egg is released from the ovaries. Thus, when women are trying to get pregnant, they are advised to monitor their ovulation (this can be done through over-the-counter ovulation monitors or sticks in which a woman urinates on to detect hormone levels in the blood, which predict ovulation). All fertility awareness methods require a woman to abstain from having sex when she is ovulating to prevent pregnancy. Other fertility awareness methods include the calendar, basil body temperature, billings, cervical mucus, and sympto- and thermal methods.

The failure rate is high with these methods because they involve a great deal of time, training, body awareness, and longer periods of planned abstinence. Fertility awareness methods tend to be unpopular in the United States for these reasons. Also, over-the-counter and prescription methods of birth control, which require little to no training and much less effort, are readily available.

The use of *spermicides* (typically made of nonoxynol-9) kills sperm, preventing pregnancy. Spermicides come in the form of liquid gel, foams, creams, and films (small thin square inserted into the vagina prior to intercourse). Spermicides loose effectiveness over time and a new spermicide must be used prior to each act of intercourse. Spermicides tend not to be as popular as some other types of birth control because they are sticky and sometimes a bit messy.

Other methods of this type include the diaphragm, cervical cap, and contraceptive sponge. Each of these methods involves the woman inserting an object that blocks the cervical opening, preventing sperm from reaching the Fallopian tubes. These methods can be effective when used correctly; however, human error with these methods tends to be greater than with other methods; thus these are less popular forms of birth control. For women who are unable to or do not wish to take hormonal forms of birth control, these methods are a suitable alternative.

The intrauterine device (IUD) is a popular international form of contraception but tends to be less popular in the United States due to a problem with IUDs in the 1970s, though it is a highly safe and effective form of birth control. It can be considered a barrier and hormonal method of birth control. The IUD is made of plastic or metal (usually copper) and comes in the form of several shapes. A medical professional places it in the uterus and prevents the implantation of a fertilized egg but typically works to prevent fertilization in the first place. IUDs release progesterone, which impair the passage of sperm. A small string hangs outside of the vagina.

The birth control pill is a highly popular and effective hormonal form of contraception, though it offers no protection against STIs. As with other forms of birth control, there are some health risks associated with the birth control pill, especially for smokers (e.g., blood clots, mood swings, weight gain, and decreased sex drive). Most of these side effects disappear over time and most women have no side effects at all. The effectiveness of all hormonal forms of birth control depends heavily on a woman taking it consistently. Other forms of hormonal birth control include Depo-Provera (injectable progesterone given every 3 months), the birth control patch (OrthoEvra—applied to the skin one week at a time), and the NuvaRing (placed into the vagina; it releases hormones).

Emergency contraception can be used if a couple forgets to use birth control or their method fails them (e.g., the condom breaks). It must be taken within a few days. Most emergency contraception is known as *Plan B*, which is a progestin-only pill. Two pills are taken together or 12 hours apart. Plan B is 99 percent effective if taken within 12 hours of intercourse and 89 percent effective is taken within 3 days. It is now available as an over-the-counter medication. Side effects include nausea, headache, and breast tenderness. It should be noted that emergency contraception is *not* abortion. Emergency contraception works by preventing ovulation, fertilization, or implantation of a fertilized egg. If implantation has already occurred, emergency contraception is ineffective and will not harm the embryo.

Voluntary sterilization is another form of birth control. This is the most popular type of birth control in the United States. More than half of all married couples use voluntary sterilization after the birth of their last child. For men, vasectomy is the male sterilization technique. The vas deferens is tied off and cut, which prevents the passage of sperm through the reproductive tract. For women, tubal ligation is popular, which involves cutting, tying, or burning the Fallopian tubes. *Essure* is a non-surgical technique called transcervical sterilization that does not require general anesthesia and takes about 30 minutes to complete. A micro-insert is placed in the Fallopian tubes (via the cervix). The insert looks like a flexible spring. It is anchored inside the tubes through flexible coils, which irritates the tubes' lining and builds up scar tissue in each tube, which prevents the passage of an egg. Most women are fully recovered within a day of the procedure. Reversal of these procedures is quite difficult and has varying degrees of success, so when an individual decides on one of these forms of birth control, he/she should consider it to be permanent.

CHOOSING A BIRTH CONTROL METHOD THAT IS RIGHT FOR YOU

Choosing a contraceptive method that is right for you can be difficult and sometimes overwhelming. Most individuals and couples use several different types over their respective life spans. For example, younger women may prefer the pill or another form of hormonal birth control and/or condoms. These methods tend to be quick, easy, and highly effective. The choice of which contraceptive method to use often depends on answers to the following questions: Are you single? Are you sexually active? Are you in a committed monogamous relationship? Do you have multiple sexual partners? Are you interested in having children one day? Are you finished having children? Do you need active protection against STIs? Does your religious/spiritual orientation direct you to one type of birth control over another or simply does not support the use of nonnatural birth control at all? As you can see, this is why individuals and couples use different forms of birth control over their life span. Individuals and couples should weigh birth control options carefully and choose the best method for them, given their specific contraceptive needs.

ABORTION

Abortion is the termination of a pregnancy. Very few women use abortion as birth control but instead use it to terminate an unwanted pregnancy. Most abortions are performed in the first trimester of pregnancy (within the first 12 weeks). There are several types of abortion, including the following: RU 486, the "abortion pill" that operates by chemically inducing an abortion up to eight weeks after a woman's last period; dilation and curettage, where a woman goes under anesthesia and her uterine lining is scraped; and evacuation, where a tube inserted through the cervix and the fetal tissue is removed by suction. The procedure does not require general anesthesia and is the most common way abortions are performed in the United States. It takes about five minutes. Induced labor is used only when a pregnancy has proceeded for 16 weeks or more. A saline or prostaglandin solution is injected into the amniotic sac. Labor happens within 12–36 hours and the fetus is born deceased.

Research demonstrates that most women do not experience negative emotional consequences after having an abortion; however, some do. Women who do are more likely to have been suffering from depression or experiencing other emotional issues. Obviously, our society continues to be highly conflicted about abortion as evidenced by this issue coming up in political campaigns so frequently. Many people separate themselves into *pro choice* and *pro life* camps. Although *Roe v. Wade* was the Supreme Court decision making abortion legal in the United States, many local courts, as well as specific policies, have chipped away at this decision, making it much more difficult for women to get an abortion.

PREGNANCY

Obviously, pregnancy can be a wanted or unwanted consequence of having sexual intercourse in a heterosexual context. When a pregnancy is planned, a couple is often happy to welcome a baby into their lives; however, when pregnancy is not planned and desired, it can be very stressful. Becoming pregnant is not always as easy as people believe it to be. As stated previously, women can only get pregnant during about 6 days during the month, which consists of the 5 days leading up to ovulation and the 24 hours after ovulation. This is because sperm can live up to 5 days in a woman's body and the ovum lives for only 12–24 hours. If sperm does not penetrate the ovum at this time, the ovum becomes overripe and cannot be fertilized. Figuring out the exact time of ovulation is difficult. It typically occurs around the middle of a woman's cycle. During heterosexual intercourse, a man ejaculates an average of 200–400 million sperm into the vagina. Sperm attempt to pass through the vagina, cervix, and uterus into the Fallopian tubes. The majority of sperm die on their journey to reach the Fallopian tubes. While sperm are in a woman's reproductive tract they undergo *capacitation*, which thins out their membranes making them thin enough to penetrate the egg's outer surface. The egg sends out projections drawing sperm to it. When a sperm penetrates the egg's outer surface, fertilization takes place. The egg's surface immediately hardens, preventing other sperm from penetrating. The fertilized egg goes through many stages of cell division, for example, zygote—one-celled organism, to a morula—multiple-cell organism, to a blastocyst—hundreds of cells. The blastocyst reaches the uterus and after 8–11 days after ovulation attaches itself to the uterine wall. Implantation occurs and the cells continue to divide. Eventually, cell layers form the *umbilical cord* (which will become the link between mother and embryo) and the *amnion* (which is the protective fluid-filled sac around the developing fetus).

Early in pregnancy several things can go wrong. About 20 percent of all pregnancies (in women under 35 years of age) will miscarry or spontaneously abort. This may be due to chromosomal abnormalities or other factors, indicating that there might be genetic issues with the embryo.

Sometimes an *ectopic pregnancy* can occur when an embryo does not make it to the uterus but instead implants in the Fallopian tube. If left undetected, the embryo can grow in the Fallopian tube and it can burst, rupturing the tube. It can be fatal if undetected. Scarring of the Fallopian tubes due to PID can contribute to a woman having an ectopic pregnancy. If detected early, ectopic pregnancies can be treated with a drug called methotrexate, which dissolves the embryo in the tube. Prior to the availability of drug therapy, ectopic pregnancies were treated by removing one of the tubes, significantly reducing a woman's chance of becoming pregnant.

Pregnancy is divided into 3 trimesters and lasts an average of 270 days. Around 6 weeks, a heartbeat is detectable on an ultra sound. During the second trimester, a woman begins to feel the fetus moving and kicking. Many women feel very connected to their pregnancy during this time. Morning sickness typically dissipates. Some women experience back pain, hemorrhoids, a swelling of the hands and feet, and an increase in appetite. During the third trimester walking, sitting, and standing may become more difficult due to her increase in size. Back pain may be ever present and there is pressure on the bladder and stomach. Increased frequency in urination, indigestion, heartburn, gas, constipation, and leg cramps are also common. Sexual intercourse is possible during pregnancy, although some women experience declining interest especially during the end of the third trimester. Couples usually utilize woman on top and spooning positions for intercourse.

During pregnancy a woman must carefully watch what she ingests as it goes directly to her developing baby. Obviously, drugs, smoking, drinking alcohol, and anything else harmful to the fetus should be avoided as it could cause significant harm. Pregnant women are also unable to take most over-the-counter drugs and need to watch their diet to prevent undue harm of the developing baby.

MISCARRIAGES

One in four (25 percent) of all conceived pregnancies end in miscarriage. This is sometimes thought of nature's way of not allowing a pregnancy with genetic or other issues to continue. Miscarriages commonly occur in the first trimester of pregnancy, mostly before 6 weeks. Miscarriages can be caused by genetic, anatomic (e.g., uterine structural problems), hormonal issues, infections, maternal autoimmune issues, drug use, and sometimes unknown causes. Sometimes, a miscarriage can occur before a woman even knows she's pregnant. For many women and couples, experiencing a miscarriage can be emotionally devastating. This is one of the reasons why many women and couples do not choose to tell people they are pregnant until after the first trimester. After the first trimester, the chances of miscarriage significantly drop.

COMMON COMPLICATIONS DURING PREGNANCY

Although most women do not experience serious complications during pregnancy, many do. Some common complications include preeclampsia group B strep, preterm labor, gestational diabetes, low birth weight, and Rh negative disease. Preeclampsia includes maternal high blood pressure, which can include swollen hands and feet and weight gain and can be very dangerous to the mother, especially if preeclampsia becomes eclampsia, which can cause convulsions and coma. Treatment often depends on the severity of the condition. If a woman is at the end of her pregnancy, labor may be induced. Group B strep is the leading cause of infections in newborns and is determined via vaginal swab, in which the cells are cultured. Testing for group B strep infection is a routine part of prenatal care and women are screened between the 35th and 37th weeks of pregnancy because testing done within 5 weeks of delivery is the most accurate. Treatment consists of being given an antibiotic during delivery to decrease the chances of passing the infection onto the baby.

Preterm labor is the leading cause of infant death. Infants are considered preterm if he/she weighs less than 5.5 pounds and is born less than 37 weeks (38–40 weeks is considered full term). One out of every nine babies are born premature. Preterm birth is the leading cause of neurological disabilities in children. Babies born early often have trouble breathing because their lungs are not developed. Thus, if a woman goes into preterm labor, she can sometimes be given antenatal corticosteroids for fetal lung development to mature the baby's lungs. Significant advances in medical care have helped save many premature babies. Infants weighing just over 1 pound have about a 20–30 percent survival while infants weighing 2.5 pounds have an 80 percent survival rate. The former are at high risk for psychomotor problems, disabilities, low IQ scores, and other issues. During pregnancy, every week counts. As you can see, there can be a significant difference in the health of a newborn depending on his or her gestational age.

Low birth weight babies can also experience complications. Low birth weight can be caused by poor nutrition, substance use (e.g., cigarettes, alcohol, drugs), STIs, having little-to-no prenatal care, and other contributing factors. Babies who are born at a low birth weight can experience respiratory problems, blindness, learning disabilities, cerebral palsy, heart conditions, as well as other complications. This is one of the many reasons why continuous monitoring and prenatal care during pregnancy is so important.

Gestational diabetes develops during pregnancy when a woman's body is not making enough insulin. It usually develops in the second trimester (typically around the 24th week of pregnancy) and is primarily treated through diet and/or insulin. Between 2 and 10 percent of pregnant women develop gestational diabetes. Some women are at higher risk for developing gestational diabetes than others. Risk factors include maternal obesity (having a body mass index over 30), previous history of gestational diabetes during pregnancy, the presence of sugar in the urine, a family history of diabetes, previously given birth to a big baby (over 8 pounds), having a baby with a birth defect or an unexplained still birth, having high blood pressure, and being over 35 years of age, though some women who develop the condition have none of these risk factors. There are other health issues associated with having gestational diabetes. Because of the high glucose levels in the mother's blood, the baby may grow too big for the birth canal and have a higher risk for breathing problems and jaundice. Women with gestational diabetes are also at risk for developing preeclampsia. Most gestational diabetes is treated through diet and exercise. The majority of women with gestational diabetes do not go on to develop diabetes after the delivery of their babies.

Most people have a protein in their blood called the *Rh factor*. If a person has the Rh factor, he/she is considered *Rh positive*. If a person does not have the Rh factor, he/she is considered *Rh negative*. There is a problem only if there is a mismatch between mother and baby (i.e., one is Rh positive and the other Rh negative). The problem happens for the woman in subsequent pregnancies because her body develops antibodies to "fight off" the Rh opposite fetus, as if the fetus were a disease or infection. In sum, this condition is easily diagnosed and treated by administering an injection of *RhoGAM* to the mother, which prevents antibodies from forming in the first place. The injection contains Rh negative blood that already has antibodies in it, which allows a mother's body to carry another Rh positive fetus.

CHILDBIRTH

Before a woman gives birth, the fetus will typically rotate positions so that the head is down. When babies do not do this, they are determined to be in the *breech* or *feet first* position. Most women experience *Braxton-Hicks contractions*, which consist of a tightening and hardening of the uterus for a few moments before the uterus relaxes. These contractions help get the uterus ready for true labor and can start as early as 5 months into the pregnancy. Although they can sometimes be so strong as to be mistaken for "real" labor, they are not true contractions and do not last long, nor increase in intensity. When contractions become regular and are around 10 minutes apart, "true" labor is said to have begun. At the beginning of labor, the cervix begins to *dilate* (becomes wider and larger). During the last month of pregnancy the cervix dilates to 1 centimeter but during active labor, the cervix must eventually dilate to 10 centimeters. The cervix must also efface (become thinned out so it does not block the baby's passage into the birth canal). Labor is divided into three stages. The start-up stage of labor lasts 6–13 hours. The woman experiences contractions, which push the fetus downward toward the cervix. Prior to active labor, the cervix developed a thick layer of mucus preventing amniotic fluid leakage and the fetus from exposure to the outside environment. During labor, the mucous plug is lost. Some women lose it a little bit at a time and for others, it comes out in one piece along with some blood, which is known as the *bloody show*. For some women, the amniotic sac (water) breaks before labor begins and for others, the doctor must break it, which effectively speeds up labor. The first stage of labor ends during the *transition phase*. The cervix is 10 centimeters dilated and contractions are severe. This stage lasts about 40 minutes. The second stage of labor begins when the cervix is fully dilated and the fetus moves through the birth canal and ends with the birth. Uterine contractions push the fetus into the birth canal, causing a strong desire on the part of the woman to push. The vaginal opening expands. This stage lasts between 30 and 80 minutes. The head can be seen through the vaginal opening, which is known as the *crowning*. The third stage of labor consists of the placenta detaching from the uterus and leaving the mother's body (known as *afterbirth*).

Some births require a *cesarean section*, in which an incision is made through the abdominal and uterine walls to deliver the baby. This may be done for many reasons but should only be done to ensure the safe delivery of the fetus and the health of the mother. C-sections are not the preferred type of delivery because a C-section is a major surgery and the mother is at higher risk for complications than in vaginal deliveries.

POSTPARTUM ISSUES

Many women experience *baby blues* after childbirth, which consists of mood swings, bouts of tearfulness and crying, and a low mood. This tends to last about 2 weeks or so after giving birth and is often attributed to the massive hormonal changes in the mother's body as her body shifts from a pregnant state to a nonpregnant state and hormones return to normal. Women experience a drastic drop-off in hormones (estrogen and progesterone), which can contribute to extreme emotional reactions. Some women experience a longer lasting low mood that can become depression. This is known as *postpartum depression*. Symptoms include appetite loss, insomnia, intense irritability and anger, overwhelming fatigue, loss of interest in sex, lack of joy in life, feelings of shame, guilt, or inadequacy, severe mood swings, difficulty bonding with the baby, withdrawal from family and friends, and thoughts of self-harm or of harming the baby. In very severe cases, some women develop postpartum psychosis, which typically develops within 2 weeks post-delivery. Symptoms include confusion and disorientation, hallucinations (seeing/hearing/feeling things that are not actually there), delusions (holding extreme faulty beliefs), paranoia (feeling like everyone is out to get you), and/or attempts to harm oneself or one's baby. Postpartum depression and postpartum psychosis can be treated by a doctor and help should be sought immediately as the condition can become life threatening. Women who have a history of depression or postpartum depression, who have a poor support system, who have financial problems, who have problems in their romantic relationship, who have pregnancy complications, who experienced stressful events leading up to the pregnancy, and/or for whom the pregnancy is unwanted may be at higher risk for developing postpartum depression (Mayo Clinic Staff, 2015).

INFERTILITY

Infertility is defined as the inability of a couple to get pregnant after 1 year of trying (if under 35 years) and 6 months (if over 35). Infertility can happen for both men and women and is often due to many reasons. For women, infertility can be due to pelvic inflammatory disease, blockage of Fallopian tubes, diminished ovarian reserve (this happens in older women when the quantity and quality of eggs significantly decreases), polycystic ovarian syndrome (in which eggs only partially develop within the ovary and women have an excess of male hormones), endometriosis (growth of endometrial/uterine tissue in the Fallopian tubes and around the ovaries), scars from STIs, structural issues with the uterus, hormone deficiencies, early menopause, and other reasons. For men, infertility can be due to a very low sperm count (man's body does not produce enough sperm), low levels of necessary hormones, scar tissue or swelling of the seminiferous tubules, where sperm are produced (often caused by mumps), as well as other issues. Infertility can be treated in many ways depending on its causes. Use of assisted reproductive technology has significantly increased over the last few decades. *Intrauterine insemination* (IUI) is one form of fertility treatment used to increase the number of sperm that reach a woman's Fallopian tubes (FTs). A man ejaculates into a cup and then sperm is directly injected into the woman's FTs. Sometimes, IUI is combined with a woman taking the drug Chlomid, which increases the number of eggs she releases during ovulation. IUI does not use hormone treatments but is typically used if a man has a low sperm count or motility (sperm's difficulty swimming to FTs) or if a woman has cervical scarring or has less receptive cervical mucus, which might prevent sperm from reaching the FTs. It tends to be a less invasive procedure than other fertility treatments because there are no hormones involved. *Invitro fertilization* (IVF) was pioneered in the 1970s. In sum, eggs and sperm are combined in a Petri dish in hopes that some of the sperm will fertilize the eggs. Once fertilization takes place, the fertilized embryos are placed into a woman's uterus in hopes that they will implant in the uterine lining. As part of the IVF process, the woman takes fertility drugs to stimulate egg production and to ready her uterine lining for optimal implantation. Once her eggs are mature enough, they are surgically removed and combined with the sperm (which is attained through masturbation). Success rates vary depending on the quality of the eggs, the doctor and laboratory (embryos are created in the lab) conducting the procedure, and thickness of uterine lining; however, most women under 35 years of age have about a 35–40 percent success rate. IVF is very expensive ($15,000 for one round) and very few states mandate that insurance companies cover it. Couples who struggle with infertility report that it is a very isolating and emotionally painful experience. Recently, technology has improved such that women can now freeze their eggs, which can extend their natural fertility beyond what it might have been. Typically, a woman's fertility begins to decline around 35 years of age and women experience another steep decline of fertility around age 40. This is a general guideline because some women under 35 experience fertility issues while some women over 40 do not. Although men typically do not experience a sharp decline to their fertility, as men get into their 50s, there is a decline in semen quality and an increase in genetic problems in their sperm.

Other options for infertile couples wishing to have children include adoption, egg donation, sperm donors, or a surrogate. Egg donation involves using a younger woman's eggs to get pregnant if the older woman wishing to be pregnant experiences poor egg quality or diminished ovarian reserve. A sperm donor might be used if a man wishing to have a child has low quality or low motility sperm. A surrogate might be used if a woman wishing to be pregnant cannot get pregnant on her own and has structural or other problems with her uterus. In all the above cases, IVF is used to get a couple (or individual) pregnant. Egg and sperm donors as well as surrogates are usually financially compensated for their role. Each of these options can help couples who struggle with infertility achieve pregnancy.

PROSTITUTION

Prostitution is a negative consequence of sex. It is defined as the practice of engaging in sexual relations for payment. Individuals who are paid for sex are called sex workers or prostitutes. Prostitutes can be male or female, gay or straight, though most prostitution is female to male where the woman is the prostitute. Prostitution is largely illegal in the United States, for the exception of areas just outside of Las Vegas, Nevada. Since prostitution is illegal in most areas of the United States, it is an unregulated industry. Sex workers are at a higher risk for violence and STIs than the general population. This is far less true when prostitution is regulated (e.g., Amsterdam in the Netherlands). Some prostitutes may be forced into prostitution. This is known as human trafficking and is defined as using coercion or force to transport an unwilling person into prostitution or other sexual exploitation against his or her will. Other types of prostitution include escort services (where a higher class of sex worker than a street prostitute is employed as a social and sexual companion) and a brothel (considered a house of prostitution where the sex acts occur within the brothel).

There tends to be a much higher prevalence of female sex workers in areas where poverty is high. Prostitution in the United States has decreased. Some suggest this is because of the ease of accessing pornography and sex on the Internet as well as societal normalization of multiple sexual contacts outside of a relationship.

COMMUNICATION ABOUT SEX WITH ONE'S PARTNER

Many people find it difficult to communicate to one's romantic partner about sex. This may be because most people did not grow up in households where they felt comfortable asking their parents and the other adults in their lives about sexual issues. Additionally, our sexual education in the United States has primarily focused on abstinence-only education. As a result, most individuals do not feel comfortable talking about sex and/or asking questions about sex. Although having sexual intercourse with another individual is an intimate act, it is often interesting that most people do so without ever directly speaking about it. For example, when two people get ready to engage in sexual intercourse, they most likely do not directly ask for sex. Instead, each couple comes up with their own language to communicate that they want sex. Some couples have "code" words, certain looks, or even specific touches that communicate that one or the other of them would like to have sex. People tend not to directly ask for sex because they fear being rejected—even long-time married couples typically have their own language to ask for sex so it is not communicated directly. We also may not be able to communicate directly about sex with our partners due to our own sexual shame. We may have been taught through our families, spiritual practices, and/or society that sex is shameful and sexual desire leads to problems. We also may have been taught body shame. Each of these things can lead to dissatisfying sexual relationships and/or difficulty communicating with our partners about sex. It can also contribute to the false notion that our partners should "just know" what we want without us having to directly communicate it.

The unfortunate consequence of not clearly communicating our sexual thoughts, fantasies, wants, and desires to our partners is that we can be left sexually frustrated, unfulfilled, resentful, and disinterested in sex with our partners. In some extreme cases, it can lead to one person pushing for sex and another person allowing himself or herself to be pushed because he or she did not have the language to say "no" to a sexual encounter. Clear communication about sex is important so that you and your partner are on the same page regarding sexual issues. Sex is an important part of romantic love for most sexually active adults. When two people are in a healthy relationship, they should feel safe enough to communicate about sex with their partners without fear of being shamed. Being educated about basic principles of human sexuality, sexual anatomy, and sexual responses helps aid successful communication about sex.

CHILDHOOD SEXUAL ABUSE, SEXUAL ASSAULT/RAPE, AND SEXUAL HARASSMENT

There are several types of sexual behavior that are considered outside the norm. They include childhood sexual abuse, sexual assault/rape, and sexual harassment. Childhood sexual abuse is far more common than we think it is. Exact statistics are difficult to determine because it goes underreported by the vast majority of those who are abused. This is because of the stigma associated with it and also abusers are typically someone whom the child knows. Research finds that 1 in 5 girls and 1 in 6 boys is a victim of child sexual abuse. Children tend to be most vulnerable between the ages of 7 and 13. Childhood sexual abuse is defined by the National Child Traumatic Stress Network as any interaction between a child and an adult (or another child) in which the child is used for the sexual stimulation of the perpetrator or an observer. Sexual abuse can include genital touching, oral-genital contact, forcing a child to look at a naked body or other sexual acts, penetration, and any other sexual act that requires manipulation or coercion of the child in a sexual way. *Incest* is a type of sexual abuse that occurs between relatives—typically father-daughter, father-step-daughter, uncle-child, grandfather-child, and so forth. Abusers tend to be very persuasive and convince a child to participate and threaten that no one will believe the child if he/she tells an adult. Children usually experience deep feelings of shame. Without intervention and support, childhood survivors of sexual abuse (especially multiple instances, those who experienced penetration, and/or those who told an adult but were not believed) are at a high risk for self-esteem issues, depression, sexually acting out, angry outbursts, feelings of isolation and loneliness, posttraumatic stress disorder (symptoms include flashbacks, psychological trauma reactions, irritability, anger, mistrust of others, nightmares), anxiety, and other fearful reactions. Studies demonstrate that those who molest children are usually known to the child and are often a relative. King (2009) distinguishes between *preference molesters* and *situational molesters*. Preference molesters have a primary sexual orientation to children and are not interested in adult sexual partners. Situational molesters have a primary sexual orientation to adults and have sex with children impulsively and regard their own behavior as abnormal. *Pedophiles* are sexually attracted to prepubescent children who provide the preferred and/or exclusive method of achieving sexual gratification. Pedophilia is considered an aberrant/abnormal sexual behavior and most societies have a strong negative reaction to those who sexually abuse and/or exploit children.

Sexual assault can be defined as any type of involuntary sexual act that involves coercion including sexual touching, being forced to engage in sexual acts against one's will, and sexual penetration. Violence is often involved, as is the case in *rape*, which usually includes forced sexual vaginal and/or anal penetration. When a victim is intoxicated and/or under the influence of alcohol or drugs, he/she cannot give consent for sexual intercourse or behavior. Women are more likely to be the victims of rape than men, though men too can be raped. According to the Rape, Abuse, and Incest National Network, 1 out of every 6 women has been the victim of an attempt or completed rape. Approximately 15 percent of sexual assault and rape victims are under age 12. Rape survivors have higher incidences of posttraumatic stress disorder, depression, and drug and alcohol abuse and are more likely to contemplate suicide. Rape is typically a crime about power and control, where the abuser demonstrates his or her dominance, though the large majority of rapists are men. Sexual arousal comes from hurting and dominating the victim. Many rapists drink alcohol before committing rape and most rapists are repeat offenders. Because victims carry so much shame and guilt (though the rape was not at all their fault) rapes are significantly underreported. Victims often feel that they face a significant social stigma in reporting what happened to them and fear that they will not be believed. Unfortunately, society will still sometimes hold a victim unfairly responsible for his or her own sexual victimization. This is unfair and completely inaccurate. Rape can occur in several contexts. *Stranger rapes* are committed by someone who is unknown to the victim, *acquaintance rapes* are committed by someone whom the victim knows, and *date rapes* are typically committed during a social encounter (date) agreed to by the victim. *Sexual coercion* is the act of forcing another person into unwanted sexual activity by physical or verbal intimidation, threats, or other types of force. For example, if one partner uses verbal insults and belittling to get the other partner to agree to have sex when that partner clearly does not want to, this would be an example of sexual coercion. There can be long-term emotional and psychological consequences for victims of sexual abuse, rape, sexual assault, and sexual coercion. Having a strong support system and seeking counseling can frequently help the victimized individual deal with the consequences of the abuse or assault.

Sexual harassment can be defined as unwelcome sexual advances that persist after the recipient has indicated that they are unwanted (King, 2009). Sexual harassment is difficult to define because it is not always clear. For example, if two friends who work at the same place exchange sexual jokes, neither may define this as sexual harassment. Sometimes (but not always), sexual harassment occurs between two individuals of different power statuses (e.g., boss and a lower-level employee). A key component of sexual harassment includes the persistence of sexual advances after an individual has made clear that these advances are unwanted. This can contribute to the creation of a hostile work environment in which an individual does not feel comfortable working (e.g., lewd comments, touching, starring, sexual innuendos). Sexual harassment can occur between men and women, women and men, women and women, and men and men. Sexual harassment is thought to be motivated by one person's need to have power over another. This is known as the "power-based" view. Most sexual harassment occurs between men (in higher positions of power) and women employees (in lower positions of power). Research demonstrates that the more a man believes highly stereotypic gender views regarding traditional roles of men and women (men in power, women are subordinates), the more likely he is to accept sexual harassment as being normal (Dietz-Uhler & Murrell, 1992, as cited in King, 2009).

CONCLUSION

As you can see from this chapter, there are many consequences to sex—both positive and negative. This chapter reviewed many of these consequences. Having sex is one of those behaviors that always comes with some consequence. These can be psychological, emotional, physical, and even economical (e.g., an unwanted pregnancy or STI). Prior to beginning a sexual relationship, one should examine the consequences carefully. There are many positive reasons to have sex; however, there are also many potential negatives, especially if one is unprepared to deal with the consequences.

REFERENCES

Brewer, G., & Archer, J. (2007). What do people infer from facial attractiveness? *Journal of Evolutionary Psychology, 5*, 39–49.

Centers for Disease Control and Prevention. (2007). Diseases and conditions. Retrieved from www.cdc.gov/diseasesconditions/.

Centers for Disease Control and Prevention. (2010). National Intimate Partner and Sexual Violence Survey. Retrieved from http://www.cdc.gov/violenceprevention/pdf/nisvs_executive_summary-a.pdf.

Centers for Disease Control and Prevention. (2011). *Youth Risk Behavior Survey.* Retrieved from http://www.cdc.gov/mmwr/pdf/ss/ss6104.pdf.

Dietz-Uhler, B., & Murrell, A. (1992). College students perceptions of sexual harassment: Are gender differences decreasing? *Journal of College Student Development, 33*, 540–546.

Frederick, D. A., et al. (2007). Desiring the muscular ideal: Men's body satisfaction in the United States, Ukraine, and Ghana. *Psychology of Men & Masculinity, 8*, 103–117.

Furnham, A., Swami, V., & Shah, K. (2006). Body weight, waist-to-hop ratio and breast size correlates of ratings of attractiveness and traits. *Personality and Individual Differences, 41*, 443–454.

King, B. R. (2009). *Human sexuality today* (6th ed.). Upper Saddle River, NJ: Pearson Education.

Laumann, E. O., Gagnon, J. H., Michael, R. T., & Michaels, S. (1994). *The social organization of sexuality: Sexual practices in the United States.* Chicago: University of Chicago Press.

MacLean, P. (1962). New findings relevant to the evolution of psychosexual functions of the brain. *Journal of Nervous and Mental Disorders,* 134(4), 280–301.

Mayo Clinic Staff. (2015). *Postpartum depression.* Retrieved from http://www.mayoclinic.org/diseases-conditions/postpartum-depression/basics/definition/con-20029130.

Miller, R. (2012). *Intimate relationships* (6th ed.). New York: McGraw-Hill.

Mullen, P. E., Pathé, M., & Purcell, R. (2000). *Stalkers and their victims.* Cambridge, UK: Cambridge University Press.

Olds, J., & Milner, P. (1954) Positive reinforcement produced by electrical stimulation of septal area and other regions of rat brain. *Journal of Comparative and Physiological Psychology,* 47(6), 419–427.

Shibley Hyde, J., & DeLamater, J. (2003). *Understanding human sexuality* (8th ed.). New York: McGraw-Hill.

Van Dis, H., & Larsson, K. (1971). Induction of sexual arousal in the castrated male rat by intracranial stimulation. *Physiological Behavior, 6,* 85–86.

Vannoy, R. (1980). *Sex without love: A philosophical exploration.* Buffalo, NY: Prometheus Books.

Walker, L. (1979). *The battered woman.* New York: Harper & Row.

Zajonc, R. B. (2001). Mere exposure: A gateway to the subliminal. *Current Directions in Psychological Science, 10,* 224–228.

4

❖

Who: Psychologists' Theories about Sex

This chapter will provide an historical context of the study of sex and the influences on sexual behavior in the United States. Notable theorists shaping American viewpoints on sex throughout history will be reviewed. Finally, how the sexual revolution and the widespread introduction of the birth control pill in 1960 forever changed sexuality and behavior in the United States will be explored. Greenberg et al. (2011), Kelly (2011), and King (2009) provide an excellent review of some of the historical influences on our current views of human sexuality. Their collective historical review includes the influences of Judaism, Greeks and Romans, Christianity, and the Victorian era and the profound effects of these perspectives on our understanding of human sexuality as well as our values about sex.

INFLUENCES OF JUDAISM

"The roots of the Judeo-Christian sexual prohibitions, as well as the sexual prohibitions of religions such as Islam, spring from ancient Jewish tribal law. Jewish law considered wives 'property'" (West, 2012, p. 28). The primary purpose of sex in ancient Hebrew times was procreation and the goal was to have several children for God and the health of one's family. Hebrew society was patriarchal (i.e., men are considered the head of the household) and there was significant concern at that time about the social consequences of sex. "Sex outside of marriage, especially for women was severely condemned and punished harshly and rape was considered a violation of another man's property" (King, 2009, p. 9). There was also punishment for homosexuality. In ancient times, Jews considered sex between husband and wife a positive bonding event and a sacred sharing between couples. They considered the mutual pleasure that sex could provide to be a gift from God and there were only a few restrictions: one, the husband must ejaculate within his wife's vagina (so as not to spill his seed, which would reduce the chances of conception) (King, 2009), and two, there was to be no intercourse when women were experiencing the menstrual cycle.

GREEKS AND ROMANS

Greeks and Romans also strongly supported marriage and having many children. Greek and Roman society was patriarchal (men and masculinity are highly valued over women and femininity). Hyper-masculinity was prized in men while modesty and chastity was prized in women. Men were allowed greater latitude in sexual promiscuity than were women. Couples were expected to procreate for the purposes of creating a strong state (society). Sex between young boys and older men was both acceptable and an expected societal norm in some circumstances. For example, King (2009) highlights that "in Greece, sexual relations between men and adolescent boys in a teacher-student relationship were not only tolerated, but were encouraged as part of the boy's intellectual, emotional, and moral development" (p. 11). This was not stigmatized as "homosexual behavior" as we often stigmatize same-sex sexual relationships today. Instead, this was considered an important stage of development for some boys departing adolescence and entering adulthood. Sexual relationships between men and boys in this context were considered in part as mentorship into manhood.

As can be seen in many ancient Greek and Roman sculptures, the human body was idealized and considered physically beautiful. Earlier permissive attitudes about men's sexual behavior later became influenced by the philosophy of *dualism*, which is the belief that body and soul are separate (King, 2009). Dualism ushered in a new phase of sexual restrictiveness and conservatism different from the sexual freedom many men experienced in earlier times. King (2009) summarized that during this time period in the Greek era, there was a strong emphasis on spiritual development and a denial of physical pleasures. As a result, Greek and Roman sexual behavior (especially for men) became more limited. King (2009) asserts that *dualism* strongly influenced early Christian attitudes toward human sexuality and sexual behavior.

CHRISTIANITY

St. Augustine was a fourth century bishop (A.D. 354–430) who had an extraordinarily negative view about sex and specific sexual acts. St. Augustine's views on sex and sexuality significantly shaped the Christian viewpoint on these topics. Prior to his entering religious life, he lived a lifestyle of sexual debauchery, which included a mistress and a son born out of wedlock, and it is also rumored that he had a same-sex affair (Boswell, 1980, as cited in King, 2009). As a result of his shame regarding his own sexually explicit behavior, he developed distinctively antisexual views and believed that all sex was sinful. Father Thomas Rauch states that "it is regrettable that St. Augustine's influence and the negative appraisal of sexuality, based on his own struggles to be chaste has so impacted negatively with Christian tradition" (www.cybercollege.com/history.htm). Catholic religious traditions involved seeking resolution from sins, which included lust and other sexual feelings. The *missionary position* (man on top) was the only sexual position sanctioned by the Church, as sex was only for married couples for the purposes of procreation and that position was deemed the most appropriate for procreation. Ironically, Masters and Johnson's research in the 1970s would reveal that women are least likely to have an orgasm in the missionary position.

Common Christian teaching included the idea that couples were not supposed to enjoy sexual intercourse as that too was considered a sin. The only reason to have sex was to have children. Experiencing lust was also considered a sign of weakness. As you can see, religious traditions have always influenced the sexual behavior of couples and society's viewpoints about sex. While the societal norms of the day limited and regulated men's sexual behavior, the idea that women had any sexual feelings was extremely threatening. For women especially, appearing sexually inappropriate (e.g., adultery) had extreme consequences (e.g., ostracism, death). Women were to embody the ideal that "godly women," or women who were most like Mary, the Mother of God, did not enjoy sex but only did so as part of their marital obligations to produce many children. King (2009) reminds us that women were still blamed for Adam's being expelled from the Garden of Eden as this resulted in the original sin of man. In the story of Adam and Eve, Eve offered Adam a bite of the "forbidden fruit." God had given Adam specific instructions not to eat from this particular fruit. He ate it because Eve gave it to him. Thus, women were viewed as temptresses and without moral restrictions; women's sexuality could destroy the moral order. This view-point, unfortunately, shapes concerns regarding women's sexuality today.

St. Thomas Aquinas, a 13th century philosopher, was another individual who shaped Christianity's teachings about sex. He spoke to the value of chastity and especially condemned masturbation. He believed that masturbation was an unnatural vice and that lust was sinful and harmful. He also believed that any sexual behavior for the sole purposes of pleasure (and not for procreation) was unclean, a sign of weakness, and a sin. Misperceptions about masturbation continued throughout the latter parts of the 20th century. Falsehoods about masturbation, including the idea that it caused hairy palms, hair loss, blindness, serious health problems, chronic fatigue, and so forth, persisted. Although today's views from the Catholic Church differ in that intercourse within the marital relationship is considered an act of bonding and mutual self-giving, the Church's former negative views of sex from ancient times still impact our acceptance of human sexual behavior today.

THE VICTORIAN ERA

The Victorian era, named for the British queen Victoria, espoused an era of sexual restrictiveness, strong moral and social codes, and emotional and sexual repression. The viewpoint that sexual expression and loose sexual behavior could cause emotional and mental disturbances was popularized during this time period (Soble, 2008, as cited in Kelly, 2011). Psychology, a relatively new science at this time, began contributing to societal views about sex, including the strict gender roles of men and women, ejaculation as physically and emotionally draining for men, menstruation considered to be an emotionally debilitating condition, and sex to be restricted and controlled. Interestingly, the Victorian era brought forth several early sexologists (people who study human sexuality from a scientific perspective) and others who significantly contributed to the field of human sexuality, which include the following individuals: Richard von Kraft-Ebing, Sigmund Freud, Magnus Hirschfeld, Henry Havelock Ellis, Helena Wright, and Robert Latou Dickinson. Each person's viewpoint will be briefly summarized. Alfred Kinsey, William Masters, Virginia Johnson, and Margaret Sanger were also significant contributors to the field and are discussed in several sections of this book.

Richard von Kraft-Ebing

Richard von Kraft-Ebing (1840–1902) was an Austro-German neurologist and psychiatrist. He published one of the first medical texts on sexual aberrations (i.e., sexual behavior that deviated from the norm) entitled *Psychopathia Sexualis* (Kelly, 2011). Von Kraft-Ebing believed that masturbation was "the cause of all sexual deviations" (p. 14) and that there were four types of sexual pathology: sadism, masochism, fetishism, and homosexuality (Kelly, 2011). He hypothesized that these were in part due to hereditary influences and based much of his work on limited, sensational case studies that would not necessarily be scientifically valid today. He believed that sex was for procreative purposes only and thought that women were sexually passive.

Sigmund Freud (1856–1939)

Sigmund Freud is one of the most influential psychiatrists ever to shape the field of psychology as well as our discourse on human sexuality. Freud was from Austria. He studied the psychosexual development of children and how it impacted adult life and psychological conditions (Kelly, 2011). Some of Freud's interest in the psychosexual development of children may have come from his own background. According to Murdock (2009), Freud was born to a relatively young mother and a father 20 years her senior. He had half-siblings from his father's previous marriage who were his mother's age. This may have shaped his ideas about how early childhood experiences impact us as adults. He entered university when he was 17 and excelled academically. He eventually went on to earn a medical degree in neurology, though he later practiced psychiatry.

Freud worked with Joseph Breuer, another influential physician of the time, on cases involving "hysterical" patients. Hysteria then meant "wandering uterus," which was originally thought to only afflict women. *Hysteria* is defined as emotional instability caused by trauma: an emotionally unstable state brought about by a traumatic experience. The term *hysteria* has been used for over 2,000 years. In psychology *hysteria* is a primary symptom characterizing disorders that have physical symptoms (e.g., headaches, pain, blindness) but have no identifiable physical cause (Hysteria, n.d.-a, n.d.-b). In fact, the causes of these disorders are thought to be psychological. Martin and Lyons (2011) reviewed several cases in the early history of abnormal psychology that include individuals suffering from *hysterical blindness* and *hysterical paralysis*, in which the patients appeared highly emotional, dramatic, and attention seeking. These individuals demonstrated a multitude of symptoms. For example, those who reported paralysis of a limb were indeed paralyzed but the cause of the paralysis was manufactured by the mind. The cause was psychological and not physical.

Freud later stated that men too could be afflicted with hysteria (Murdock, 2009). At this time, Freud was interested in somatization as well, which includes physical ailments, body complaints, pain, and/or psychoneurological symptoms (e.g., amnesia) that have no known physical cause but may be caused by psychological concerns. In his work with Breuer, he discovered that talking to patients about their fears, anxiety, and concerns had a significant impact on their recovery. He became interested in what would later be known as the *talking cure* or *psychoanalysis*. Psychotherapy developed from the talking cure.

Freud's theory of psychoanalysis has significant implications for our views on sex and sexuality. He developed his theory at a time when the Victorian era values of sexual restrictiveness and sexual repression were evident in everyday life. This is only one of the many reasons his theory was controversial at the time. Murdock (2009) asserts that "Freud's ideas laid the foundation for the profession of psychology and the practice of psychotherapy as we know it today. Most of the prominent theories of counseling and psychotherapy either incorporate Freud's ideas or were formulated in reaction to them" (p. 33). Following is a description of his theory. The parts most relevant to our views on human sexuality will be highlighted.

Psychoanalysis

Freud began to develop his theory of *psychoanalysis* through his exploration of the patients in his practice and their presenting concerns. Freud saw many women and children with debilitating anxiety, recurring frightening dreams, and hysterical illnesses. He concluded that the root of his patients' neuroses (extreme anxiety) was sexual repression. He strongly believed that many problems in adulthood have their beginnings in childhood—usually prior to the age of 6 (Murdock, 2009). "For Freud, human behavior is produced by conflicts between genetically built-in drives, the instincts of self-preservation, sex, and destruction. In his view the dominant force in human behavior is the sexual instinct which is innate" (p. 34).

Freud believed that from the time we are born, we have sexual (also known as *libidinal*) energy swirling inside us that influences our behavior and reactions. Because society condemns overt sexual expression—it especially did so in the Victorian era—human beings must find socially appropriate outlets for these unacceptable influences. Freud proposed that individuals deny the existence of these unacceptable influences to the point in which we are completely unaware that they exist. Freud would say that these feelings and thoughts then become *unconscious*. He believed that our *unconscious* influences us in significant ways but we are completely unaware of what is in our unconscious minds. A large part of psychoanalysis has to do with the psychotherapist helping the patient reveal what is in his or her unconscious. Freud believed that "evidence of the unconscious was found in everyday occurrences such as forgetting, mistakes, 'slips of the tongue,' and dreams" (Murdock, 2009, p. 34). Slips of the tongue are mistakes in language. For example, if a person says the name of one person (e.g., Julie) when he or she really mean the name of another (e.g., Kathy), this would be known as a slip of the tongue. Freud generally thought this to reveal some unconscious sexual thoughts or the true feelings on the part of the individual making the "slip" (Tran, 2013). Today, in Freud's honor, slips of the tongue are also referred to as *Freudian slips*.

Structure of Personality

Freud believed that there were three basic divisions in the mind (Murdock, 2009): *id*, *ego*, and *superego*. Newborns are born with intact ids. Babies seek immediate gratification for their needs and they learn their environments by putting everything in their mouths. The id operates on a totally unconscious level and is guided by the *pleasure principle* (Murdock, 2009), which seeks pleasure and avoids pain. The id's needs are immediate and must be satisfied right now. The next personality structure to develop, according to Freud, is the ego. The ego develops to help restrain instinctual sexual drives, as society will not tolerate the raw sexual, immediate needs of the id. The ego operates on the *reality principle* (Murdock, 2009). While the id does not operate in reality nor is it conscious, the ego does operate in reality. It represents the most rational, thoughtful part of us. This part of our personality has adapted to live in society in a balanced and socially acceptable way. Finally, the superego is the third part of our personality. The superego represents our internalizing society's rules, norms, and moral standards for our behavior. Our parents teach us right from wrong and we internalize certain values given our upbringing and the environment where we grow up. The superego represents our sense of morality and/or rightness/wrongness. It helps us to behave in moral and socially acceptable ways and serves to balance our negative unconscious (id) forces. When we behave in ways inconsistent with our superego we may feel shame and guilt.

Freud believed that we all develop from childhood to adulthood through a series of psychosexual stages, primarily focusing on sexual development. Freud's focus on sex as a primary motivating force of human behavior shocked the Victorian era professional community

(Murdock, 2009). According to Murdock (2009), other controversial ideas included Freud's belief that humans are inherently sexual creatures, infants and children have sexual urges, humans are inherently bisexual, and that gender identification results from an innate tendency toward maleness or femaleness along with the way certain developmental crises are resolved (e.g., Oedipal complex) (p. 41). In each stage, an individual has an unconscious conflict he or she must work through. Successful resolution of this conflict results in the person moving onto the next stage. A failure to resolve the conflict means the person remains *fixated* or stuck in the present stage.

Freud's psychosexual stages include the following: oral, anal, phallic, latency, and genital stages. Each stage is associated with an erogenous (pleasure) zone. The *oral stage* lasts from birth through 1 year. Infants get their needs met through sucking (e.g., breast, bottle). Pleasure is derived from feeding and oral exploration of the environment. Infants put everything in their mouths, which is how they begin to learn about their surroundings. The *anal stage* is from 1 to 3 years old. Satisfaction is gained from the functions of elimination (Murdock, 2009, p. 41). Children this age become quickly fascinated with urination and defecation in themselves and others. Potty training traditionally begins around the end of this phase and parents and children frequently struggle to gain power during these interactions surrounding potty training. This is also the time children begin to be expected to live by society's rules and social norms. The *phallic stage* (3–6 years) is focused on the genitalia. Genitalia is the primary erogenous zone. Children this age are very interested in the differences between boys and girls. They frequently want to know why boys have a penis and girls have a vagina. They begin to ask questions regarding how babies are made, why genitals are different, and what it means to be a boy or a girl. Freud believed that boys have an *Oedipus complex* and girls go through something similar. Named for characters in Greek mythology, these complexes describe children's same-sex desires and feelings for their opposite-sex parents. Freud believed that little boys unconsciously sexually desired their mothers while little girls unconsciously sexually desired their fathers. Because these feelings are socially unacceptable, children must learn to quickly repress them into their unconscious (so that they are not aware of these feelings) so they can identify with the same-sex parent (boys identify with dad and girls identify with mom); they may therefore lead socially acceptable lives. Freud also believed that boys and girls feel competition with their same-sex parents and may unconsciously compete for the opposite-sex parent's attention.

The Oedipus complex derives from the Greek mythological story of Oedipus. (Murdock, 2009). Oedipus's parents, King Laius and Queen Jocasta, found out from an oracle (fortune teller) upon their infant son's birth that this child would kill his father. As a result, the child was left on the side of the road to die; however, the child was found and raised to adulthood. Unknowingly, Oedipus eventually marries his mother and kills his own father. As soon as he discovers this, his mother commits suicide and he gouges his own eyes out so that he is blinded. Both Oedipus and his mother are horrified and disgusted by their behavior as their incestuous union is forbidden by society. This tale highlights the societal taboo against incest—sex between close blood relatives is taboo in every society. Thus in using this Greek myth to explain the unconscious sexual feelings boys have toward their mothers, Freud is illustrating that because incest is such a cultural taboo, part of the conflict of this particular psychosexual stage is to repress (block something from one's mind) these unacceptable feelings and identify with their fathers. He hypothesized that boys fear their father's power. Boys fear that should their fathers discover their secret sexual feelings toward their mothers, their fathers would retaliate by cutting off their son's penises. He termed this *castration anxiety*. Since boys do not want to be castrated by their fathers, they repress into their unconsciousness any sexual feelings they have toward their mothers and identify with their fathers.

Freud did not seem to fully understand girls and women's psychosexual development. His theory is incomplete when it comes to describing their resolution of the Oedipal stage. He stated that "psychology is unable to solve the riddle of femininity" (Freud [1964], p. 16, as cited in Murdock, 2009). He believed that girls had *penis envy* and that girls struggled with negative psychological implications of not having a penis. According to Murdock (2009), he hypothesized that female homosexuality was due to unresolved penis envy. He believed that women felt inferior because the penis was superior to the clitoris and the only way that women could get close to having a penis was to have a male baby and thus he concluded that this is one reason mothers and daughters have such complicated relationships with one another (Murdock, 2009). In an attempt to help clarify the female psychosexual experience, Carl Jung, a follower of Freud in his early days (he later broke with Freud), developed the *Electra complex* to explain women's psychosexual development in the phallic stage. Jung believed that similar to boys, girls have sexual feelings toward their fathers, which becomes apparent during the phallic stage. He hypothesized that the Electra complex is heightened when girls discover they have no penis.

This is when they most strongly desire their fathers, as they are very disappointed to not have a penis. Similar to boys, girls fear their mothers' power and are in competition with them for their father's attention. They also become aware that their sexual desire toward their fathers is unacceptable; thus they repress it into the unconscious and identify with their mothers. Successful resolution of the Oedipal and Electra complexes allows children to develop a mature, adult, sexual identity (Murdock, 2009).

Fixation

Becoming fixated at a stage implies that the psychic conflict an individual was supposed to resolve was not done so successfully and individual becomes fixated or stuck in that stage. Freud believed that when an individual was fixated at a particular stage, certain behaviors were apparent. For example, a person fixated at the oral stage might excessively chew gum, smoke, or be highly immature. A person at the anal stage might be obsessively organized and rigid or extremely careless and sloppy. Someone fixated at the phallic stage might be unhealthily attached to the opposite-sex parent. Finally, fixation at the latency stage might imply someone who will never be sexually fulfilled while being fixated at the genital stage might be expressed through an individual's total inability to enjoy sex or have satisfactory romantic relationships (McLeod, 2008).

Concluding Comments on Psychoanalysis

As you can see by this extensive review of his theory, Freud's ideas remain both influential and controversial. Freud's ideas about children's sexuality, childhood, and adult sexual repression significantly shaped our understanding of childhood development. Although he had many critics, several of his former followers went on to develop theories in contrast to his and believed that he focused too much on sex. Freud's work has had a lasting impact on the field of psychology and the psychology of sex.

Magnus Hirschfeld (1868–1935)

Magnus Hirschfeld was a German Jewish physician who studied homosexuality. He believed that "justice through science" would promote more tolerance toward the homosexual community and eliminate hostility toward this group. He also studied the transgender population and wrote the book *Institut* publishing his findings. Hirschfeld was interested (and later American sex researcher Alfred Kinsey would follow in his footsteps) in sexual variety among human beings. Today, he would be considered a gay rights activist. Kelly (2011) states that "Hirschfeld was one of the first professionals to take a stand on rights for people who were gay or lesbian. He risked personal persecution and anti-Semitic repercussions for saying that people with same-sex sexual orientation constituted an intermediate third sex that deserved the same rights and privileges as heterosexuals" (p. 38). Hirschfeld also argued against the prevailing claims about the negative effects of masturbation, believing them to be exaggerated and unfounded (Bullough, 2003, as cited in Kelly 2011, p. 15). Just before World War II, the Nazis burned and banned many of his books.

Henry Havelock Ellis (1859–1939)

Henry Havelock Ellis was a British physician and foundational sex researcher. His ideas would later be echoed in Alfred Kinsey's work. According to Kelly (2011), Ellis "spent decades studying all available information on human sexuality in the Western world and on the sexual mores of other cultures" (p. 16). He published a six-volume series between 1896 and 1910 entitled *Studies in the Psychology of Sex*. His books recognized the significant variation in human sexual behavior. Ellis concluded the following: Both men and women masturbate and that it is normative behavior, sexual orientation is more fluid than how it is currently labeled, recognizing that sexual orientation is not necessarily absolute (i.e., people are not 100 percent hetero or homosexual but somewhere in between), women are as capable as men of great sexual desire, the male and female orgasm are similar, and sexual behavior and values are largely determined by cultural and social influences (Kelly, 2011). These ideas were in direct opposition to the strict moral codes of the Victorian era. Ellis also wrote the first English medical textbook on homosexuality entitled *Sexual Inversion*. He also wrote the first objective study of human sexuality as he did not characterize it as a disease, crime, or immoral act (Kelly, 2011). Ellis is credited with coining the term *autoeroticism*, which refers to the practice of masturbation in both sexes and by people of all ages (Kelly, 2011). Ellis also had more sexually liberal views regarding women and believed that women could experience sexual pleasure and that doing so was psychologically healthy.

Helena Wright (1882–1982)

Helena Wright was a British physician who specialized in gynecology, birth control, and family planning. She was a pioneer in both England and internationally. Wright's (1938) book *The Sex Factor in Marriage* was especially popular in the United States and helped to solidify her reputation as an international figure in women's reproductive health. Wright was an outspoken supporter of both abortions and adoptions, often helping women arrange for one or the other. She advocated for the medical professions' responsibility in educating women about contraception. She faced significant opposition to her liberal views regarding birth control for women; however, she was able to persuade some of the English bishops to allow the use of contraception between married couples. Wright went on to establish several birth control clinics in the United Kingdom. In her role as chief medical officer at the Kensington Centre, she changed the training model of doctors and nurses including for the first time, education about family planning and women's contraception. She was also instrumental in getting the British government to think about including family planning in the National Health Service, though full inclusion of family planning in the National Health Service would not happen until 1974.

Margaret Sanger (1879–1966)

Margaret Sanger was an iconic birth control activist, sex educator, and nurse in the United States. She is responsible for forming Planned Parenthood (known first as the American Birth Control League), supporting safe family planning methods for women, helping to usher in the birth control pill, and educating women about their reproductive health. She had training as a nurse. Sanger opened the first birth control clinic (staffed by all women) in the United States, which was illegal at the time. She was arrested. Much of her early work happened in New York City. She also opened a birth control clinic in Harlem staffed entirely by African American medical personnel. She is known as the founder of the birth control movement (Chana & Steward, 2003).

Although both her parents were Roman Catholic, she took significant issue with the Catholic Church on the grounds that the church was run by men who set doctrine for women's sexual behavior. Her father became an atheist, abandoning his own Catholic roots. Her mother had 18 pregnancies, with 11 live births in 22 years and died at age 49. We can hypothesize that this significantly impacted Margaret's views on birth control as she spent much of her childhood and adolescence caring for her siblings and taking care of the household. She was the 6th out of 11 children. In her work as a nurse, she often tended to the working class and poor and saw firsthand how many children women had that they did not want nor could afford (Chana & Steward, 2003). It was said that she associated poverty, depression, and social ill will with large families and she came to believe that birth control would help liberate women from unwanted pregnancies and change the social order, elevating the working classes. She viewed birth control as a free speech issue and sought to educate women, in mass on birth control options. She published several newsletters circulating her views that women should be the "master of their own bodies." She popularized such terms as *family limitation* and *birth control.*

The Comstock Law of 1873 was meant to stop trade in "obscene literature and immoral articles that ended up targeting obscenity, dirty books, birth control devices, abortion, and information on sexuality and sexually transmitted diseases" (Johnson Lewis, n.d.). Margaret Sanger often acted in opposition to this law, which led to her arrest more than once. Despite the law, she continued to publish newsletters and educational information on contraception and family planning. However, in 1938, a judge lifted the federal ban on birth control ending the use of the Comstock Law to target birth control information and devices (Chana & Steward, 2003; Johnson Lewis, n.d.).

In her travels to Europe, she discovered that other countries had more progressive birth control views. In the Netherlands, she discovered the *diaphragm*, a new method of birth control that was much more effective than the suppositories and douches she had been disseminating in her clinics in the United States. She quickly began importing diaphragms to the United States, though these were seized by the government. In her promotion of birth control and contraceptive education, Margaret Sanger was arrested multiple times. Her trial received considerable attention and as a result, the birth control movement gained popularity. She even began receiving consistent (but anonymous) contributions from John D. Rockefeller. He wanted to support her cause but did not want to publically expose himself to controversy. She served as the first president of the International Planned Parenthood Federation, until she was 80 years old. Margaret Sanger was instrumental in securing funding for clinical trials of the birth control pill from philanthropist Katharine McCormick and lived to see legalization of the birth control pill in 1960. In addition to her work on birth control she was a strong advocate for openly discussing women's sexuality. She was heavily influenced by Henry Havelock Ellis's book *The Psychology of Sex* and met with him while she was in England. Sanger and Ellis were convinced that women should be able to enjoy sex without fear of pregnancy. Margaret Sanger frequently blamed the Catholic Church for their limited views on sexuality and for discouraging conversations about women's sexuality and birth control. Because today women can receive an abortion in many Planned Parenthood clinics, it is mistakenly believed that Margaret Sanger supported abortion. She was opposed to abortion as she believed that life began at conception. She was much more interested in promoting birth control and believed that abortion caused a significant health risk to the mother.

Margaret Sanger is the author of several books and educational pamphlets. She was extraordinarily influential in bringing the plight of women facing unwanted pregnancies to the national landscape. Though controversial, she significantly shaped the discussion on birth control and opened multiple clinics helping women achieve what she believed as their contraceptive rights to control when pregnancy happened.

Robert Latou Dickinson (1861–1950)

Robert Latou Dickinson was an obstetrician and gynecologist. He was an active researcher in women's sexual health and published many of his findings. He was chief of obstetrics and gynecology at the Brooklyn Hospital and the president of the American Gynecological Society. He was a sketch artist and often (with his patient's permission) sketched his patients' genitalia. He was also one of the first physicians to get detailed sexual histories from his patients. Alfred Kinsey was strongly influenced by his work, as we will see later in this chapter. In later years, Dickinson closed his medical practice and became a public health educator and advocate for contraceptive rights, though his writings were often limited by the Comstock Laws. In 1932 he published an influential book entitled *A Thousand Marriages: A Medical Study of Sex Adjustments*, based on his gynecological practice teaching women how to achieve orgasm (Kelly, 2011). In this book he utilizes his sex histories from 1,000 married women. In 1933, he published *Human Sex Anatomy*, the first modern book that held illustrations of sexual positions. He studied the female response during masturbation and was one of the first gynecologists to induce orgasm in female patients using an electric vibrator (Wallechinsky & Wallace, 1981). He utilized the case studies seen in his own practice to inform his writings.

Alfred Kinsey (1894–1956)

Alfred Kinsey is arguably one of the most influential sex researchers in the United States. He was born to parents Alfred Kinsey Sr. and Sarah Ann. His father was a college professor, but his parents had little money. Kinsey himself was an unhealthy child and fell prey to several medical conditions, including rickets, rheumatic fever, and typhoid fever. His parents were conservative and devout Christians and his father was known to be extremely strict. As a young boy, despite his physical limitations, Kinsey joined the Boy Scouts of America and went on many camping trips, which later proved to be influential in his future career path. Kinsey's father wanted him to become an engineer; however, Kinsey was interested in biology and nature. He followed his father's wishes for 2 years but later quit his study of engineering and confronted his father about his desired career as a biologist. The two actively fought about Alfred Jr.'s decision to pursue a career in which his father did not approve. As a result, his father kicked him out of the house. Kinsey went on to study biology against his father's wishes and later earned his doctorate. Kinsey went on to study gall wasps at Harvard as a doctoral student. His work with gall wasps was highly influential and he achieved some success as a scientist in this area. One of the things he took from his study of the mating practices of gall wasp was the immense variation within the species. He later applied the notion of exploring the depth of variation among human sexual behavior to his research on sex (Goodman & Maggio, 2005).

Kinsey married Clara Bracken McMillen in 1921 and they had four children. It took them over 6 months to consummate their marriage as intercourse was painful for both of them. This impacted Kinsey deeply and in his own early sexual experiences with Clara, he began to research human sexuality to help explain their sexual problems. He was disappointed in the lack of scientific study, which sparked his interest and transition to the field of human sexuality. Kinsey became a professor at Indiana University, where he taught the first ever human sexuality course. Students had to be married to take the course and several moved up their weddings so that they would be married and qualify to take the course prior to the beginning of the semester. He shocked the class by putting diagrams of human genitalia on the overhead projector. While teaching this course, he began taking extensive sexual histories of students. Clara and Kinsey had an old abandoned car in their backyard and often allowed married students to use the car to have sex with one another, as there were no coeducational dormitories at the time (Goodman & Maggio, 2005).

When the administration found out that Kinsey was taking students' sexual histories, they made him choose between taking students' sexual histories and teaching the course. Kinsey quit teaching the course and began researching human sexuality by taking sexual case histories from students, faculty, neighbors, and whoever would volunteer to give them. He received outside funding for his research on human sexuality. He founded and directed Indiana University's Institute for Sex Research (Kelly, 2011). He formed a research team and trained them in his method of taking sexual histories, which sometimes consisted of over 500–1,000 questions. Questions included content such as age at first sexual desire, experiences with masturbation, numbers of sexual partners, how many orgasms someone experienced, types of sexual desire experienced, and sexual orientation. Kinsey utilized the case study method of research and sought to get as many different types of people from as many different groups as he and his team could. Thus, Kinsey interviewed homosexuals, a limited number of African American men and women, prisoners, prostitutes, church members, fraternities and sororities, and so forth. His research was expensive and time consuming and his outside funding sources began to demand that he take random samples of the population as opposed to attempting to get more subjects. Kinsey refused and thereby lost his funding source.

During his research Kinsey often sexually experimented with his own research staff. He convinced them to have sex with one another and he himself found that he was bisexual. He and his wife engaged in extramarital sexual relationships, which were subsequently absorbed into his research.

Kinsey's work was highly controversial in that sexual issues were still taboo in the United States during the 1940s and 1950s. Resultant from Kinsey's research were two very popular massive publications entitled *The Kinsey Reports*. The first volume explored men's sexuality: *Sexual Behavior in the Human Male* (1948); the second volume (the most controversial) explored women's sexuality, entitled *Sexual Behavior in the Human Female* (1953). These volumes sold out. Although many people criticized his work and feared that exploring women's sexuality would destroy the moral order, many others bought the volumes, went to see him speak, and developed a more open dialogue about human sexuality. For the first time, America had an idea of what "normative" sexual behavior was. They no longer had to guess what types of sexual behavior were out there as it was clearly documented in Kinsey's research. Kinsey found that masturbation and oral sex were far more common than most people believed. He also found that both men and women had more than one sexual partner upon marriage. He also explored homosexuality and developed a theory that sexual orientation does not consist of dichotomous categories (i.e., heterosexual or homosexual). He believed that it made more sense to describe human sexuality on a continuum. He developed a scale measuring sexual orientation ranking from 0 to 6. Zero was exclusively heterosexual and 6 was exclusively homosexual. Most individuals did not fall strictly at a 0 or 6 but instead fell closer to one end or the other. This finding may have paved the way to our beginning to broaden our views regarding sexual orientation. Kinsey's work has been seen as foundational to the sexual revolution, which is discussed below.

Despite his seminal works, Kinsey died disappointed and disillusioned. His research was largely halted due to lack of funding because his funding source did not agree with his research methods. His research team was disbanded and Kinsey reportedly experienced cardiac health issues and severe depression. Kelly (2011) discusses some problems with his methods, including only using samples of convenience (i.e., only people who would volunteer to give sexual histories). This is a problem because there may be differences between those subjects willing to give histories and those unwilling to do so. These two groups may have very different sexual experiences. One major controversy in his research was his use of a known pedophile who abused several children. Kinsey kept all subjects anonymous and only identified them by a number. Kinsey used this subject's journal, which recounted his sexual abuse of children and the children's sexual reactions. Kinsey reported that this data came from multiple sources but in fact it had only come from the pedophile's journal. This was disturbing to the general public when this was revealed and significantly tainted his reputation and acceptance of his research findings. His research pool was also criticized for not including many African Americans and other groups of color. Others also suggested that homosexuals and prostitutes may have been overrepresented in his research sample. Despite these significant methodological flaws, Kinsey's work is still foundational in the way we understand human sexuality and sexual behavior today.

William Masters (1915–2001) and Virginia Johnson (1925–2013)

In many ways, Masters and Johnson's research took up where Kinsey's research left off. Kinsey explored the frequency of occurrence of certain sexual behaviors. Masters and Johnson brought individuals into the laboratory and recorded their bodies' physiological responses before, during, and after sex. Before Masters and Johnson's work, we did not know for certain the male and female's responses to sexual stimulation and orgasm. According to Kelly (2011), Masters and Johnson's work focused on two areas: the physiology of human sexual response and the treatment of sexual dysfunction. Kelly (2011) and King (2009) describe the sophisticated instrumentation used to study the human body's responses to sexual intercourse. They brought 382 women and 312 men aged 18–89 into the laboratory. Their resultant publications included *Human Sexual Response* (1966) and *Human Sexual Inadequacy* (1970). As you will see below, both were foundational to the field of human sexuality and sexology (the scientific study of sex) in different ways.

Masters and Johnson used tools to measure penile and vaginal responses to sexual stimulation. As a result of their efforts, they developed a four-stage model of the sexual response cycle. King (2009), Kelly (2011), and Greenberg et al. (2011) review the sexual response cycle.

> *Excitement phase*: In both men and women there is a vasocongestion response (blood rushing to the genitals) within several seconds. In men, this causes an erection and in women this causes vaginal lubrication. Both men and women experience an increase in heart rate and blood pressure. Some individuals experience a sexual flush in which the chest "blushes" and the skin takes on a pinkish tinge. There is also a tightening of muscles. In men the testicles are drawn upward toward the body. In women, there is a swelling of the clitoris and labia (lips) minora and vagina. The vagina also begins to elongate. Also, a woman's breasts may increase in size.

> *Plateau phase*: This is a state of heightened arousal and sets the stage for orgasm. In men, the diameter of the penis increases and the testicles become fully engorged. The Cowper's glands of the penis secrete a few drops of clear fluid at the top of the penis (King, 2009). For women, the inner two thirds of the vagina continue to elongate and expand. The tissues surrounding the vagina continue to swell (King, 2009). For many women, the clitoris may also disappear behind the clitoral hood.

> *Orgasm*: Men and women describe the experience of orgasm similarly. There is a series of muscular contractions in the lower pelvic muscles surrounding the anus and primary sexual organs. Men ejaculate semen. Women's vaginal lubrication usually increases during orgasm. Women's vaginal walls also tighten during orgasm heightening sexual pleasure for both individuals.

> *Resolution phase*: For both men and women, there is a decrease in blood pressure and heart rate and the body returns to its normal resting state. Men have a refractory period, in which they are unable to have another orgasm. The refractory period for young men tends to be shorter than for older men. Women do not have a refractory period and can be multiorgasmic.

After developing this model, Masters and Johnson began working on treating individuals with sexual dysfunctions, including male erectile disorder (a man's inability to achieve or maintain an erection), premature ejaculation (ejaculating too soon in the sexual experience for both partners to experience sexual satisfaction), hypoactive sexual desire (low sexual desire), orgasmic disorder (inability to achieve orgasm), vaginismus (the vaginal muscles tightening or snapping shut, preventing any type of insertion or intercourse), and dyspareunia (pain during intercourse). They developed such methods as the *squeeze technique* to prevent premature ejaculation, where the man himself or his partner gently squeezes the penis between the shaft and corona (the rounded projected border at the top of the penis) (King, 2009) prior to ejaculation. *Sensate focusing* is a treatment that decreases the performance anxiety often associated with sexual issues. Typically, the couple is given a series of sexual exercises with the goal of increasing communication, physical and emotional awareness, and trust. Couples are allowed to touch one another (nonsexually at first). They communicate about what they like and what feels good. They each gather information from the other about specific touching likes and dislikes. Eventually, the couple moves to more sexual touching (genital touching, still communicating with one another) and they continue onto sex if their previous exercises have been successful. Couples use techniques such as placing one's partner's hand over one's own and showing the other person how to touch are important. Non-genital aspects of sex are emphasized including, hugging, kissing, and massage. Sensate focus is highly effective in treating some of the sexual dysfunction that stems from *performance anxiety* (a strong concern or fear regarding how one is performing an act that usually impedes the ability to do it satisfactorily). It also tends to significantly improve communication about sexual issues between couples. Masters and Johnson developed several successful techniques in the treatment of sexual dysfunction that are widely used today.

THE SEXUAL REVOLUTION

The sexual revolution in the United States was a period of significant social change. It coincided with the end of the civil rights movement. It is known as a period of *sexual freedom*, which contributed to the relaxing of the current sexual norms of the time. There were several contributing factors to this movement, including the wide acceptance of the birth control pill in the 1960s and women's changing role in society, the normalization of premarital sex, the women's movement, the legalization of abortion, and the beginnings of acceptance of sexual orientations other than heterosexual. Although, Kinsey, Sanger, and many of the other researchers listed above preceded the sexual revolution their earlier contributions served as the foundation for the changing sexual norms that grew out of the movement (Chana & Steward, 2003).

Widespread acceptance of the birth control pill allowed women to plan their reproductive lives. For the first time, women did not have to fear pregnancy. As a result, within one generation after the pill, there were large numbers of women entering the work force, going to college, and going on for graduate degrees, law school, and medical schools (Chana & Steward, 2003). Employers no longer feared that women would get pregnant and leave their positions. As a result, many women chose to delay marriage and child bearing and instead chose to focus on attaining higher education and long-term careers. Previously, these things were not open to most women. The women's movement also supported women expressing their sexuality. Women were encouraged to view sexuality for themselves and not just for the pleasure of men. During this same period of time, the *Stonewall riots* occurred in New York, which served as the beginning of the gay rights Movement. The Stonewall incident began when police began harassing those in attendance at this gay bar. The attendants at the bar fought back and did not put up with harassment as they had for years. After fending the police off, they continued to take a stand. They returned to the bar and had a peaceful march to protest their continued negative treatment. They gay community began to fight back against the negative stereotypes projected onto them such as being portrayed as sexual freaks, pedophiles, criminals, and aberrant members of society. The women's movement also began to support lesbians and moved away from understanding women's sexuality as being solely for the purposes of reproduction. Women began to speak out against Freud's notions of penis envy and women being portrayed as inferior to men, intellectually, psychologically, and emotionally.

During this time the media also began producing more sexually explicit movies. Additionally, the 1970s saw the rise of popular pornographic films including the iconic *Deep Throat*. Each of these influences shaped the sexual revolution. Many of the sexual restrictions that existed prior to this movement no longer do as a result of the sexual revolution. The sexual revolution fundamentally changed the way our society views sex, sexuality, and sexual behavior.

CONCLUSION

This chapter has provided a historical context for our understanding of human sexual behavior today. We have reviewed the particular individuals who have contributed to human sexuality research as well as the historical underpinnings of current understanding of human sexuality. As you can observe, each of these influences has had powerful effects on our sexual behavior as well as society's sexual values as we experience them today.

REFERENCES

Boswell, J. (1980). *Christianity, social tolerance, and homosexuality: Gay people in Western Europe from the beginning of the Christian era to the fourteenth century.* Chicago: University of Chicago Press.

Bullough, V. L. (2003). Magnus Hirschfield, an often overlooked pioneer. *Sexuality and Culture, 7*(1), 62–72.

Chana, G. (Writer) & Steward, D. (Director). (2003, February 17). The pill [Television series episode]. In A. Brown (Producer), *The American experience.* United States: Public Broadcasting Service.

Freud, S. (1964). New introductory lectures on psycho-analysis. In J. Strachey (Ed. and Trans.), *The standard edition of the complete psychological works of Sigmund Freud* (Vol. 22, pp. 1–182). London: Hogarth Press. Original work published in 1933.

Goodman, B. (Writer), & Maggio, J. (Director). (2005, February 14). Kinsey [Television series episode]. In C. Allan (Producer), *The American experience.* United States: Public Broadcasting Service.

Greenberg, J. S., Bruess, C. E., & Conklin, S. C. (2011). *Exploring the dimensions of human sexuality* (4th ed.). Sudbury, MA: Jones and Bartlett.

Hysteria. (n.d.-a) In *Bing Encyclopedia online.* Retrieved from http://www.bing.com/search?q=hysteria+definition&qs=AS&pq=hysteria+de&sc=8-11&sp=1&cvid=dbacc25b27f14c47a8e35820b742e3d4&FORM=QBLH.

Hysteria. (n.d.-b). In *The Free Dictionary.* Retrieved from http://medical-dictionary.thefreedictionary.com/hysteria.

Johnson Lewis, J. (n.d.). *Comstock law.* Retrieved from http://womenshistory.about.com/od/laws/a/comstock_law.htm.

Kelly, G. F. (2011). *Sexuality today* (10th ed.). New York: McGraw-Hill Higher Education.

King, B. R. (2009). *Human sexuality today* (6th ed.). Upper Saddle River, NJ: Pearson Education.

Martin, B., & Lyons, C. A. (2011). *Abnormal psychology* (4th ed.). Redding, CA: BVT Publishing.

McLeod, S. (2008). *Psychosexual stages.* Retrieved from http://www.simplypsychology.org/psychosexual.html.

Murdock, N. L. (2009). *Theories of counseling and psychotherapy: A case approach.* Upper Saddle River, NJ: Prentice Hall.

Soble, A. (2008). *The philosophy of sex and love: An introduction* (2nd ed.). St. Paul, MN: Paragon House.

Tran, A. (2013, November). *Slips-of-the-tongue errors* [Cartoon]. Retrieved from http://mercercognitivepsychology.pbworks.com/w/page/3301 5683/Slip-of-the-Tounge%20Errors.

Wallechinsky, D., & Wallace, I. (1981). History of sex surveys: A thousand marriages part 1. In *Trivia Library*. Retrieved from http://www .trivia-library.com/a/history-of-sex-survey-a-thousand-marriages-part-1 .htm.

West, R. (2012). *The ancient roots of our Judeo-Christian sexual prohibitions.* Retrieved from http://www.cybercollege.com/history.htm.

Wright, H. (1938). *The sex factor in marriage: A book for those who are or are about to be married.* New York: The Vanguard Press.

5

❖

When: Sex throughout
the Life Cycle

Part of understanding human sexuality is comprehending that we are each
born with a sexuality that is individual to each of us. Sexuality is a part of
our identity as individuals. As I have highlighted throughout the text,
human sexuality is a complex concept incorporating our thoughts,
feelings, behavior, gender identity, whom we find ourselves attracted to
(sexual orientation), our views about sex, as well as many other factors.
Human sexuality is present throughout the lifespan. As you read in
Chapter 4, Freud developed specific stages of *psychosexual development*,
which Kelly (2011) describes as factors that form a person's sexual feelings,
orientation, and patterns of behavior. Erik Erikson (1968) was a famous
psychologist studying human beings' *psychosocial development* from birth
to death. He devised a lifespan model of psychosocial development in
which he explored how we form individual identities and accomplish the
tasks of each stage all the way through older adulthood. He believed that
the task in each stage was for an individual to gain a positive sense of self
socially, emotionally, sexually, and psychologically, enabling each of us
to develop emotionally intimate interpersonal relationships throughout
the lifespan. This chapter will explore how human sexuality changes
throughout our lives as well as particular factors that influence our sexuality. We will examine the following developmental phases: early infancy,

early childhood, school age years, puberty, adolescence, emerging adulthood, young adulthood, middle age, and the elderly years.

EARLY INFANCY (0–1 YEARS)

It might surprise you to know that baby boys have been shown to experience erections in the womb and girls can have vaginal lubrication within
24 hours of birth (Calderone, 1983; Langfeldt, 1981, as cited in King,
2009). Children become interested in their body parts and in self-
stimulation. They enjoy touching themselves and learning about their
own (and others') bodies. When they touch their genitalia and learn that
it feels good (due to the numerous nerve endings existent in the genital
area), their self-stimulation becomes purposeful. In examining sexuality
in children, it is important to note that children understand sex and sexuality much differently than do adults. For example, until children learn
differently, grabbing a stranger's breast is the same as grabbing that same
stranger's ear. In very early childhood, they do not differentiate between
the two and are very curious about different body parts. Research demonstrates that a healthy sexuality often begins in childhood and is drawn from
children's early attachment relationships with caregivers.

Attachment, in the context of human development, describes the emotional, social, psychological, affectional, and interpersonal bond between
caregiver and child. Attachment theorists find that the strength of the
attachment relationships in early childhood often predicts the attachment
relationships in adulthood—including romantic relationships. The attachment relationship is formed in infancy between the primary caregiver (e.g.,
mother or father) and the infant. Strong attachment relationships are critical to the social, emotional, and psychological development of the child.
Attachment is formed in several ways. Caregivers who consistently
respond to their child's needs, cries, bids for attention and affection, and
desire for social interaction tend to have strong attachment relationships
with their children. Touching, hugging, laughing, and cuddling are critical
to the healthy development of children. This was especially illustrated
with Harry Harlow's research on monkeys. Harry Harlow raised rhesus
monkeys with inanimate surrogate mothers (nonhuman mothers made of
plastic and wire). Harlow had two types of inanimate wire mothers: one
had a bottle of milk attached so the baby monkey could nurse, the other
had no bottle but was wrapped in soft terry cloth. Harlow discovered
that as soon as the monkey satisfied its hunger with the milk bottle, it
immediately left the wire mother for the "mother" dressed in a soft cloth.

The monkeys appeared to be seeking *contact comfort.* (touch and physical comfort babies need to survive).

Another researcher who underscored the critical view that strong attachment relationships with caregivers are necessary for survival is René Spitz. Spitz used direct observation of children to study the effects of maternal and emotional deprivation on infants. In his work he found that infants deprived of contact comfort (even if they received food and adequate medical care) became sick, depressed, and often died. Those who lived often showed significant developmental delays. He observed babies growing up in orphanages without their mothers. His work helped solidify Harlow's findings. Thus, from Spitz and Harlow we learned the importance of hugging, touching, and cuddling in early childhood by primary caregivers.

John Bowlby, a British psychiatrist, is credited with discovering attachment. Infants are completely helpless at birth and their survival depends on those around them to take care of them. Attachment relationships become the secure base at which infants can explore their environments. Mary Ainsworth (a student of Bowlby) took Bowlby's research a step further and named the specific types of attachment relationships she noted in her research of Ugandan infants and their mothers. Ainsworth discovered a reliable and predictable way to measure the strength of the attachment relationship between caregiver and infant, called the *strange situation*. In the strange situation, "the mother [or father] sits with the infant in a comfortable room until a stranger enters; she and the stranger talk a while and she leaves when the infant is not looking, leaving the infant alone with the stranger until the mother returns" (Cobb, 2001, p. 218). Ainsworth noted that the differences in the way infants responded to their mothers' return were reflective of certain types of attachment. She named four types of attachment relationships: Secure, anxious-avoidant, anxious-resistant, and disorganized (which was discovered much later).

Securely attached infants feel safe and secure when with their primary caregiver. They feel free to play contentedly on the floor only occasionally checking to see if the caregiver is nearby. When a stranger enters, the baby may look at the primary caregiver briefly (as if checking to make sure the stranger is OK) but continues to play. If the primary caregiver leaves, the infant is distressed and may cry. Although they may allow a stranger to hold them, they are not completely consolable until the primary caregiver returns. Upon the caregiver's return, the child runs over, snuggles, calms down, and then returns to playing. Sixty-five percent of infants are securely attached (Cobb, 2001). Secure caregivers respond appropriately, promptly, and consistently to the infant's needs.

Anxious-avoidant infants may also play happily when their primary caregiver is present but engage in fewer "checking in" behaviors. They glance over to their caregivers much less than securely attached infants, almost as if they do not completely trust their caregivers. They show little distress when their caregiver leaves them with a stranger but also show little response to their caregivers when they return. These infants may in fact turn away from their caregivers. Twenty-five percent of infants show this pattern (Cobb, 2001). *Anxious-resistant* infants appear wary and stay close to their caregivers in new situations but are not easily comforted by nor feel secure with their caregivers. They are extremely distressed at their caregivers' absence but are not comforted by the caregiver's return. They may cry to be picked up but want to be put down immediately and continue to be fussy. They struggle to return to playing. Approximately 10 percent of infants have this attachment pattern.

In their interviews with expectant mothers Diane Benoit and Kevin Parker (1994, as cited in Cobb, 2001) found that the expectant mother's attachment relationships with their own mothers was predictive of the attachment relationship they would have with their new child. They found that this affect was multigenerational (i.e., the predictive patterns of attachment relationships went back several generations). This has important implications for sexual development. Because our first physical contact with the world is often through our caregivers, how we view touching and cuddling is shaped by these early interactions. Our comfort with our own bodies is also shaped by these interactions both positively and negatively.

Finally, let's return to Erik Erikson's model of psychosocial development to help us understand the specific developmental tasks of each stage. Erikson's model has significant implications for our sexual development as the end goal of each stage is to complete a developmental task that brings us closer to understanding ourselves, being comfortable with our identities, and developing close interpersonal relationships. The first stage, in infancy, involves gaining *trust* in one's self and one's environment. If infants are unable to do this, they instead develop *mistrust*. Thus, at the end of this stage infants have developed either a sense of trust in their world or a sense of mistrust. If mistrust is developed, this sets the children up to have problems in their interpersonal relationships, most especially their intimate romantic relationships. Trust is developed through infants having secure attachments to caregivers, having caregivers respond to their infants' needs, and infants being allowed to safely explore their environment.

EARLY CHILDHOOD (2–6 YEARS)

Children this age become especially curious about others' bodies, as well as their own. Children's behavior becomes increasingly sexualized around the age of 2, reaching its peak from 3 to 5, then dropping off around 5, and continuing to decrease up to puberty (King, 2009), when it peaks again. Children are very interested in the differences in genitalia between boys and girls and why boys urinate standing up while girls sit down. They may undress in front of others, play games involving exposing one's body and genitals, touch others' genitals, masturbate, and ask questions about sex (King, 2009). These are normal behaviors and parents should not react with shock and disgust lest they teach their young children body shame or shame about normal curiosity about one's and others' bodies. At this age, genital penetration or aggressive sexual behavior is not normal and may be indicative of abuse (Friedrich et al., 1991, as cited in King, 2009). Sexual curiosity is normal and not harmful to a child's development but negative parental reactions can be very harmful and give children the idea that they are "bad" or doing something "wrong." Most kids engage their sexual curiosity with same-sex children because children typically segregate themselves into same-sex friendships when they are around 7 years old. This has few implications for sexual orientation and should be considered a normal part of childhood development. In other words, just because a 6-year-old girl engages in sexual curiosity (e.g., looking at her same-sex friend's genitals) does not mean she will become a lesbian later in life. Experts suggest that when parents discover their child masturbating, the parents should not strongly react but instead should socialize the idea that touching one's genitals should be done privately at home (not in public). It is also suggested that parents should ignore the behavior when seen at home. Punishment or shaming can have significant negative consequences. For example, shaming or punitive parental behaviors can teach children to have shame about their bodies and/or sex and will decrease the likelihood that the child will feel comfortable asking the parent about sex in the future.

The time period above covers two of Erikson's stages: toddlerhood and early childhood. In the toddlerhood stage, the developmental conflict includes developing a sense of either *autonomy* (independence) or *shame and doubt*. Children who are encouraged to explore their environments and are rewarded for their new discoveries typically develop a sense of autonomy, which is built on the earlier stage's fundamental sense of trust. A sense of autonomy will become important as children learn to have a sense of confidence in themselves and their abilities. If children do not develop a sense of autonomy, they will feel shame and doubt in who they are and their ability to operate independently in the world. The next stage in this age range is early childhood. The developmental conflict is *initiative versus guilt*.

SCHOOL AGE YEARS (7–11 YEARS)

Freud hypothesized that children go through a period of latency when they are far less concerned with sexual issues. "Studies have found that American children do engage in less overt sexual behavior at this time (Friedrich et al., 1991, as cited in King 2009) and most parents and teachers believe that sexual interest at this age is unusual or a problem" (Ryan, 2000, as cited in King, 2009, p. 248). By age 7 or 8 most children have developed a sense of modesty and wish for privacy when going to the bathroom or undressing. It is also clear that most children have internalized many values about sexual behavior and understand that this is not something that is supposed to be discussed with or shown to parents. Although Freud hypothesized that his latency stage is reflective of children's temporary lack of interest in sexual issues, other researchers find that children may be just as interested in sexual issues as they were in earlier childhood and that they may have just learned to hide their interest and behavior from adults (Ryan, 2000, as cited in King, 2009). Children continue to play "doctor" games with other children, especially in same-sex peer relationships. They may also masturbate. King (2009) points out that most parents react negatively when they find their children engaging in sexual exploration games. Girls are treated more harshly than boys and boys often have more tolerance from parents in exploring sexually and masturbating. Again, it cannot be overstated that when parents react negatively to their children's normative curiosity about sex, they can cause the child to feel shame, guilt, and a sense of wrongness about sex and sexuality that can last a lifetime.

Erickson's next stage is middle childhood. The developmental conflict is *industry versus inferiority*. During this stage children accomplish particular tasks and develop certain skills that provide the basis for self-esteem. These tasks and skills center around being able to stay current with their peer group's physical development (running, playing ball, climbing, etc.)

as well as certain academic and social skills. Around this age, children begin to learn the things they have a special talent for and they also learn the things that they may not be as good at as other members of their peer group. If children fail to develop necessary skills, they may suffer from self-esteem issues and feel inferior to others. These negative feelings and sense of self could last a very long time and have implications for the next stage of development.

PUBERTY (11–15)

In the United States, puberty is considered a time of excitement and great change. It marks the transition from childhood to adolescence. Adults expect more things from adolescents than they do from children. Adolescents are expected to follow certain rules and social norms. For example, most parents expect their teenagers to do their homework and chores on a more independent basis than they did when the adolescent was younger. Adolescents are often given more independence but certain expectations for behavior are to be followed (e.g., getting a later curfew but remaining in contact with the parent via phone if they will be late for any reason). This is also the time when adolescent behavior can have adult-like consequences (e.g., pregnancy, car accident, criminal behavior) and when the peer group becomes significantly influential over an adolescent's choices and behavior. Freud described puberty as a time when adolescents' sexual attraction and lust are consciously directed at nonfamily members. This is the first time that sexual lust looks more like it does in adulthood.

Much of this sexual awakening is due to the significant physical changes the body is going through. Puberty is a two-part maturational process. The first part (called *adrenarche)* begins between 6 and 8 years and the second (called *gonadarche*) occurs in early-to-mid adolescence (King, 2009). During adrenarche the adrenal glands secrete the androgen hormone dehydroepiandrosterone, which is then later converted to estrogen and testosterone (King, 2009). During gonadarche the pituitary gland secretes FSH (follicle stimulating hormone) in high doses, which stimulates sperm production in boys and the maturation of ova (eggs) in girls (King, 2009). The end result of this stage is that boys can ejaculate, girls can menstruate, and both develop *secondary sexual characteristics* (e.g., breast development, facial hair, pubic hair, deepening of the voice for boys). When these changes begin to take place, children begin to view themselves as adolescents about to enter adulthood. These physical changes often coincide with behavioral changes in the adolescent.

Girls' Pubescent Development

As the amount of estrogen (hormone) increases in the body, girls begin to develop breasts (first in the form of breast buds—which appear as bumps on the chest). Girls also grow in height earlier than boys, which typically accounts for the discrepancy we see in height in junior high school children. Girls grow taller earlier. Boys typically begin to catch up and then surpass girls in high school. Boys start approximately 2 years later than girls in height development but continue growing about 2 years after most girls have stopped. Girls may also see a broadening of their hips and thighs as a result of development of fatty deposits in these places. Girls develop pubic and underarm hair as a result of increased male hormones in the body, secreted (released) from the adrenal gland in the brain. The onset of a girl's first period is called *menarche* and typically occurs between the ages of 11 and 14, although this varies from girl to girl. Increases in estrogen cause the vaginal walls to thicken and become more elastic. Girls also experience more vaginal lubrication, especially during sexual arousal. Girls also begin releasing vaginal discharge throughout the month. This discharge ranges from clear fluid to white, thick fluid. This is normal and is indicative of where a young woman is in the stages of ovulation (release of an egg each month).

The menstrual cycle occurs in four phases and the average length is about 28 days, though this can significantly vary from woman to woman. The four phases are preovulatory (days 5–13), ovulation (day 14), postovulatory (days 15–28), and menstruation (days 1–4). Girls are born with all the eggs they will need (about 300,000). King (2009) describes each stage succinctly. During the preovulatory stage (days 5–13), the pituitary gland (a small pea-sized gland in the brain that serves as the "master gland" during puberty as it is responsible for much of the pubescent development) secretes high levels of FSH, which in turn secretes the hormone estrogen. Follicles are immature eggs (ova). Estrogen signals the release of luteinizing hormone (LH), which makes the lining of the uterus grow (thicken) to prepare for the implantation of an egg. When this phase is nearly at its end, estrogen levels peak and the pituitary gland triggers a release of LH from the pituitary gland called the LH surge.

During ovulation (day 14), the LH surge (and a sharp increase of FSH) signals ovulation to occur within 12–24 hours of the LH surge. A mature follicle (egg) moves to the surface of the ovary (the organs in women that contain the eggs/ova). At *ovulation* the follicle ruptures (follicles are the "container" holding the eggs within each ovary; they help protect the egg from harm) and the mature egg is released from the ovary, which eventually makes its way into the Fallopian tube (a female reproductive structure that eggs travel through on their way to the uterus). During the postovulatory phase (days 15–28), large amounts of the hormone *progesterone* are secreted, which stops LH from being released. In other words, progesterone serves as the shut off switch for LH. The uterine lining (called the *endometrium*) is thick. Progesterone prepares the uterine lining for the implantation of a fertilized egg. If sperm has fertilized an egg, it travels through the Fallopian tubes and implants in the thick uterine lining. This will eventually develop into a fetus; however, when sperm first fertilizes an egg, it is known as an embryo. Most of the time, fertilization does not occur and in the absence of fertilization, the egg disintegrates and is absorbed by the body. As a result, there is a rapid decrease in estrogen and progesterone, which signals the menstrual cycle.

During menstruation (days 1–4), the thick uterine lining is sloughed off and shed over several days (3–6). "Menstruation is the discharge of sloughed off endometrial tissue, cervical mucus, and blood (about 4–6 tablespoons over the entire menstrual period)" (King, 2009, p. 62). The loss of estrogen results in the pituitary gland once again releasing FSH and thus beginning a new cycle. The length of the entire menstrual cycle is approximately 28 days, although as was stated before there is quite a bit of variability from woman to woman. Women are most fertile around ovulation. There are only specific days of the month in which a woman can get pregnant, although because not every woman has a 28-day cycle and few women regularly monitor their ovulation cycles, many do not know when they are the most fertile. Thus, if a woman does not want to get pregnant and she is sexually active, she should take precautions to avoid pregnancy.

King (2009) points out that girls' feelings about the changes their bodies are going through, especially the menstrual cycle, often depend on how well informed they are about these normal changes as well as others' attitudes around them about the menstrual cycle. For example, if it is described as disgusting and gross, young women may be more likely to adopt these negative attitudes. If it is described as a positive and exciting change, young women are more likely to feel more positive about getting their period. They may be less embarrassed and more likely to ask questions and feel more comfortable with all of the changes that puberty brings. Because girls all develop at different rates, some girls may feel self-conscious and shame about their quickly or slowly developing bodies. Faster maturing girls are more likely to hang out with older peers, date earlier, have intercourse earlier, and be introduced to drugs and alcohol (i.e., engage in riskier behaviors). This is because as soon as a girl begins to go through puberty, she is looked at like a woman. Because women's bodies are frequently *objectified* (looked at as an object) early-developing girls may feel self-conscious and may be more likely to succumb to some of the negative aspects of peer pressure (e.g., having sex earlier). Many girls this age also begin to negatively judge their own bodies and feel badly about themselves if they do not "measure up" to societal ideals of thinness and beauty. This can have negative consequences for the development of a healthy positive self-esteem and sense of self.

Boys' Pubescent Development

Changes in boys include growth of the testicles and scrotum, increases in testosterone, and growth of the penis, prostate gland, and seminal vesicles (structure where sperm will be contained within the testicles) (Biro & Dorn, 2005, as cited in King, 2009). Boys' genital growth typically begins around age 11 or 12 and finishes around 15. Boys can ejaculate approximately 1 year after the penis begins to grow (King, 2009). Boys may experience erections that they find difficult to control (at first) and *nocturnal emissions* (also known as a "wet dream"), in which the boy may ejaculate in his sleep and wake up with semen on his pajamas. These are often embarrassing events for boys but are less so when they are informed about the normal changes their bodies are going through. During puberty, some boys may develop breast buds (similar to girls) called *gynecomastia*, as a result of an increase in the levels of estrogen boys experience during the early parts of puberty. This too can cause boys shame and embarrassment if they are not told what is happening to them. This usually disappears by the mid-teens. Pubic hair, underarm hair, and facial hair also coincide with genital development in boys. Boys also experience a deepening of their voices. As was mentioned earlier, early-developing girls often have a more difficult time in adolescence than do late-maturing girls. The opposite seems to be true for boys. Early-maturing boys are often more popular than later-maturing boys. This is because society reinforces the notion that boys/men should be tall, strong, and athletic. Early-maturing boys meet this ideal sooner than their later-maturing counterparts. As a result, they may be more popular and more athletic, earning a higher status among their peers.

When Should Parents Talk to Their Children about Sex and What Should They Say?

Parents often struggle with what to tell their children about sex. They may wonder, "How do I answer my child's questions in developmentally appropriate ways?" Some parents are so uncomfortable that they either never talk to their children about sex or do so once and leave the rest up to the school. Parents should realize that they can easily pass their shame and discomfort regarding talking about sex onto their children. The transmission of sexual knowledge can be multigenerational (over the generations). For example, if a mother's mother was uncomfortable talking about sex to her, she may pass the same attitude to her own children. Children learn so much from their parents, including their morals and values regarding sex and sexual behavior. Children respond to parental disproval regarding sex, and may sometimes interpret a negative response as self-shame or feel that they themselves are bad. Thus, parents should think about their responses to their children's questions and take care with their answers. Since every child is different, parents should take into account what they know about their own child and their child's stage of development and understanding before engaging in talks about sex. It is usually recommended by psychologists that parents not wait until adolescence to talk about sex.

Most young children turn to their parents as sources of information about sex; however, by the time they are teens, fewer than 10 percent are still turning to their parents for sexual information (Kaiser Family Foundation, 2000, as cited in King, 2009; Stodghill, II, 1998). Children and teens rarely feel comfortable talking to their parents about sex if parents respond in punitive (punishing), threatening, defensive, intrusive, or embarrassing ways. Children and teens are more likely to talk to their parents about sex if they feel like they will be heard and that their parent is open to their feelings. This means that many parents need to first clarify and understand their own views, issues, values, and morals about sex. Also, parents should consider educating themselves about the basic concepts of human sexuality so that they feel prepared to answer their children's questions. There are many children's books parents can review to help them understand developmentally appropriate ways in which to talk to their children about sex. Also, as parents teach children about sex, they are also socializing their values and morals about sex and sexual behavior (e.g., "In this family, we believe that you should only have sex with someone you love" or "In this family we believe that sex should only be had within marriage").

Many parents fear that having open dialogues with their children about sex will lead children to have sex earlier. This is an unfounded fear as research demonstrates that children who are educated about sex are no more likely to have sexual relations, get pregnant, or contract STDs (sexually transmitted diseases) than those children who have not had a sex education (Grunseit et al., 1997). In fact, it might be argued that when children have more information about sex, they may be more inclined to delay intercourse because they are well informed about the positive and negative consequences. Parents should make it a point to have regular discussions with their children about sexual issues beginning in childhood and continuing into adolescence and young adulthood. For example, with very young children, (e.g., ages 2, 3, 4), parents may wish to teach them the proper names of all of their body parts, including their genitalia. Sometimes, parents are uncomfortable with proper names; however, when parents come up with cutesy names for genitalia they may be sending children a powerful message about body shame. For example, we never come up with pseudonyms for *ear* and *nose*. Therefore, why do we do so for *vagina* and *penis*? When we do this, we are teaching children something about the "secretive" nature of genitalia and we are setting it apart from other body parts. Additionally, parents eventually have to reteach the proper names for genitalia as the child gets older anyway so it may make more sense to begin with the proper name in the first place.

In early childhood, children also need to learn that their bodies belong to them and no one, adult or child, has the right to touch them without their permission. In this way, parents can begin teaching about stranger-danger and allowing their children to develop a sense of body privacy and body security. As children begin to touch themselves and other children, parents can teach them which body parts should be touched in private (genitalia) and which body parts can be touched in public (ear, face, etc.). In this way parents are teaching their children the social norm of privacy as well as individual ownership over one's body without teaching the child sexual shame about any body part in particular. Young children also ask about how babies are made. Parents should try to explain this in a developmentally appropriate way without using old standbys such as "the stork brought you" because children will quickly see through this. Again, this conveys the message that there is something "secretive" or "dirty" about how babies are made. It might be that the more myths we come up to explain this, the less our children learn to trust our explanations of sexual issues, which could pave the way for them not talking to us about sex as they get older.

Sexual issues discussions should be just that—discussions and not lectures. As children get older they will notice more things. They will ask about sexual orientation, premarital sex, pregnancy, and STDs. They may even ask parents personal questions about their own sexual experiences. Parents should be prepared to deal with these questions honestly but in ways the parents themselves are comfortable. Parents should not convey a sense of negativity or be punitive in their discussions with their children about sex. Also, the tone of the discussion is important. Parents should think about when both parent and child are most relaxed: In the car? In front of the TV? Roan (1993, as cited in King, 2009) makes a critical point for parents to keep in mind. He states the following: "The most important message is that nothing a child does will be made worse by talking to the parent about it. There is [no] way of dealing with sexuality unless the parent has created the atmosphere of love and caring. Unless that atmosphere is there, nothing works. The child will lie" (p. 275). Finally, as children get older, parents should accept that even if they have open discussions about sex with their child or teen, there are simply some things that teens may prefer to keep private or figure out themselves. In some ways, this is part of becoming an adult. Teens frequently tell things to their parents when they are ready. It is the parents' job to create a loving, supportive atmosphere where discussions of sex can happen but sometimes it is the teen himself or herself that may determine the timing of the discussion. Parents should be ready to listen. Children and teens will learn a great deal from their parents about sex— whether or not parents talk about it. Children's sexual attitudes generally reflect their parents' attitudes about sex. Parents help to socialize sexual and social scripts, sexual morals and values, and frequently shape their child's sexual behavior and understanding of sex. It is a significant and critical responsibility.

ADOLESCENCE (13–17)

Adolescence clearly marks the time between childhood and adulthood. Most teenagers have begun the process of puberty, which continues through about mid-adolescence. This time coincides with Erikson's adolescence stage. The developmental task of this stage is *identity versus role confusion and self-questioning*. Teenagers begin to question who they are (identity), what their purpose is, why they are here, and what should be their path in life? According to Erikson, the developmental conflict at this stage has to do with a teen figuring out who he or she is. This is also linked with understanding one's strengths and weaknesses and purpose in life. Teens often begin thinking about higher education and career paths seriously at this age. They may also question or solidify their religious faith and/or political beliefs. This is also the time when many teens begin to form romantic relationships and start to date. Some experiment with sexual intercourse while others do not. Kinsey (1948) and Kinsey et al. (1953, as cited in King, 2009) found that 82 percent of teenage boys masturbated to orgasm, as had 20 percent of girls. We can hypothesize that with the relaxing of some sexual norms as well as the amount of information on sex many teens have via the Internet, even more may engage in regular masturbation.

It is also during this time that our *social* and *sexual scripts* become expressed through our behavior. Gagnon and Simon (1999) describe social scripts as a complex set of learned responses to a particular situation that is formed by social, cultural, familial, and peer influences. Sexual scripts are learned from these same influences and shape our ways of thinking, feeling, and acting sexually. For many people, these scripts serve as a standard by which we judge our sexual behaviors and those of others. They also contain our values and morals surrounding sex. Our sexual scripts are shaped from infancy throughout adulthood.

Many adolescents begin to experiment sexually with different types of sexual behavior, including kissing (though most have kissed a romantic partner prior to adolescence), sexual touching (genital, breast), and sexual intercourse for some. There are several predictors for the early sexual behavior of adolescents, including race, age, religious beliefs, peer group influences, and education about sex. African American and Caucasian boys are more likely to engage in sexual intercourse earlier than are their Latino and Asian American counterparts. Very religious and conservative teens are less likely to have had sex by their senior year in high school. Peer groups can socialize the norm of having sex or not having sex. For example, the number of teens reporting sexual intercourse in high school decreased in the 1990s. It was hypothesized that this was due to the spread of HIV and a decrease in popularity for sexual activity within the peer group. Finally, older teens (junior/senior in high school) are more likely to have had sex (over 60 percent have had sex prior to graduating from high school) than their younger freshmen/sophomore counterparts (Eaton et al., 2006, as cited in King, 2009). Today's attitudes toward premarital sex tend to be more permissive than they were in the 1940s; however, depending on one's background, attitudes about premarital sex are still diverse. Some believe it is permissible as long as two people are in a committed, monogamous relationship, whereas others still believe that sex should only be within a marriage.

EMERGING ADULTHOOD (18–25 YEARS)

In the 1960s, most people got married and started a family between the ages of 18 and 25 years old. Today, this is no longer the case. The average age of marriage for women is 26 and 28 for men. Many individuals are delaying marriage (or not getting married at all). The United States is experiencing a decline in marriage rates, for the purposes of higher education and career opportunities. Additionally, adulthood has changed (from what we considered it to be in 1960). Due to economic hardship, graduating college students frequently have to go home and live with their parents for a few years, as there are fewer jobs for new grads than there were in earlier generations. Also, the philosophy in 1960, when people got married around 18–25 years of age, was that as a couple, you built your lives together and it was completely acceptable to start married life without much in terms of financial savings or property. Today's philosophy seems quite opposite to that. One often hears young unmarried singles discuss wanting their career and finances in place prior to getting married. Also, many young people want to own their own home before walking down the aisle. As you can see, this is a distinct change in attitudes, which may also account for the increase in marital age as well as the decrease of heterosexual marriage rates.

Erikson's stage, called emerging adulthood, involves solving the developmental task of achieving *intimacy and connection with others versus feeling alone and isolated.* Individuals during this time often desire a romantic relationship, whether through marriage, cohabitation, or romantic dating relationships, as well as close connections with family and friends. Young adults who have connections with others feel well grounded, emotionally secure, and well loved. Young adults without significant relationships in their lives frequently feel isolated, disconnected, and withdrawn from their environments, making it difficult to feel as if they are making an impact on the world around them. Sometimes, this can lead to one becoming depressed.

YOUNG ADULTHOOD (26–39 YEARS)

As you can see, young adulthood has been extended through the end of the 30s age range. This is because people are living longer and having children later in life. By the end of young adulthood, many adults are either married, in long-term or cohabitating relationships, or seeking long-term romantic relationship fulfillment. Cohabitation became popular in the 1970s and remains increasingly popular today. Some see cohabitation as a necessary part of getting to know one's partner prior to marriage and some cohabitating couples chose not to marry. Interestingly, however, research finds that married couples who cohabitated prior to their marriage have an increased chance of divorce. Some researchers hypothesize that this is because cohabitating socializes the value that the relationship is "temporary." Although we may not know the reason behind why couples who cohabitate prior to marriage are more likely to divorce, cohabitation is here to stay and is popular with many couples, especially among college-aged students. More recent findings indicate that older cohabitating couples (versus college-aged cohabs) may be more likely to eventually marry.

Many couples are having children during this time in their lives. It may also be the time when they begin to assume responsibility for aging parents. One resultant phenomenon of adults waiting to have children is the increase in fertility issues experienced by some couples. As is commonly known, most women experience a sharp drop in fertility around age 35. Because women are born with all the eggs they will ever have, there is no opportunity to replenish eggs, unlike sperm, which regenerates every 30 or so days. Many women in their mid-30s to early 40s experience what is called *ovarian failure*, which means that their remaining eggs may not be healthy enough to achieve or maintain a pregnancy. Infertility (the inability to conceive after a sustained period of trying—usually a year or more) is often a very painful and emotionally devastating experience for couples wanting to have children and finding themselves unable to do so on their own. Couples often turn to fertility treatments to help them conceive a child. There are many types of infertility. For example, infertility on the part of the male is called *male factor infertility* and infertility on the part of the female is known as *female factor infertility*; when the reasons the couple is infertile are unknown it may be called *infertility due to unknown factors*. However, today's fertility treatments are reasonably successful for many couples. Fertility treatments include *invitro fertilization*, *intrauterine insemination (artificial insemination)*, as well as many others, which were discussed in Chapter 3. Fertility treatments are often very expensive and not covered by most insurance companies. Couples who utilize fertility treatments often struggle with the emotional consequences of infertility for years before being successful in having children. Most people who struggle with infertility eventually do have families through the use of the above treatments, adoption, or deciding to end their pursuits to have children and accept family life without children.

MIDDLE AGE (40–59)

Many younger people are surprised to find that middle-aged and older adults still engage in and enjoy sex with their partners. In Western culture, adults are often viewed as being nonsexual. In movie depictions of sex, we always see young, perfect bodies. Wrinkles and sagging skin are not seen as sexy, but instead, viewed as something to be covered up and hidden. Because sex was historically viewed as for the purposes of procreation, it would make sense that middle-aged and older adults would not have a need for sexual intercourse because the majority of these couples have already had (or do not want to have) children. However, as we have learned throughout this text, sexual intercourse is more than just for the purpose of procreation. Sex fulfills our need to feel physically and emotionally connected to our partners (physical and emotional intimacy) and our need to touch and be touched and contributes to a healthy sense of self. A healthy sex life within a relationship helps to enhance the bond between partners and this is true over the entire lifespan. Women experience physical changes as well that impact their sexuality. For example, as women enter their 40s, their supply of ova is nearly depleted. As a result, they may experience irregular periods. A woman's ovaries begin to wither (atrophy), and she goes through *menopause* (the ceasing of the menstrual cycle). Other physical changes women experience include decreases in estrogen and progesterone (which may cause *hot flashes*—where the body temperature briefly increases and then rapidly decreases; she may sweat, get headaches, feel nauseous, and have sleep disturbances.). To combat vaginal dryness, women are encouraged to use vaginal lubricants (e.g., KY jelly) and/or estrogen-based creams. Most women do not experience a drop in sexual desire, nor the desire to have sex. This remains consistent with their sex drives in earlier adulthood. In 2000, there was a medical trend encouraging women to deal with some of the more uncomfortable physical effects of menopause, with *hormone replacement therapy* (HRT). HRT has been found to help women deal with menopausal symptoms, such as vaginal dryness, sleep disturbances, and hot flashes, and was found to have a protective benefit against heart disease, Alzheimer's disease, and colon cancer (King, 2009). However, long-term studies found that HRT in some women significantly increased their risk of getting breast cancer with long-term use. Other studies did not support the benefit against heart disease, as was previously found in early trials. In fact, King (2009) reports that an 8-year study on HRT was halted at 5 years because of the negative effects of HRT (in the drug called Prempro), including increased risk for heart disease, stroke, blood clots, breast cancer, and ovarian cancer (Lacey Jr. et al., 2002, as cited in King, 2009; Manson et al., 2003). As a result of these significant risks most women decline to use HRT and some look to homeopathic (natural) methods (e.g., herbs) to deal with some of the negative side effects of menopause. HRT is now only recommended on a short-term basis as opposed to the longer-term use that caused so many problems in the early 2000s.

As with the menstrual cycle, women's attitudes toward menopause are frequently dependent upon what they heard about it growing up, from their peers and the media. Some women are thrilled to not have to contend with menstruation anymore and see menopause as an exciting gateway into a new time in their lives with more opportunities to focus on themselves. Other women may struggle with aging and what they see as their physical decline. Society often struggles to see older women as sexy and attractive and some older women unfortunately buy into this unfair depiction of older women. Menopause should be viewed as a natural and normal part of the aging process and not the end of one's usefulness in life, nor the end of one's attractiveness. Thus, whereas some women embrace this part of their lives, others struggle with what getting older means.

Erikson's adulthood stage states this developmental task to be *generativity versus stagnation*. Erikson believed that realizing that generativity (making your mark on the world, creating a legacy that outlasts your life on earth [children, writing a book, etc.]) and positive interpersonal relationships versus feeling stagnant and unfulfilled is an important part of solidifying adulthood. His emphasis is that adults should continue trying to reach their career and interpersonal goals while still recognizing that connections with others fulfills us. In some ways, his conceptualization of the tasks of this stage informs us that although career fulfillment is important, it is our connections with others that will fulfill and sustain us. Additionally, adults during this stage think about ways to contribute to their environments in meaningful ways. They often ponder how they can make their contributions to have a lasting impact.

OLDER ADULTHOOD (AGE 60+)

As we age, so do our bodies. Older adults experience several physical changes impacting their sex lives. For example, after men ejaculate, they experience a refractory period (a period of rest) in which they cannot achieve an erection or ejaculate for a period of time. In very young men (e.g., 18 years old) the refractory period may not be that long. For example, an average refractory period for a young man might be an hour or few hours. An average refractory period for a man in his 50s might be a day. Thus, when a man in his 50s has sex, once he ejaculates, he may not be ready to ejaculate again until the next day. The refractory period differs significantly from man to man. Men begin to show a gradual decrease in testosterone from adolescence onward. Men in their 50s have about half the testosterone they did as young adults. As a result they may experience the following physical changes: decreased sensitivity in the penis, taking a longer time to become erect, having a more difficult time maintaining erection, a less firm erection, shrinkage of the testicles, a less forceful ejaculate, a longer refractory period, a decline in body muscle mass, reduction in bone density, decline in facial hair, an increase in vocal pitch (higher voices), and a decline of sperm production (King, 2009). Many men also experience vascular and other health issues (e.g., high blood pressure, stroke, diabetes, prostate issues) that can impact sexual performance. Any health issue that causes a reduction in blood flow to the penis may cause men problems achieving and maintaining an erection. This can cause self-image problems for older adult men as society has always stereotyped the male ideal as virile, sexually dominant, and always wanting sex. Many men have taken Viagra (a drug that increases blood flow to the penis allowing men to achieve and maintain an erection) to compensate for these issues. Men with extreme health issues should consult with their doctors prior to taking Viagra as it can cause problematic consequences for some men. Some men may feel empowered at this time in their lives. They may see this time period as one of decreasing financial and familial responsibility and an opportunity to focus on things they may not have had time to in the past. Also, they may look forward to retirement. For some men, however, the opposite may be true. They may see their physical decline as evidence of their declining manhood. They may struggle with the physical and emotional changes to their lives. A man's reaction to his advancing age is individual to the man himself.

Many of the physical changes women experience due to aging were discussed in the previous section. Many of these changes begin when a woman is middle aged and continue into older adulthood. As was stated earlier, how a woman deals with these changes as well as her advancing age is frequently dependent on her role models (e.g., mother), peer group, and media influences. When women deal with these changes in positive ways, most continue to feel good about themselves regardless of the physical changes they go through. Women who deal with advancing age in this manner typically feel empowered. Women who struggle to deal with these changes are more prone to depression, isolation, and self-esteem issues.

In the film documentary *Still Doin' It: The Intimate Sex Lives of Women Over 65*, several women over 65 discuss their sex lives. The film shows a wide variety of experiences, from women who are sexually active to those who believe that they are "over the hill" and should not be having sex anymore. Other women in the film say they miss sex a great deal but do not have regular partners, in which to have intercourse. One woman featured in the film is dating and having intercourse with a partner who is 35 years her junior and another woman discusses her experience with masturbation. She talks about how much she enjoys it and it makes her feel connected to herself. We rarely explore older adult sexuality. Most older adults report consistently enjoying sex and having satisfying sex lives, especially those who have a consistent sexual partner. Additionally, older adults state that they are more patient with their sex lives and are more likely to enjoy the total experience versus just having sex to have orgasms. Older adults tend to view sex as a total, holistic, bonding experience. King (2009) reports that Janus and Janus (1993) found very little evidence of any decline in sexual activity through their early 60s. "In the AARP study, 60% of men aged 45+ masturbated and a majority of women said that self-stimulation was an important part of their sexual pleasure. Fifty-one percent of 45+ men and women had sexual thoughts, fantasies or erotic dreams at least once a week" (Jacoby, 2005, as cited in King, 2009, p. 263). As you can see, clearly most older adults maintain an active sexual life in thought and/or behavior. Again, sexuality is with us from birth to death and is clearly present over the entire lifespan. There are several predictors of a healthy sex life over the lifespan. They include the following: positive feelings about sex and one's own sexuality, consistent sexual experiences, frequency of masturbation, physical health, availability of sexual partner(s) (King, 2009). For those older adults who have positive feelings about sex and their own sexuality, sex in older adulthood is simply a normal extension of who they were as younger adults. *Use it or lose it* is often the philosophy surrounding a healthy sexuality over the lifespan. When older adults who were sexually active as younger adults continue having a healthy sex life, they maintain satisfactory sexual relationships. One factor indicative of this is masturbation. Research demonstrates that those older adults who consistently masturbated as younger adults are more likely to have an active sex life into older adulthood. Finally, older adults, especially women who reported having a regular sexual partner, were more likely to maintain an active sex life. Since women continue to outlive men, many older adult women who would like to have sex may not. Additionally, as men get older, many unmarried heterosexual men tend to prefer younger partners, leaving older adult heterosexual women without suitable romantic partners.

Many older adults find this is to be an exciting time because (if they had children) the children are all grown up. They may be facing retirement and decreasing responsibility. They may feel that they can engage in activities for which they did not previously have time (e.g., travel). Much of the experience of older adults is dependent upon one's physical health. For example, if an older adult is relatively healthy and has not experienced any significant health threats, they may embrace this period in their lives.

In contrast, an older adult who has had significant health difficulties and has experienced a reduction in lifestyle activities due to health issues may have negative feelings about getting older.

Erikson's last psychosocial stage is *maturity* and involves individuals accepting their life as they've lived it as well as integrating the lessons life has taught them. It also involves wanting to give back to subsequent generations. The developmental conflict in this stage is *ego integrity versus despair*. Erikson describes this as achieving a sense of ego (self) integrity and relative peace with one's life versus feeling a sense of despair and regret. One might feel despair if he or she had unfulfilled dreams, had a lack of connection to others, or was never able to figure out who he or she is or his or her purpose in life. Erikson believed that older adults who have lived full and satisfying lives face older adulthood with dignity and a sense of self-satisfaction. They are better able to enjoy their age and stage in life. Older adults who feel unfulfilled on multiple levels may struggle with feelings of depression and isolation and despair that their chance to achieve their dreams and desires may be gone.

SEXUAL DISORDERS AND DYSFUNCTION OVER THE LIFESPAN

Every adult experiences some type of sexual dysfunction at some time in his or her life. The dysfunction tends to last for short periods of time. For example, individuals may suffer from low or *hypoactive sexual desire* due to stress, physical tiredness, illness, or problems in the relationship with their partners. On a temporary basis, sexual problems do not usually cause problems; however, when they continue, they can cause an individual or a couple significant distress. Sexual dysfunction tends to include more normative, treatable sexual issues. Sexual disorders include more aberrant (outside of the norm) sexual behaviors. Below are some common sexual problems and their treatments divided by gender. The more serious sexual disorders were reviewed in Chapter 3.

Male Sexual Dysfunction

If you remember, sexual desire (as defined in Chapter 4 under Masters and Johnson's sexual response cycle) has to do with the wish for, motivation to have, and drive to have sex. It indicates a person's willingness to engage in sexual behavior (Levine, 2003, as cited in King, 2009). Hypoactive sexual desire, as defined above, describes a sexual problem characterized by a consistent lack of sexual fantasies, desire, or motivation to have sex.

Individuals avoid opportunities to have sex. This is often most disturbing for men because society has a view that men are always supposed to desire sex. In some ways, hypoactive sexual desire (HSD) is difficult to treat because getting an individual to desire sex when he or she does not is hard to do. HSD is sometimes associated with stress, anger at one's partner, depression, and negative feelings about sex in general. Most often cognitive behavioral techniques are used to explore a person's thought processes about sex and to build new positive associations around sexual thoughts and behaviors. *Sexual aversion disorder* is considered an extreme form of HSD. An individual becomes sex phobic (terrified of having sex or any sexual thoughts). Sexual aversion disorder is most commonly found in individuals who may have experienced sexual abuse, restrictive gender roles, or an extremely conservative upbringing around issues of sex. For example, they may have been taught that sex is nasty, gross, or a sin.

Erectile disorder is specific to men and involves a man's difficulty in achieving or maintaining an erection. Men suffering from erectile disorder (ED) are not able to maintain an erection long enough for a satisfactory sexual performance for themselves or their partners. Most men with ED find it extremely demoralizing to deal with as they may see it as a lack of their own masculinity and their ability to perform as a man. This attitude frequently makes ED much worse. Most men experience ED occasionally and occasional problems are usually little cause for concern; however, consistent problems typically take a very negative toll on the man and his partner. Dunn et al. (2002) and Simons and Carey (2001, as cited in King, 2009) state that about 2 percent of men under age 40 and about 10 percent of men aged 55 have ED. ED is more common in older men, as aging decreases blood flow to the penis, as do common vascular disorders that affect older men. Other common causes include problems in the relationship between partners (e.g., anger, mistrust, negative feelings), stress, and performance anxiety (when a man is overly focused on his sexual performance, this can lead to anxiety while having sex, which can cause erectile problems). Common treatments include cognitive behavioral therapies, an exploration of the person's sexual scripts, and any problems that may exist in the relationship between two partners. The teasing procedure is also employed: The sexual partner touches the man until he becomes erect, then he or she lets the erection go soft, and then bring the man to erection again with manual stimulation. This teaches the man that he does not have to use his erection quickly and shows him how to slow down. Viagra and sensate focus (see Chapter 4) are also other treatments for male sexual dysfunction.

Premature ejaculation involves a man's inability to control when he ejaculates. Premature ejaculation is persistent and leads to an unsatisfactory outcome for both the man and his partner. It typically causes the man and his partner interpersonal difficulty and negative feelings. Most causes of premature ejaculation are psychological and are more common in younger men. Think about this; when most young boys start masturbating, they typically do so quickly so as not to get caught by others. As they get older and begin having sexual intercourse, they have to learn to slow down to prolong the sexual experience for themselves and their partners. Some men struggle to do so. Treatments include cognitive behavioral therapy, the squeeze technique (see Chapter 4), and drug therapy.

Male orgasmic disorder (or *ejaculatory incompetence*) refers to a man's inability to attain orgasm and ejaculate into a woman's vagina. Most of these men are able to reach orgasm through masturbation or oral stimulation. Masters and Johnson (1970) found that this disorder in men was largely due to having a very strict, religious upbringing, fears of getting a woman pregnant, or being dominated by their mothers. Other reasons may be due to performance anxiety and significant concerns about pleasing their female partners (Apfelbaum, 1989, as cited in King, 2009). Male orgasmic disorder is taught using the *bridge maneuver*. King (2009) describes the technique like this. The man is taught to masturbate alone, then in the presence of his female partner, then the female partner manually stimulates the man to orgasm. When this works consistently, the female manually stimulates the male to near orgasm and then quickly inserts the penis into her vagina. Over time, the man overcomes his fears and then he can successfully ejaculate into his partner's vagina.

Sexual pain disorder (*dyspareunia*) involves recurrent and persistent genital pain during intercourse. It is usually due to physical (not psychological) problems. For example, in uncircumcised men, sometimes the foreskin covering the penis may become too tight (known as *phimosis*), which can cause painful intercourse. Sometimes, during rough sex, a couple may inadvertently bend the erect penis. Other causes include fibroid (scar tissue) buildup around the penis. Another related condition called *priapism* involves a man having an erection that lasts for hours or days. This is very painful and can be caused by tumors, a Viagra overdose, an infection, some antidepressants, and so forth. It is most commonly treated with drug therapy to decrease the erection. Sexual pain disorder is usually treated by discovering and fixing the physical problem that causes the pain.

Female Sexual Dysfunction

Hypoactive sexual desire, sexual aversion, female sexual arousal disorder, and *sexual pain disorder* all have the same definitions as listed above in the section on male sexual dysfunctions. Some of the reasons for the above disorders may also be similar to those for men (e.g., sexually repressive/ conservative upbringing, sexual trauma/abuse, restrictive gender roles). For women, however, these issues may not be taken as seriously by the woman herself or by the medical professional because of the gender-biased view that women are not supposed to desire sex as much as men or that the woman may be overexaggerating her symptoms. As a result, women are more likely to suffer silently than men, who are more likely to seek help for issues impacting their sex lives. For women, sexual pain disorder may be due to physical or psychological causes, for example, *vaginismus,* defined as a recurrent/persistent problem in which any attempt to insert anything into the vagina (a finger, tampon, or penis) provokes vaginal muscle spasms and the vagina snaps shut upon attempted insertion. This is treated by a behavioral therapy called *systematic desensitization.* Systematic desensitization involves a series of relaxation techniques where the woman learns to relax. She may be asked to visualize a peaceful scene (e.g., a beach) and then while relaxed imagines gentle, pleasurable insertion of a desired object into her vagina. Gradually, it is accompanied by in vivo exposure, where a series of dilators are used in a relaxing atmosphere. This allows the woman to slowly overcome her fears about vaginal insertion. Her partner may be asked to be involved during the final phases of treatment; he or she may be the one gently inserting the dilators. Eventually, the couple works their way up to intercourse.

Female orgasmic disorder is the absence of orgasm following normal sexual excitement, which the female finds disturbing. In other words, a woman is able to become sexually excited and aroused. She desires sex but cannot seem to achieve an orgasm. This may be due to many factors; most are psychological. Female orgasmic disorder can be primary or secondary, meaning that a woman may never have been able to achieve orgasm (primary) or she had a history of achieving orgasms previously and now cannot (secondary). Therapists will explore whether the woman's vagina is adequately lubricated, if she is receiving appropriate sexual stimulation (as it frequently takes women a bit longer to become lubricated than it takes the man's penis to become erect), and if there has been enough time for foreplay or sexual excitement to build. For most women, a key to their sexual excitement is clitoral stimulation as most need this for orgasm. Additionally, most women do not have orgasms with every sexual intercourse episode. Sometimes, women may experience orgasmic disorder if they have negative feelings about their partners, are distracted during sex (e.g., making out the grocery list), are not in the mood, do not feel an intimate connection with their partners, have negative attitudes about sex, were the product of a conservative/sexually restrictive upbringing, feel that they are not supposed to enjoy sex, are experiencing physical tiredness, illness, or stress, or have a history of sexual abuse. Additionally, some women may experience problems in achieving orgasm if they have a negative body image (e.g., gained weight, just had a baby). It is usually recommended that the couple take more time with foreplay, the woman begin masturbating paying special attention to clitoral stimulation, and that she communicate with her partner about what feels good sexually. For many women, sexual satisfaction is closely related to how connected they feel to their partners.

CONCLUSION

As you can see, sexuality is a lifespan experience. Although we experience it differently depending on our age and stage in life, it has critical value to our lives regardless of the developmental stage in which we currently exist. Though sex and sexuality change over the lifespan, they are always critical parts of who we are as individuals. As highlighted throughout this book, sexuality is a part of our identity, though its expression can change as we change throughout our lives.

REFERENCES

Apfelbaum, B. (1989). Retarded ejaculation: A much misunderstood syndrome. In S. R. Leiblum & R. C. Rosen (Eds.), *Principles and practice of sex therapy: Update for the 1990s* (pp. 168–206). New York: Guilford Press.

Benoit, D., & Parker, K. C. H. (1994). Stability and transmission of attachment across three generations. *Child Development, 65*(5), 1444–1456.

Biro, F. M., & Dorn, L. D. (2005). Puberty and adolescent sexuality. *Pediatric Annals, 34,* 777–783.

Calderone, M. S. (1983). Fetal erection and its message to us. *SIECUS Report, 11*(5/6), 9–10.

Cobb, N. (2001). *The child: Infants and children.* Mountain View, CA: Mayfield Publishing.

Dunn, K. M., et al. (2002). Systematic review of sexual problems: Epidemiology and methodology. *Journal of Sex & Marital Therapy, 28,* 399–422.

Eaton, D. K., et al. (2006). Youth risk behavior surveillance—United States, 2005. *Journal of School Health, 76,* 353–392.

Erikson, E. (1968). *Identity: Youth and crisis.* New York: Norton.

Friedrich, W. N., et al. (1991). Normative sexual behavior in children. *Pediatrics, 88,* 456–464.

Gagnon, J., & Simon, W. (1999). Sexual scripts. In R. Parker & P. Aggleton (Eds.), *Culture, society and sexuality: A reader* (pp. 31–40). New York, NY: Routledge.

Grunseit, A., et al. (1997). Sexuality education and young people's sexual behavior: A review of studies. *Journal of Adolescent Research, 12,* 421–453.

Jacoby, S. (2005, July/August). Sex in America. *AARP The Magazine,* 62–68, 98–99.

Janus, S. S., & Janus, C. L. (1993). *The Janus report on sexual behavior.* New York: John Wiley & Sons.

Kaiser Family Foundation. (2000). *Sex education in America: A view from inside the nation's classrooms.* Menlo Park, CA: Author.

Kelly, G. F. (2011). *Sexuality today* (10th ed.). New York: McGraw-Hill Higher Education.

King, B. R. (2009). *Human sexuality today* (6th ed.). Upper Saddle River, NJ: Pearson Education.

Kinsey, A. C. (1948). *Sexual behavior in the human male.* Philadelphia, PA: W.B. Saunders.

Kinsey, A. C., et al. (1953). *Sexual behavior in the human female.* Philadelphia: W.B. Saunders.

Lacey Jr., J. V. et al. (2002). Menopausal hormone replacement therapy and risk of ovarian cancer. *Journal of the American Medical Association, 288,* 334–341.

Langfeldt, T. (1981). Sexual development in children. In M. Cook & K. Howells (Eds.), *Adult sexual interest in children* (pp. 99–120). London: Academic Press.

Levine, S. B. (2003). The nature of sexual desire: A clinician's perspective. *Archives of Sexual Behavior, 32,* 279–285.

Manson, J. E., et al. (2003). Estrogen plus progestin and the risk of coronary heart disease. *New England Journal of Medicine, 349,* 523–534.

Masters, W. H., & Johnson, V. E. (1970). *Human sexuality inadequacy.* Boston: Little, Brown.

Roan, S. (1993, July 12). Are we teaching too little, too late? *Los Angeles Times,* pp. E1, E4.

Ryan, G. (2000). Childhood sexuality: A decade of study. Part I. Research and curriculum development. *Child Abuse & Neglect, 24,* 33–48.

Simons, J. S., & Carey, M. P. (2001). Prevalence of sexual dysfunctions: Results from a decade of research. *Archives of Sexual Behavior, 30,* 177–219.

Stodghill, II, R. (1998, June 15). Where'd you learn that? *Time,* 52–59.

6

❖

Where: Sex around the World

We know that sex, sexual behaviors, and sexual values are significantly shaped by culture and societal expectations. This chapter will explore how sex, gender roles, sexual behaviors, and sexual values differ among several different cultures around the world. The first part of this volume has explored these topics from a Western and U.S. point of view. This chapter will look at cultural differences in sexual expression around the world.

GENDER AROUND THE WORLD

In the United States, we view gender as a binary concept (i.e., male or female, masculine or feminine). As discussed in previous chapters, our society is not good accepting that most men and women have both masculine and feminine traits. Other cultures vary with their acceptance of masculine and feminine traits within the same individual. For example, the Mandan and other North American Plains Indians accepted the *berdache*, or two-spirit people (Williams, 1992). Two-spirit people embodied both masculine and feminine traits as well as held masculine (e.g., hunting) and feminine (child care) roles. Segal (2003) states that research shows four different forms of gender role variation around the world including: (1) having neither masculine nor feminine distinct categories, (2) having a binary concept of gender (i.e., two distinct types) but labeling the boundaries of gender in very different ways than Western society does, (3) having a basic binary concept

of gender but allowing individuals with one distinct set of biological characteristics (e.g., female) to step outside of society's gender construct into the
other (e.g., female acting in traditional male roles), (4) having a residual category where societal gender constructs do not fit neatly into any of the above
categories. All cultures have at least masculine and feminine categories;
however, how these categories are defined and expressed varies widely across
cultures around the world.

Let's go back to the berdache (two-spirit) people of the North
American Plains Indians. Some two-spirit people had visions in which
they were told of their two-spirit status. They were then allowed to wear
clothing of the opposite gender (e.g., a pre-adolescent boy would wear
women's clothing and engage in traditionally feminine daily activities).
The two-spirit individual would also be expected to have a special role in
weddings, childbirth, child naming, and warfare (Williams, 1992, as cited
in Segal, 2003). Thus, the role of the two-spirit individual in this culture
was highly regarded and respected. Another example of diverse gender
expression comes from the Chukchee of northern Siberia at the beginning
of the 20th century (Bogoras, 1909, as cited in Segal, 2003). Shamans are
healers and magic workers highly respected in a given society. They can
be male or female and can have other males or females as spouses.
In Chukchee culture, Shamans become healers when they themselves re-
cover from a serious illness. It was said that if a Shaman had a same-sex
spouse, the Shaman would begin a process of changing sex that would also
encompass the changing of external genitalia. This was a powerful process
and is symbolic of this culture's more flexible view of gender and gender
roles for Shaman who were considered *special* and held a higher status in
society than most. In Chukchee culture, it was also acceptable for an individual to have a gender transformation (change gender) on a temporary
basis (i.e., for a limited period of time) and then return to his or her original gender. The term *couvade* or *couvade syndrome* has been found in
the Amazon people (Gregor, 1985, as cited in Segal, 2003) as well as in
Melanesia (Blackwood, 1935; Meigs, 1976, as cited in Segal, 2003), where
men take on female characteristics of pregnancy during their partner's/
wife's pregnancy, such as increased emotionality, childbirth pains, and
taking on the same food and sexual restrictions as the pregnant spouse.
This typically continued until the child was weaned.

The Tewa people in the southwestern United States had a third gender
known as a *kwido'* (Jacobs & Cromwell, 1992, as cited in Segal, 2003).
Kwido's are morphologically male and can have sex with men or women.
Kwido's are made so by *spiritual powers* and are considered to be a separate
gender from either male or female. Kwido's hold superhuman status and

were considered sacred. The Tewa people are one such group, which has a three- or four-gender system. Similarly, in Tahiti there existed a person occupying a non-masculine non-feminine position in society (Segal, 2003). These people were called *mahu* and were often morphologically male; however, either special men or women could hold *mahu* status. Mahus could have sex with men or women and sexual orientation is not generally considered or labeled as we do in Westernized societies. As you can see, gender around the world can be a fluid and flexible construction. Remember that *gender* is socially and culturally constructed. In other words, each society defines gender and gender roles for itself. Biology (e.g., biological sex) often shapes gender but biology does not have to dictate definite gender roles.

GENDER ROLES AROUND THE WORLD

Gender roles and economic activity are interrelated. "In every society, human beings appear to associate some activities with women and others with men" (O'Brian, 2003, p. 91). Economic activity envelops work for survival supplies (e.g., food, shelter) as we; as other areas of trade and commercial production. Commercial production is tied to cash. For example, if women of a certain tribe weave baskets, these baskets can be sold for cash to support the members of the tribe. Economic activities are based both in the household and outside of it. For example, if a woman is engaged in child care, there are certain items she will need (e.g., diapers, food, children's clothes) that come from these activities. Many societies differentiate between "women's work" (e.g., child care and homemaking activities) versus "men's work" (work outside the home). Because most societies are patriarchal, "women's work" (and their roles stemming from such work) is often devalued while "men's work" is often viewed as more important. When some women become mothers, their role does shape the activities they pursue, as it often needs to be combined with child care activities (O'Brian, 2003). *Compatibility theory* suggests that women specialize in activities that do not interfere with infant care—so work fits in around the demands of child care (e.g., breastfeeding) (O'Brian, 2003). The theory suggests that this may be one reason why men were more free to choose dangerous economic roles (e.g., the collection of honey or hunting) because their role was traditionally not compromised by child care activities.

It is easy to see how in many societies, gender and activity are strongly linked, with many tasks assigned on the basis of one's gender (and therefore one's gender role) (O'Brian, 2003). It is important to remember that gender roles are socially constructed and fluid—they can shift over time. It remains true that the performance of particular roles (e.g., laborer) is strongly linked to one's definition of male (and masculinity) and female (femininity). One can see then how one's gender role and expression of that role (e.g., through role performance and dress) come to shape one's gender identity over time. It tends to be true in the majority of societies around the world that women's gender roles have less status than men's; however, in societies where women and men contribute more or less equally to production, women have a social status more similar to men. It is also true that cross-culturally, more men are likely to be engaged in heavy-labor activities than women.

Gender roles often change based on "the larger economy, the work people do in the home, the work they conduct outside of it, and ideas about status" (O'Brian, 2003, p. 95). These influences shape what are considered appropriate roles for men and women. Social scientist O'Brian (2003) surmises that as the commercial market demands more of women (or what women make), homemaking activities drop in status while activities in the commercial marketplace increase in status. In this way, women's gender roles shift. One pattern seen as some cultures transition from rural to urban life is that men who work away from their rural homes become more invested in urban life than women who live in urban environments. Therefore, rural women who remain in activities close to home may become devalued by their husbands and children as urban life becomes more valued. This shift has been seen in many developing nations around the world. Thus, "while people continue to conduct their economic activities even though the economic systems in which they live change, these processes will have a range of effects on their own gender roles and on their participation in their family and community life" (O'Brian, 2003, p. 95). These are some of the ways that socially and culturally prescribed gender roles change over time.

GENDER ISSUES AROUND THE WORLD

Some cultural groups with strong preferences for boy babies (i.e., males in general) may practice the *infanticide* (routine abortion or killing) of female babies. For example, selective abortion is often practiced in certain Asian countries (e.g., China) because there is a strong preference of having sons over having daughters (Brown, 2003). Additionally, in many cultures, when daughters marry, their families are expected to provide a dowry (gifts or payment to the husband's family) upon the time of her marriage. Fatal neglect is also practiced to decrease the number of female children. Countries known for male-selection practices include rural North India, certain parts of China, and the Yanomami of South America (Brown, 2003). For example, the Yanomamo viewed a wife's giving birth to a daughter as a "wifely misdeed" in which a husband might severely punish the wife through a beating. This encouraged mothers to practice female infanticide.

Some cultures celebrate the transitions from childhood to adulthood. For women, these events might include menarche (the onset of a girl's first menstrual period when she departs childhood and enters womanhood), the celebration of a girl's virginity, ritual defloration (proof of virginity loss from a girl's husband—blood on the bed sheets or a bloody cloth indicating the breaking of the hymen), marriage, and childbirth. For boys, life transition events might include the onset of puberty (i.e., his moving from childhood to manhood), first sexual experience (if outside marriage), marriage, fatherhood, and other rites of passage to manhood.

In some parts of the world, female genital mutilation (FGM) (formerly known as female circumcision) is performed. There are several types, but in all types the clitoris (organ whose sole purpose is for sexual pleasure in women) is removed. Some types of FGM include partial or complete removal of the clitoris, inner and outer labia, and vulva. In many cultures this is considered an important rite of passage marking the transition from childhood to womanhood and is thought to preserve sexual purity and virginity. It is done between the ages of 0 (infancy) up through age 15. There are no health benefits. It is often performed using a razor blade or sharp rock and frequently done on several young female children at the same time. Sometimes, anesthesia is used but in more rural settings, girls are held down or sat on as the procedure is performed. A small hole is left for sexual intercourse and menstruation. It is most frequently performed by a female elder in the village/community. Sometimes, girls are sewn up and when she gets married, her husband reopens her genitalia through intercourse. Additionally, women may be repeatedly sewn up and ripped open during childbirth; this is known as re-infibulation. This is a common occurrence in some northeastern African countries (28 African countries), a few Middle Eastern countries (e.g., Yemen, Kurdis communities, Saudi Arabia), some cultural groups in Central and Southern Asia, North America, and Europe. In North American and Europe, FGM may be practiced by immigrants from the above-stated parts of the world. In many countries, FGM has been outlawed although criminal prosecution is rare and laws are not consistently enforced. Women having undergone FGM are at high risk for major health complications including infertility, frequent urinary tract infections, organ damage, death in childbirth, painful intercourse, and other types of sexual dysfunction, as well as many other physical problems and psychological issues (e.g., posttraumatic stress disorder, depression). Girls frequently have no choice and many female relatives fear that if their female children do not participate in FGM, they will not be able to marry and will be ostracized from their communities. Most Westernized countries have laws banning the transportation of girls overseas to participate in FGM; however, these laws are difficult to enforce because victims of FGM are told not to tell anyone or they will be killed. They also may risk being ostracized and/or excommunicated from their communities. Some male and female relatives oppose FGM; however, other members of the community may wait until the opposing relative is out of town and subject the girl to the procedure despite objections. There has been international outcry regarding FGM and attitudes in some parts of the world are slowly changing; however, it is estimated that over 800 girls internationally are subjected to FGM on a daily basis.

COURTSHIP AND MARRIAGE RITUALS AROUND THE WORLD

There are vast cultural differences in dating and mating rituals, especially in the selection of a spouse. Mate selection differences include the range of individuals that are marriage eligible, if individuals have a voice in the selection process, gifts or transactions accompanying marriage, and culturally appropriate motives for marriage (Hendrix, 2003). "Marriages around the world vary in many ways, including their intimacy or aloofness, the extent and form of violence, the level of husband dominance, the division of labor, divorce freedom, level of divorce, and the number of permitted spouses of either sex" (Hendrix, 2003, p. 71). Westernized marriages tend to have a large degree of freedom—including the freedom of mate selection, divorce, intimacy, and individuals having the freedom to choose their own spouses. In other cultures around the world, there may be far less freedoms. In terms of spouse selection, many non-Westernized societies allow parents (especially fathers), families, and communities to dictate this process. For example, in traditional Japan, parents had a significant role in who their children married and the children themselves had no voice in the selection process. Typically, individuals met their spouses on their respective wedding day (Hendrix, 2003). Other cultures have a more blended model, where the parents choose the spouse but allow children veto power. In this blended model, men often had more veto power than did women. Broude and Greene (1983, as cited in Hendrix, 2003) found that out of 142 cultures around the world, only 12 had fully free choice for both sexes and only 16 had fully arranged marriage for both, which means that most cultures may have a more combined approach to spouse selection. Twenty of these cultures had greater freedom for men while only two had more freedom for women.

Some research suggests that as free choice in spousal selection increased, the role of the extended family in the couples' lives decreased (Goode, 1967, as cited in Hendrix, 2003; Parsons, 1951). "Some cultures with extended families, such as India today, do have explicit ideologies against romantic love and free choice which bolster the authority of family elders in arranging marriages" (Derne, 1994, as cited in Hendrix, 2003, p. 72). In societies where there is more freedom of choice, courtship rituals (e.g., dances) are less supervised, which also reflects less concern over the control of sexual activity (Hendrix, 2003). Equality of men and women in mate selection and in sex matters is usually reflective of a greater tolerance of premarital sex and predictive of societies in which marriages are more likely to be love based. Some studies have found that "in societies with more male dominance, arranged marriage tends to occur in the absence of large extended family structures. However, in societies with more sexual equality, elders are more likely to arrange marriages if there are extended families" (Hendrix, 2003, p. 72). Clearly, there is a complex relationship between the role of the extended family, male dominance, and the impact of mate selection on different societies. In research on heterosexual mate selection criteria, most societies found that females tended to prefer ambitious mates with good financial prospects, with few exceptions to this pattern, while males tended to prefer features associated with reproductive value or fertility such as youth and beauty (Hendrix, 2003). Other research suggests that there is some variation in this pattern when social structure varies. For example, in less developed countries and countries where there is less sex equality, the above criteria rarely vary.

One factor common across cultures is the rule that close relatives should not marry and have children. There is a strong cultural taboo against incestuous relationships. Most cultures restrict mate selection in a number of ways. For example, some cultures express preferences that mates be of similar ages, social status, and racial/ethnic backgrounds. Other cultures encourage partners to "marry up" and increase one's (and one's family's) social, economic, and community standing by choosing spouses of higher status. Selecting spouses within one's own social category is known as *homogamy*. "Homogamy occurs in part because of structural factors such as residential and age segregation in communities, but also because of individual preferences and group pressures" (Hendrix, 2003, p. 73). Social theorists, for example, Parsons (1951), believe that mate selection preferences based on similarity (see above) help maintain the structure of

society; since racial/ethnic groups differ in their values and lifestyles, inter-
marriage would tend to weaken or dilute the values and lifestyles of these
various social categories (Hendrix, 2003). This type of marriage is thought
to maintain social and economic categories (e.g., middle class). The literature does suggest that for individual couples, marital adjustment may be
easier and more lasting when spouses share similar values and lifestyle.
"Traditional, less diverse, cultures are often structured more along kinship
lines with people being grouped into extended families, or even larger
groups tracing descent from a common ancestor" (Hendrix, 2003, p. 73).
These cultures restrict couple parings by type of cousin—that is, a cross-
cousin in which one is linked via a cross-sex sibling link in a previous
generation. In other words, there is a genetic link between the couple
but not strong enough to be genetically damaging as in the case of incestuous relationships. Cross-cousin marriage is thought to perpetuate relationships among kin groups thereby stabilizing social structure as marriage is
thought to reorganize social structure (Radcliffe-Brown, 1950, as cited in
Hendrix, 2003). Cross-cousin marriage too, then, limits who one can
marry, as an individual can only marry a distant cousin. This was thought
to promote cooperation and strong family alliances among couples and
families as it strengthened kinship bonds. Close-cousin marriages are now
more typical in rural societies. This type of cousin marriage is called *gener-*
alized exchange and is more likely in cultures with patrilineal descent than
with matrilineal kin groups based on female ancestors (Homans &
Schneider, 1955, as cited in Hendrix, 2003). First-cousin marriage is far
more likely to be acceptable in societies with a centralized political
hierarchy (e.g., one ruling party in which all decisions are made at the
top—Communist China) than in simpler un-centralized hierarchies
(Ember, 1975). Also, marriage among first cousins is often found in larger
societies (population over 5,000) and in societies with recent extensive
population loss (e.g., large numbers of people left the area). It is hypothesized that first-cousin marriage becomes allowable to make up for the
shortage of available spouses (Hendrix, 2003).

Marriage has been defined as "a transfer of rights in the new spouse.
These rights include: sexual access, rights to claim offspring, and rights to
the spouse's labor" (Radcliffe-Brown, 1950, as cited in Hendrix, 2003,
p. 107). Marriage and its definition and expression are strongly influenced
by cultural norms and values and thus vary significantly across cultures.
Marriage consists of rights and behaviors (Radcliffe-Brown, 1950, as cited
in Hendrix, 2003). According to social scientist Murdock (1949), cross-
culturally, marriage tends to include the following: a socially approved sexual relationship and resulting childbirth, economic cooperation and

sharing, coresidence of spouses, expected duration for some years, and a ritual transaction marking entrance into the marriage itself. One must keep in mind, however, that there is significant variation to how marriage is expressed around the world. Marital age and length also differs significantly by culture. For example, in some cultures girls marry just prior to puberty while the average marital age for women in the United States is 26 years old (and 28 for men).

FORMS OF MARRIAGE

Traditionally, marriage has occurred between members of the opposite sex; however, prior to the acceptance of gay marriage in several states in the United States, other cultures sanctioned same-sex marriage as well as marriage between multiple males and females (polygamous marriages). The literature on marriage cites four primary types of marriages across cultures in preindustrial societies, that is, prior to the Industrial Revolution, which occurred between 1750 and 1850: monogamy (one wife, one husband), 16 percent; polygyny—two or more wives, one husband (83.5 percent); polyandry—two or more husbands, one wife (0.5 percent); group marriage—two or more husbands with two or more wives (0.0 percent).

Polygyny appears to be declining today. There are many subtypes of polygyny; however, the norm within polygamous marriages was and is sexual monogamy among partners. In traditional polygamous societies, men typically marry only one wife at a time but may accumulate more over a lifetime. Polygamy requires more wives than husbands; thus a balanced sex ratio prevents widespread polygamy (Hendrix, 2003). Additionally, polygamy is more likely to occur in societies where men can financially provide for each wife; thus poorer men were less likely to routinely practice polygamy. "While many might assume that polygymous sexuality involves multiple simultaneous partners, most cultures have stringent regulations which have been interpreted as reducing sexual rivalry and jealousy among cowives (Murdock, 1949, p. 75, as cited in Hendrix, 2003) but also preventing cowives from organizing against the husband" (Blumberg & Pilar Garcia, 1977, pp. 137–139). Regulations included the following standards:

(1) The senior wife has authority over the others which provides a mechanism for dispute resolution and aids the husband in controlling the wives; (2) wives live, eat, and sleep separately, or are preferentially sisters. Separate residences reduce interaction and interdependence among wives thereby reducing conflict. Sisters were thought to have less conflict than non-related women; (3) wives take turns

with the husband. [Polygamous] husbands and wives do not sleep, eat, recreate, and have sex all together. Most cultures specify a period of rotation in which the husband spends time with each wife in turn. Thus, in many cultures, [polygamous] interaction is similar to monogamous interaction—one on one—but in a social manner. (Blumberg & Pilar Garcia, 1977, pp. 137–139)

General polygyny is most common in Africa and is associated with female food production (White, 1988, as cited in Hendrix, 2003). Cowives provide and prepare the food while caring for infants and young children, which profits the husband and does not drain his resources and increases his status. For some societies, polygyny may be an adaptive practice where there has been a shortage of men/male partners. In this way, polygyny allows for population growth (i.e., having children) and the provision of women without being damaged by a shortage of male partners.

Polyandry is the rarest form of marriage and occurs mostly in Asia (Hendrix, 2003). Polyandry is fraternal in that a woman marries full brothers or a clan of brothers. For example, in Toda, a caste of India, when the eldest son married a woman, his younger brothers married her also. The oldest brother was the social father of her children (Queen & Habenstein, 1974, pp. 18–47, as cited in Hendrix, 2003). Most researchers believe that polyandrous societies exist due to scarcity of resources (e.g., male food production), because it allows brothers who have inherited land and/or other resources to cooperate in food production while limiting their fertility by sharing a wife (Lee, 1982, as cited in Hendrix, 2003). In this way, the family unit has more resources, more food producers, and fewer dependents. Research finds that "polyandry is never the most common form of marriage in a society because it exists usually when there is a high male mortality in warfare or when men marry much later than women" (Hendrix, 2003, p. 109). It develops when a society begins to outstrip its environmental resources. The literature suggests that the different forms of marriage are not necessarily due to the balance of power between men and women or as a result of religious teachings but instead may be due to practical adaptations and ways of surviving that develop from a particular set of social and environmental stressors and practices (Hendrix, 2003).

SEXUAL ATTITUDES AND PRACTICES AROUND THE WORLD

Different cultures interpret sexual behavior and sexuality in different ways. Individuals develop beliefs, values, and a set of behaviors from members of the culture in which they grew up (Broude, 2005). Social scientist Broude gives the example of a society prizing virginity among unmarried girls: it may teach the value that girls should be chaste until marriage. In this way, culture determines this viewpoint. A second perspective promotes the belief system that sexual beliefs and practices are systematically related to other aspects of culture and behavior (p. 177). For example, if a society has no reliable means of birth control, this society may prize virginity until marriage, thereby minimizing the chances that a male will impregnate an unmarried female and disappear (Broude, 2005). A third perspective assumes that sexual behaviors and attitudes are guided by and grounded in biology. In other words, sexual behavior is largely determined by our need to reproduce and survive. Each of these perspectives shapes each culture's views on sex and sexuality differently.

Attitudes toward sex vary across the world. Most societies have viewed sex as dangerous and/or negative at least some of the time (Broude, 2005). One can hypothesize that certain sexual behaviors will derive from this. For example, societies that overwhelmingly subscribe to this belief system teach their members (especially women since they are the ones giving birth) sexually restrictive practices (e.g., virginity until marriage). Societies where there is equal medical care for men and women as well as birth control may view the negative consequences of sex as less serious and more manageable. Broude (2005) summarizes the attitudes of several cultures about sex and its dangerousness. The Tibetan Lepcha culture views sexual activity as wholesome, fun, and a necessary part of human life (Gorer, 1938, as cited in Broude, 2005) while sexual secretions are seen as dangerous in some culture groups like the Kurd. Kurd men bathe after sex because fluids produced during sex are viewed as dirty (Bourde, 2005). The Kimam of New Guinea believe that sperm has healing qualities but sex itself can stunt the growth of boys (Serpenti, 1965, as cited in Broude, 2005). In only 34 cultures (of a 41 percent sample worldwide) is sex viewed as safe all of the time. Broude reports that in 15 percent of a sample of 34 societies, sexual activity is always considered dangerous. She states that Ethiopian Konso males believe that the vaginas of some girls can snap off a man's penis while the Azande of Zaire believe that the mere sight of a woman's anus or genitalia can injure a man. Finally, the Bhil of India believe sex to be sacred and not engaged in for pleasure. As you can see, the "dangerous" aspects of sex seem to shape the perspectives of many different cultures on sexuality and sexual activity. Obviously, beliefs about whether sex is beneficial or dangerous shape sexual behavior, beliefs, and practices. "In cultures where people believe that sex is dangerous, extramarital affairs for women are condemned and the incidence of both premarital and extramarital sex is low. It is common to find taboos associated with menstruation in societies that equate sex with danger" (Broude, 2005, p. 178). Broude finds that attitudes about sex are not predictably related to beliefs about the desirability of frequent sexual activity within a marriage. Thus, although a particular cultural group may believe that sex is outwardly harmful, it may advocate frequent sexual relations between husband and wife. So it seems that most societies that view sex as harmful do not necessarily restrict sexual activity within marriage between spouses.

PREMARITAL SEX

Attitudes about premarital sex range from totally acceptable to totally unacceptable with a slight majority of cultures tending to disprove of premarital sex for girls. It appears as if the double standard about girl's/women's sexual behavior (i.e., having more social, physical, or psychological restrictions on it) is cross-cultural. Broude reports that in a worldwide survey of 141 cultures, 45 percent at least tolerate premarital sexual activity on the part of unmarried females while 55 percent disapprove of premarital sex for most if not all girls. Boys' premarital sexual activity tends to be more tolerated. For example, in a sample of 57 cultures, 63 percent approve of sexual activity for unmarried boys, while only 33 percent disapprove of premarital sex (Broude & Greene, 1976, as cited in Broude, 2005). Thirty-four percent of a sample of 141 societies strongly disapprove of premarital sex for girls and 23 percent strongly condemn premarital sex for boys (Broude & Greene, 1976, as cited in Broude, 2005). In these cultures engaging in premarital sex usually merits some strong societal or familial consequence (e.g., forced marriage, whipping, or even death).

HOMOSEXUALITY

Since the beginning of human history, there have been records of sexual and affectionate relationships between same-sex couples (Cardoso & Werner, 2005). "Records [of homosexual acts] have come from myths, political histories, legal documents, literature, and religious injunctions. Peruvian Mochican culture's potter depicts homosexual acts over 2000 years ago, the African Khoi-San culture has rock drawings of homosexual intercourse that are thousands of years old, and many other cultures have evidence of homosexual acts as well including Mesopotamia, Egypt, India, China, Japan, ancient Greece and Rome, and throughout Europe " (Cardoso & Werner, 2005, p. 204).

Male Homosexuality around the World

According to social scientists Cardoso and Werner (2005), most cultures have noted homosexuality's uniqueness within their respective societies but emphasize that different cultures define homosexuality in different ways. They also state that much more is written about male homosexuality than female homosexuality. This could be because most societies do not readily accept or acknowledge female sexuality and because most of the writers of history were male (because of the large-scale oppression and sexism against women) this was simply a neglected area. Cardoso and Werner (2005) review a classification system for male homosexuality, which includes three categories: the *pathic* (*passive*) or *gender-stratified* system, the *pederasty* or *age-stratified* system (includes societies with *mentorship* or *ritualized* homosexuality), and the *hemophilic* or *egalitarian* system, which can be subdivided into *adolescent homosexuality*, *comrade*, and *gay* systems. The egalitarian system the least common type of homosexuality found across cultures. Systems of female homosexuality may be similar to or different from this.

In gender-stratified systems of homosexuality, men who take on pathic (passive or receptive) roles in sexual relationships are distinguished from typical men, but the men who take on *active* (insertor) roles are not. Cardoso and Werner (2005) state that this system is widespread in all the world's continents and that in many societies pathics are known for their special ceremonial roles. They may be known as a Pathic Shaman. If you remember from earlier in this chapter, Shamans are held in high regard in the societies of many cultures. Pathic Shamans are also known as *soft men* and communicate with supernatural beings. They are allowed same-sex marriage and are considered special in these societies. They may adopt female characteristics, hairstyles, dress, and traditionally female tasks and speech. This is noted among the Siberian Chukchee people (Murray, 2000, as cited in Cardoso & Werner, 2005). Gender-stratified homosexuality is also common in Latin America (e.g., Brazil).

In age-stratified systems of homosexuality (which have also been identified in all continents except the Americas), *mentorship* is common (Cardoso & Werner, 2005). In the mentorship system, an older male takes on a boy as his protégé to teach him the arts of politics, religion, warfare, and other tasks of manhood. Boys may become apprentices around 10 years of age and continue in the *passive* role until 25 and/or they marry a woman. These men can then take on an apprentice of their own (Cardoso & Werner, 2005). In ancient Greece, men continued these relationships even after they married women. "In some societies, like the Etoro, these homosexual activities were more common and considered far superior to heterosexual sex that might be totally prohibited for two thirds of the year. Lengthy and complex rituals assured that insemination would give the boys male strength" (Herdt, 1984, p. 206; Murray, 2000, as cited in Cardoso & Werner, 2005). In Japan, during the 13th through 17th centuries, older Buddhist monks held active homosexual relations with passive younger postulants (i.e., those studying to be monks). This also happened with older and younger Samurai warriors. The *passive* recipients were often feminized or made more effeminate for the sexual pleasures of powerful older males. Cardoso and Werner (2005) report that West African Mossi chiefs often kept boys for sexual purposes, especially for Fridays when sex was forbidden with women. This was also seen among the Ashanti people, who kept male slaves and treated them as female lovers. Finally, in many societies (e.g., China, Korea, Japan, Rome, Egypt, Iraq) boys took on women's roles in theatrical productions and served as prostitutes, a practice which led some (including Shakespeare's England) to denounce the theater (Murray, 2000, as cited in Cardoso & Werner, 2005).

Cardoso and Werner find that in egalitarian systems, power differences between *active* and *passive* partners do not exist or are downplayed. For example, in many societies adolescent friends engage in homosexual play (e.g., African Nyakyusa boys live apart in separate villages) and sleep with each other. This was also true among the Yanomami Indians, as intervillage homosexuality was encouraged and a youth was likely to marry his "best friend's" sister (Cardoso & Werner, 2005). This system also existed among the Australian Aborigines in that adolescent males might have sex with their future brothers in law. We find this system in many other cultures as well, including many Melanesian and Polynesian societies, including Tikopia, Samoa, Tahiti, and Hawaii. Some of these relationships continued over a lifetime despite marriage to women. Cardoso and Werner (2005) report that the rarest system is our modern *gay* system in which exclusive gay men engage in sex with other exclusive homosexuals throughout their lives. This system has become increasingly popular in many cultures around the world but it is viewed as a more modern take on historical homosexual relationships. These are the most common ways homosexuality has been demonstrated in various societies; however, they are not the only ways. Other ways homosexual relationships occurred were through war when homosexual rape was used to humiliate one's defeated enemies (Duerr, 1993, as cited in Cardoso & Werner, 2005). Homosexual rapes in prison settings are well documented. Keep in mind that different types of homosexuality are found within the same culture.

Female Homosexuality around the World

Social scientist and scholar Kendal (1998, as cited in Cardoso & Werner, 2005) highlights that it has always been very easy to ignore or minimize female homosexuality for several reasons, including most societies' greater tolerance for physical affection between women (versus men), the minimization and denial of women's sexuality and sexual expression, and most societies' focus on sexual intercourse being defined as penial-vaginal. For example, Basotho women in Lesotho believe that sex is impossible without a penis; thus, women can *have sex* with their husbands but simultaneously maintain affective ties with women (which may include genital grinding). Kendal also notes that many cultures have described women taking on traditional male roles of warrior and husband but it was unclear if these roles involved lesbian sex. We do find some clear descriptions of lesbian relationships in the literature, including the Chukchee, who describe some women who adopted male dress, speech, and work activities and married other girls. There are also records of gender-stratified female homosexuality in ancient China and Japan. For example, the Han emperor Cheng (32–7 BC) and his wife shared a female student's sexual favor together as a couple (Murray, 2000, as cited in Cardoso & Werner, 2005). "During the Tokugawa period (1615–1867 CE) lesbianism was common in the shoguns' harems, and there are references to women dressed as males who sought female prostitutes. Additionally, Japanese theater companies had female actors who took on male roles and had sex with other female actors" (Cardoso & Werner, 2005, p. 208). Age-stratified homosexuality occurred as part of initiation ceremonies among the Kaguru of Tanzania and there is significant documentation of the ancient Greek poet Sappho, from the island of Lesbos, who addressed women in language used specifically to describe homosexual relationships between men (Cardoso & Werner, 2005).

As you can see, homosexuality has probably been around as long as human beings have. There are different types, different definitions, and different levels of societal acceptance. Most societies—both current and ancient—place a unique value on same-sex relationships but it is clear that both male and female homosexuality has existed throughout history. Our understanding of same-sex relationships and their significant cultural and social influences continues to evolve.

RAPE AND SEXUAL AGGRESSION AROUND THE WORLD

Unfortunately, sexual aggression occurs all around the world. These damaging acts occur between adults and children, men and women, men and men, between family members and non–family members, and between romantic partners. Historically, rape has existed in a variety of contexts. For example, across the world, public rapes have occurred in wars and ethnic conflicts as a way to demoralize and victimize the enemy's women—which has negative consequences for both men and women. Rape was used (and still is) as a form of terrorism. A few examples of this included the rape of Muslim women in the First Crusade, rape in Japanese concentration camps, rape in camp brothels in World War II, rape and murder of women by U.S. soldiers in Vietnam, Chinese soldiers raping and impregnating Tibetan women in 1949 as a means of ethnic cleansing and humiliation for Tibetan men, and Serbian soldiers' raping of Bosnian Muslim women with the intention of impregnating them (Campaign Free Tibet, 1994; Drakulic, 1994, as cited in Zimmer-Tamakoshi, 2005; Perpinan Sr., 1994).

In U.S. and other cultures, date rape and acquaintance rape occurs frequently on college campuses. Social scientist Zimmer-Tamakoshi (2005) reports that one study of students at 32 U.S. institutions of higher education showed that 28 percent of the women had experienced a rape or rape attempt since age 14 and that 8 percent of men admitted to having committed at least one rape (Koss et al., 1987, as cited in Zimmer-Tamakoshi, 2005). Social scientists suggest that rape and sexual aggression is the means some men use to demonstrate their masculinity and adopt masculine power roles. In U.S. college culture, women are often lured through drugs and alcohol and depicted as "asking for it." Men who object to sexual aggression are often depicted as effeminate and weak. College communities often support this behavior and sexual aggression against women by failing to prosecute it and prevent it from happening in the first place by making sexual assault against women socially unacceptable. Too often, college police and administrators look the other way and minimize women's victimization.

Another type of rape is intimate-partner rape. Within these harmful relationships, partner violence is also common. Social scientists Finkelhor and Yllo (1985, as cited in Zimmer-Tamakoshi, 2005) find that women are more likely to be raped, injured, or killed by current or former partners than by other assailants. Although violence in intimate relationships can be perpetuated by both partners, in heterosexual relationships, women are more likely to be more seriously injured and suffer repeated rapes and violent acts perpetuated against them than are men (Mahoney & Williams, 1998, as cited in Zimmer-Tamakoshi, 2005). Same-sex partner violence is also high (e.g., 38 percent of gay and 48 percent of lesbian couples experience violence). Social scientist West (1998, as cited in

Zimmer-Tamakoshi, 2005) has explored differences between ethnic groups in the United States and found that "other groups with high partner violence and sexual abuse are some Latino groups, African and Asian Americans and American Indians. African American men reportedly abuse their wives four times as often as European Americans and their wives are twice as likely to engage in severe acts of violence in return. Puerto Rican men are reportedly 10 times more likely than Cuban men to assault their wives[;] however, intimate violence is hidden in wealthier communities making it difficult to be sure that the difference is so significant" (Zimmer-Tamakoshi, 2005, p. 231). Cross-cultural statistics reflecting sexual assault and violence are difficult to get because most societies do not readily report this information and most individuals do not readily discuss it. Additionally, child sexual abuse is far more common around the world than is reported. As will be discussed in the next section, although acts of violence and sexual assault against women occur cross-culturally, they are more common in societies with strict gender roles, are non-egalitarian (not equal among the sexes), and actively denigrate women (and often children as well).

It is well documented that there is a close relationship between pornography and violence against women and children (Russell, 1998, as cited in Zimmer-Tamakoshi, 2005). Russell defines pornography as "material that combines sex and/or the exposure of genitals with abuse or degradation in a matter that appears to endorse, condone, or encourage such behavior. Pornography is different than 'erotica' in that erotica includes 'suggestive or arousing material' that is free of sexism, racism, and homophobia and is respectful of all human beings and animals portrayed." She further states that "adult pornography depicts women's bodies in ways that suggest that sexual harassment is harmless and that women enjoy being raped and sexually degraded" (Zimmer-Tamakoshi, 2005, p. 231). Russell argues that these images predispose some males to desire rape and find violence against women sexually arousing.

Rape and sexual aggression occur everywhere in the world; however, they do not occur to the same extent in every society and are not judged the same way (Zimmer-Tamakoshi, 2005). In egalitarian societies, where sexual equality is more of a value and able-bodied adults, regardless of gender, play a role in the production of food and other necessities, sexual aggression is more rare than in societies that are considered non-egalitarian. For example, among the Ituri forest foragers in Africa, the Kalahari desert foragers in southwest Africa, and the Kaulong gardeners in New Guinea, rape is far less common (Zimmer-Tamakoshi, 2005). We tend to see a rise in rape when a society's resources (e.g., food, jobs, housing) are being depleted. Child sexual abuse may be less common in egalitarian societies as well; however, due to lack of reliable statistical data, it would be difficult to state this fact definitively. In non-egalitarian societies, violence against women "is part of power complexes in which men use violence and sexual aggression to display their masculinity and induct younger men into masculine power roles" (Zimmer-Tamakoshi, 2005, p. 233). Zimmer-Tamakoshi highlights that victims of violence include women, male and female children, men in subordinate ethnic groups, groups, classes, or other statuses who suffer sexual abuse directly (themselves) or indirectly (e.g., their partners are sexually assaulted because they cannot protect their families from those in power). Interestingly, although the United States might be considered a gender-egalitarian society, rates of rape in the United States are among the highest in the world (e.g., 3 times higher than in the UK or Sweden and 5–10 times higher than in France, Belgium, or Japan) (Ellis, 1989, as cited in Zimmer-Tamakoshi, 2005). Social scientists have hypothesized that high levels of sexual aggression in the United States are consistent with America's violent society. In other words, violent behavior and sexual assault may go hand in hand.

Cross-culturally, it is found that there is a close relationship between sexual aggression and societies that are organized around masculine violence and hierarchy. Zimmer-Tamakoshi states that the more complex a violent society, the more sexual aggression and other forms of violence will also be complex in victims and expression. She finds that violence against women is part of a larger context of normative male violence. Thus, in countries and cultures where cultural ideals promote violence as evidence of masculine strength, and anything feminine is defined as weak, there are greater incidences of sexual assault and violence against women. Sexual aggression and violence are always a means of social control, hierarchy, and inequality. Domestic violence, rape, sexual slavery, and sexual harassment, whether in the United States, Zimbabwe, or the Philippines, are located in relationships of power, dominance, and privilege (Zimmer-Tamakoshi, 2005). In this way, these values engender a powerful culture of violence and the acceptance of violence against women and children.

ROMANTIC ATTACHMENT PATTERNS AROUND THE WORLD

In earlier chapters, we explored types of attachment between caregivers and infants (e.g., secure, insecure). We also discussed how the types of attachment patterns we develop in childhood are predictive of our romantic relationship attachment patterns in adulthood (e.g., securely attached children are more likely to develop secure attachments in their romantic relationships). A large-scale cross-cultural study explored attachment relationships around the world. Specifically, the researchers studied the question, "Are men universally more dismissing than women in their romantic attachment relationships?" Gender differences were explored across 62 cultural regions (Schmitt, 2003). Men are typically thought to be more dismissing of romantic attachment relationships. The following cultural regions were included in the study: North America (8 cultural regions), South America (5 regions), Western Europe (9 regions), Eastern Europe (9 regions), Western Europe (11 regions), Southern Europe (6 regions), Middle East (4 regions), Africa (7 regions), Oceania (3 regions), South/Southeast Asia (5 regions), and East Asia (4 regions). Participants represented 62 cultural regions in 56 countries of the world located on 6 different continents and 13 islands. The researchers found that in Western cultures, men were significantly more dismissing than women of attachment relationships. In non-Western cultures men were sometimes only slightly more dismissing than women. For example, in some African and Oceanic cultures (e.g., Ethiopia, Tanzania, Botswana, Zimbabwe, and Fiji) women were slightly more dismissing than men. Some social scientists suggest that in cultures where environmental and reproductive stressors are high, women might be more likely to engage in short-term mating patterns, which may encourage them to develop a more dismissing romantic attachment orientation (Belsky, 1999; Chisholm, 1996; Gangestad & Simpson, 2000; Schmitt, 2003). These studies found that gender differences in dismissing romantic attachment are not at all universal. "In a few cultures women were equal to men in romantic dismissiveness. In most cultures when men do prove more dismissing than women, the difference is usually only small in magnitude. Variation in gender differences across cultures was associated with several sociocultural differences including the similarity of mortality rates among men and women. In other words, in cultures where men *and* women had high mortality rates, (and also fewer resources and higher fertility rates) both sexes were more similar in adopting a more dismissing relationship style" (Schmitt, 2003, p. 327). There were some limitations of this study, which included a limited sample size for some cultural groups, not all cultural groups around the world being included, and the use of college students for some cultural groups, which may not be a representative sample of each individual society within a culture. What we can include is that many things contribute to developing a dismissing attachment style in romantic relationships; thus, we cannot assume that gender (i.e., male) is the primary predictor of a dismissing attachment relationship orientation.

ROMANTIC LOVE AROUND THE WORLD

Definitions of romantic love are diverse; therefore, we cannot assume that "romantic love" as practiced in the United States is universal. Social scientists Hatfield and Rapson (2005) explain that Western definitions of love include distinguishing between passionate love, which can be defined as a state of intense longing for union with another including strong physiological, emotional, and psychological responses (it is associated with fulfillment and ecstasy and its non-fulfillment is associated with feelings of emptiness, anxiety, and despair), and companionate love, which can be defined as affection and tenderness we feel for those with whom our lives are deeply entwined (it combines deep feelings of attachment, commitment, and intimacy). Hatfield and Rapson (2005) find clear evidence that passionate love and sexual desire are cultural universals and contain feelings that seem to have existed at all times and in all places (Brown, 1991; Buss, 1988a,b; Hatfield & Rapson, 1993). They define *companionate love* (also referred to as true love or marital love) as a warm, far less intense emotion that combines feelings of deep attachment, commitment, and intimacy. It also encompasses feelings of affection and tenderness that we feel for certain individuals with whom we share a sense of interdependence. Passionate love and sexual desire are often characteristic of the early stages of a romantic relationship, whereas companionate love characterizes couples who have been together for a long period of time.

CULTURAL UNIVERSALS IN PARTNER CREDENTIALS

In many societies around the world, men and women report wanting similar things in a mate (Hatfield & Rapson, 2005). In one large-scale cross-cultural study, social scientist David Buss (1989, as cited in Hatfield & Rapson, 2005) asked over 10,000 men and women from 37 countries, located on 6 continents and 5 islands, to state what characteristics they most wanted in potential mates. Geographical areas included countries in the following regions: Africa, Asia, Eastern and Western Europe, North America, Oceania, and South America. Study participants were asked to review over 18 traits and to rate the desirability or importance of each trait in choosing a mate. Results showed that, in general, men and women stated that they wanted many of the same things. The most important trait was love followed by a dependable character, emotional stability and maturity, and pleasing disposition. Men and women ranked these the four most desirable traits in that order. They differed in their order on the following traits (however, not by much—for example, if men ranked sociability at 7, women ranked it at 6): good health, education and intelligence, sociability, desire for home and children, ambition and industriousness, favorable social status or rating, good financial prospect, and similar religious and political background. There were more significant differences in rankings between men and women on the following traits: good looks (men ranked this trait at 10 whereas women ranked it at 13), similar education (men ranked this at 14 whereas women ranked this at 11), good cook and housekeeper (men ranked this at 12 whereas women ranked this at 15), and, finally, chastity (defined as no previous sexual experience: men ranked this at 16 whereas women ranked this at 18).

CONCLUSION

As you can see from this chapter, there are many cultural differences as well as similarities in sex, mating rituals, marriage, romantic attachment patterns, and definitions and acceptance of homosexuality around the world. We should also keep in mind the significance of culture and society and just how much these influences shape our values, behavior, and thoughts about sex and sexuality. Clearly, culture has a significant influence in shaping the study of sexuality as well as sexual behavior.

REFERENCES

Belsky, J. (1999). Modern evolutionary theory and patterns of attachment. In J. Cassidy & P. R. Shaver (Eds.), *Handbook of attachment* (pp. 141–161). New York: Guilford Press.

Blackwood, B. (1935). *Both sides of Buka passage: An ethnographic study of social, sexual and economic questions in North-Western Solomon Islands.* Oxford: Clarendon-Oxford University.

Blumberg, R. L., & Pilar Garcia, M. (1977). The political economy of the mother-child family: A cross-societal view. In L. Lenero-Otero (Ed.), *Beyond the Nuclear Family Model* (pp. 99–163). London: Sage.

Bogoras, W. (1909). *The Chukchee.* Jessup North Pacific Expedition, Memoirs of the American Museum of Natural History. Leiden: E.J. Brill.

Broude, G. J. (2005). Sexual attitudes and practices. In *Encyclopedia of sex and gender: Men and women in the world's cultures* (Vol. 1, pp. 177–186). New York: Kluwer Academic/Plenum Publishers.

Broude, G. J., & Greene, S. J. (1976). Cross-cultural codes on twenty sexual attitudes and practices. *Ethnology, 15,* 409–429.

Broude, G. J., & Greene, S. J. (1983). Cross-cultural codes for husband-wife relationships. *Ethnology, 22,* 263–280.

Brown, D. E. (1991). *Human universals*. Philadelphia, PA: Temple University Press.

Brown, M. F. (2003). *Who owns native culture?* Cambridge, MA: Harvard University Press.

Buss, D. M. (1988a). Love acts: The evolutionary biology of love. In R. J. Sternberg & M. L. Barnes (Eds.), *The psychology of love* (pp. 100–118). New Haven: Yale University Press.

Buss, D. M. (1988b). The evolution of human intrasexual competition: Tactics of mate attraction. *Journal of Personality and Social Psychology, 54*, 616–628.

Buss, D. M. (1989). Sex differences in human mate preferences: Evolutionary hypotheses tested in 37 cultures. *Behavioral and Brain Sciences, 12*, 1–49.

Campaign Free Tibet. (1994). We have no rights, not even our bodies. In M. Davies (Ed.), *Women and violence: Realities and responses worldwide* (pp. 133–136). London: Zed Books. Adapted and reprinted from a report compiled for Campaign Free Tibet.

Cardoso, F. L., & Werner, D. (2005). Homosexuality. In *Encyclopedia of sex and gender: Men and women in the world's cultures*. (Vol. 1, pp. 204–215). New York: Kluwer Academic/Plenum Publishers.

Chisholm, J. S. (1996). The evolutionary ecology of attachment organization. *Human Nature, 7*, 1–38.

Derne, S. (1994). Structural realities, persistent dilemmas, and the construction of emotional paradigms: Love in three cultures. *Social Perspectives on Emotion, 2*, 281–308.

Drakulic, S. (1994). The rape of women in Bosnia. In M. Davies (Ed.), *Women and violence: Realities and responses worldwide* (pp. 176–181). London: Zed Books.

Duerr, H. P. (1993). *Obszünitüt und Gewalt: Der Mythos vom Zivilisationsproze*. Frankurt am Main, Germany: Suhrkamp Verlag.

Ellis, L. (1989). *Theories of rape: Inquiries into the causes of sexual aggression*. New York: Hemisphere.

Ember, M. (1975). On the origin and extension of the incest taboo. *Behavior Science Research, 10*, 249–281.

Finkelhor, D., & Yllo, K. (1985). *License to rape: Sexual abuse of wives*. New York: Holt, Rinehart, & Winston.

Gangestad, S. W., & Simpson, J. A. (2000). Toward an evolutionary history of female sociosexual variation. *Journal of Personality, 58*, 69–96. *Biological foundations of personality: Evolution, behavioral genetics, and psychophysiology* [Special Issue].

Goode, W. J. (1967). *World revolution and family patterns*. New York: Free Press.

Gorer, G. (1938). *Himalayan village: An account of the Lepchas of Sikkim*. London: Joseph.

Gregor, T. (1985). *Anxious pleasures: The sexual lives of an Amazonian people*. Chicago: University of Chicago Press.

Hatfield, E., & Rapson, R. L. (1993). *Love, sex, and intimacy: Their psychology, biology, and history*. New York: HarperCollins.

Hatfield, E., & Rapson, R. L. (2005). *Love and sex: Cross-cultural perspectives*. Lanham, Maryland: University Press of America.

Hendrix, L. (2003). Courtship and marriage. In *Encyclopedia of sex and gender: Men and women in the world's cultures* (Vol. 1, pp. 71–76). New York: Kluwer Academic/Plenum Publishers.

Herdt, G. H. (1984). *Ritualized homosexuality in Melanesia*. Berkeley: University of California Press.

Homans, G. C., & Schneider, D. M. (1955). Kinship terminology and the American kinship system. *American Anthropologist, 57*(6), 1194–1208.

Jacobs, S. E., & Cromwell, J. (1992). Visions and revisions of reality: Reflections on sex, sexuality, gender and gender variance. *Journal of Homosexuality, 23*(4), 43–69.

Kendal, L. (1998). When a woman loves a woman in Lesotho: Love, sex and the (western) construction of homophobia. In S. O. Murray & W. Roscoe (Eds.), *Boy-wives and female husbands: Studies in African homosexualities* (pp. 223–242). New York: Palgrave.

Koss, M. P., Gidycz, C. A., & Wisniewski, N. (1987). The scope of rape: Incidence and prevalence of sexual aggression and victimization in a national sample of higher education students. *Journal of Consulting and Clinical Psychology, 55*(2), 162–170.

Lee, G. R. (1982). *Family structure and interaction* (2nd ed.). Minneapolis, MN: University of Minnesota Press.

Mahoney, P., & Williams, L. M. (1998). Sexual assault in marriage: Prevalence, consequences, and treatment of wife. In J. L. Jasinski & L. M. Williams (Eds.), *Partner violence: A comprehensive review of 20 years of research* (pp. 113–162). Thousand Oaks, CA: Sage.

Meigs, A. (1976). Male pregnancy and the reduction of sexual opposition in the New Guinea Highlands. *Ethnology, 15*, 393–407.

Murdock, G. P. (1949). *Social structure*. New York: The MacMillan Company.

Murray, S. O. (2000). *Homosexualities*. Chicago: University of Chicago Press.

O'Brian, R. (2003). Economic activities and gender roles. In *Encyclopedia of sex and gender: Men and women in the world's cultures* (Vol. 1, pp. 91–96). New York: Kluwer Academic/Plenum Publishers.

Parsons, T. (1951). *The social system*. New York: The Free Press.

Perpinan, M. S., Sr. (1994). Militarism and the sex industry in the Philippines. In M. Davies (Ed.). *Women and violence: Realities and responses worldwide* (pp. 149–152). London: Zed Books.

Queen, S., & Habenstein, R. W. (1974). *The family in various cultures* (4th ed.). New York: Lippincott.

Radcliffe-Brown, A. R. (1950). *African systems of kinship and marriage*. London: Oxford University Press.

Russell, D. E. H. (1998). *Dangerous relationships: Pornography, misogyny, and rape*. Thousand Oaks, CA: Sage.

Schmitt, D. P. (2003). Universal sex differences in the desire for sexual variety: Tests from 52 nations, 6 continents, and 13 islands. *Journal of Personality and Social Psychology, 85*, 85–104.

Segal, E. S. (2003). Cultural constructions of gender. In *Encyclopedia of sex and gender: Men and women in the world's cultures* (Vol. 1, pp. 3–10). New York: Kluwer Academic/Plenum Publishers.

Serpenti, I. M. (1965). *Cultivators in the swamps*. Assen, The Netherlands: Van Gorcum.

West, C. M. (1998). Lifting the "political gag order": Breaking the silence around partner violence in ethnic minority families. In J. L. Jasinski & L. M. Williams (Eds.), *Partner violence: A comprehensive review of 20 years of research* (pp. 184–209). Thousand Oaks, CA: Sage.

White, D. R. (1988). Rethinking polygyny. *Current Anthropology, 29*, 529–572.

Williams, W. L. (1992). *The spirit and the flesh: Sexual diversity in American Indian culture*. Boston: Beacon Press.

Zimmer-Tamakoshi, L. (2005). Rape and other sexual aggression. In *Encyclopedia of sex and gender: Men and women in the world's cultures* (Vol. 1, pp. 230–246). New York: Kluwer Academic/Plenum Publishers.

Part II

Scenarios

In this section, the reader is presented with five different case study scenarios in which individuals and couples are struggling with a common issue in sexuality. These scenarios are directly related to the topics we discussed in the book. Each scenario is followed by an analysis of the dilemma in the case study.

 ### *Scenario 1*

Kenneth and Jackie, both 19, meet at a college fraternity party. Kenneth catches Jackie's eye from across the room and he walks over to her. They spend much of the night talking to one another and dancing. They find out that they have several friends and interests in common and even grew up in neighboring towns. Jackie feels comfortable with Kenneth because they have so much in common and he seems like a nice guy. She asks him if he has a girlfriend and he tells her that he is single. Jackie tells him that she is single too, having broken up with her high school boyfriend 4 months ago. Kenneth asks Jackie if she wants to leave the party so that they can continue talking undisturbed. Jackie is happy to be asked and the two of them end up at an all-night diner, where they continue their conversation.

Kenneth tells Jackie that he and his longtime college girlfriend broke up 3 weeks ago and he tells her that he caught her cheating on him. He tells Jackie that he is still trying to "wrap his head around" what happened because he was convinced that they were going to end up getting married at some point in the future. Kenneth states that he never thought he would find anyone he wanted to be in a relationship again, which is why he is so happy to have met Jackie. Jackie is thrilled that Kenneth is opening up to her. Kenneth sits next to Jackie in the booth and they hold hands and kiss throughout their meal. Kenneth tells Jackie that she is special and states that he is very attracted to her.

Kenneth asks Jackie about her breakup with her boyfriend and she tells him that they "grew apart" and that it had been tough going for a year because he was a freshman at a different university last year when she was a high school senior. Jackie admits that she was in some ways relieved by the breakup because it freed her up to more fully enjoy college life without feeling like she had to make time for her boyfriend. Jackie and Kenneth then begin to discuss their common experience of having serious relationships in high school.

Kenneth asks Jackie if she would like to go back to his residence hall. Although Jackie is excited, she knows that if she goes back to his room, they might have sex. She tells Kenneth that she wants to spend more time with him and admits to being highly attracted to him as well. She really likes Kenneth and is looking forward to getting to know him better. The couple goes back to Kenneth's room and end up having sex. Although Kenneth promises to call Jackie the next day, he never does. Kenneth never contacts Jackie and ignores her texts to him and her request to be friends on Facebook. Jackie is devastated because she really liked Kenneth and thought that they were beginning a relationship together. She is angry at herself for having sex with him the first night they met.

ANALYSIS

The situation depicted above is unfortunately all too common. When individuals decide to have sex, they frequently do so without talking about their expectations for what happens after intercourse. People often fear that if they make their wishes known to their potential partner (especially early on in the encounter—for example, "I just want to hook up [have sex]. I don't want a relationship" or "I like you a lot and hope that this turns into a serious relationship") they will scare the other person off. Although this fear may be valid, when we do not make our feelings and wishes known early in a relationship encounter, it is easy to end up having hurt feelings or misunderstandings because the two individuals having sex may have different expectations for what happens afterward. Often, individuals struggle to have a dialogue about sex prior to the encounter itself. Even though taking one's clothes off is very intimate, it seems that this is far less intimate than having honest conversations about our sexual needs, relationship wants, and continued expectations. In the above scenario,

Jackie might have told Kenneth about her desire to date him prior to their having sex. Doing so would at least have put her expectations forward allowing Kenneth to understand that Jackie wanted more from him than one brief sexual encounter. Kenneth could then have clarified that he was not interested in a relationship at this time, if that was the case. Because individuals often feel shame and embarrassment about their sexual desires and behavior, people are more likely to lie. Additionally, Kenneth may have just wanted to have sex and not been interested in a relationship with Jackie, especially given that he just got out of a long-term relationship 3 weeks ago. If Jackie had explained that she was interested in the possibility of an ongoing relationship, Kenneth might have lied and stated he was too, just to have sex with Jackie. When we have sex with someone we can risk getting emotionally hurt; however, this is even more likely to happen when we do not state our expectations prior to having sex. As Chapter 3 discusses, we are not taught to talk about sex or be clear about our thoughts and feelings regarding sex. This often comes at a cost because the risk of misunderstandings and hurt feelings is high when we do not clearly communicate our desires prior to having sex. Although Jackie may have been afraid of scaring Kenneth off, she might have saved herself being hurt had she told him about her developing feelings for him. This typical example also highlights some gender differences that can happen in heterosexual relationships. Although this may not be true for all women, many women tend to be more relationally oriented than men at earlier ages while men may be more likely to feel comfortable having a sexual relationship outside of a relationship. These gender differences do not apply to everyone but they are something to keep in mind when understanding the dynamics of the above scenario.

 ### Scenario 2

Denise, 28, has been single for several years while she was finishing up her master's degree in biology. Many of her friends had started getting married and having children and she wanted to start looking for a serious relationship. She began asking friends if they knew any single guys to set her up with. Her friend Margaret told her that she works with a guy named Jason who seems "pretty cool" and tells Denise that he's pretty cute. Margaret asks Denise if she wants her to set them up on a blind date and Denise excitedly agrees.

Denise is from a midsized town in the Midwest. She recently moved to a big city for a new job and is excited to begin her life in a new city. She and Margaret were acquaintances in college and rediscovered each other on

Facebook. Denise was happy to reconnect with Margaret because then she wouldn't feel so isolated in her new city. Margaret is warm and encouraging and states that she is sure that Denise and Jason will absolutely hit it off.

Prior to their date, Jason, 31, called Denise and they had several phone conversations. Denise finds Jason to be charismatic, funny, and smart. She begins to really look forward to the date. Jason tells Denise that he is ready to "settle down" and admits that he is looking for "the one." They share their common experience of being single while many of their friends are getting married and having children. Denise and Jason talk about potential places to meet and Jason suggests a popular restaurant. They agree not to exchange pictures prior to the date because they both want to be surprised about the other person's physical appearance. Denise tells Jason that she is attracted to him already and both agree that they are excited to be able to finally meet in person after weeks of talking on the phone and texting.

Denise considers herself to be a cautious person, which is why she was nervous about trying online dating. One of the reasons Denise moved to the city was because she would not need a car. She takes public transportation wherever she goes. She and Jason meet for lunch and have a pretty good time. Denise finds that Jason dominates the conversation and spends more time talking about himself than getting to know her. She is ambivalent about going out with him again but has talked herself into giving it another shot should he ask her because she doesn't know that many people in her new city. Because Denise did not have a car, Jason offered to take her home. Denise felt relatively comfortable with Jason (and trusted Margaret's recommendation regarding his character); she agreed to let him drive her home.

When they arrived at her apartment, he invited himself inside stating that he needed to go to the bathroom. When they get inside of Denise's apartment he forces Denise to have sex with him, despite her repeatedly telling him no.

ANALYSIS

As discussed in Chapter 3, date rape and sexual assault happens to one out of every four women. Men can certainly be victims of date rape and sexual assault as well; however, since they are less likely to report it, our statistics regarding the frequency of this crime are less accurate for men. This is a difficult case to explore because we frequently are tempted to blame the victim for her circumstances—by being critical of Denise's judgment in allowing Jason to come back to her home. The truth is that Denise did not do anything wrong. In the dating world, we meet someone we like and have to make a decision to trust him or her eventually. Relationships cannot develop where there is no trust between two people and trust develops over time but often begins in the early stages of a relationship. As is often the case, Jason did not show any signs of sexual aggression on the date and Denise felt comfortable with him, especially given that he was recommended to her by someone she knew. Date rape often occurs this way and is the ultimate example of when one person disregards the rights of another and forces the other person into a sexual encounter she (or he) did not want. If you look back in your own dating/relationship life, you may recollect that many of us have been in potentially threatening situations where the above scenario could have occurred. Getting into a car with Jason left Denise was more vulnerable than what she realized; however, this does not mean that she made a poor decision, nor does it mean that her rape was her fault. Sexual assault is never the victims' fault. When an individual is raped, sexually abused, or sexually assaulted, he or she loses trust in himself or herself and in the world around them. Individuals who have been raped are left feeling vulnerable and frequently judge themselves harshly. This is why seeking counseling after a rape can be very helpful, along with surrounding oneself with supportive people who can affirm the individual and validate his or her feelings. Individuals never ask to be raped, no matter what they are wearing, if they were out at night or not, if they allowed an individual to come into their home, or any of the other justifications some in society may use to blame the victim for his or her own assault. Denise can benefit from talking about what happened with trusted others and should strongly consider pressing charges against Jason. She may be at risk for developing posttraumatic stress disorder and experiencing other anxiety-related symptoms. Although reporting the incident to the police may involve a significant emotional ordeal for her, this is probably a past, present, and future pattern of behavior for Jason (as research demonstrates that those who commit date rape are likely to do it several times, especially if their victims never press charges). Denise should try not to blame herself and work on learning to trust herself and others again, though it will be difficult. A frustrating truth is that date rape is not always preventable. Obviously, the majority of individuals who engage in dating rituals do so without becoming victims of sexual predators like Jason; however, the "Jasons" of the world unfortunately exist and can only be stopped if legal action is taken against them.

 ### Scenario 3

Bryan, 17, is a popular high school junior. He is on the honor roll, has lots of friends, and is a talented baseball player. Bryan has limited dating experience.

He feels that although he has dated several high school girls, he is strongly attracted to boys. He has not shared these feelings with anyone because he does not really know how to talk about it. Bryan had a friend from junior high who came out as gay when he was 15 and now lives his life as an openly gay high school student but he and Bryan have not been close for a long time and his friend does not go to his high school.

Bryan admits that he is confused and thinks he might be gay but he has also heard that bisexuality means being attracted to both boys and girls. He wonders that because he had a girlfriend when he was a freshman and they had a limited sexual relationship if he might be bisexual. He begins thinking about his attraction to men. He has had crushes on a few of his teammates, though he has never told them. He finds himself looking at some of his teammates in the locker room. He is afraid that if his teammates find out that he might be gay, they will ostracize him and that he might become the victim of bullying. Several members of his team make "gay jokes" all the time and use derogatory language about gay men as a way of teasing and insulting one another. He has started to feel unsafe around them. He is questioning his sexual orientation but is really unsure if he is gay or bisexual.

Bryan does not know whom to talk to. He has thought about contacting his friend from junior high but does not want him to tell anyone and the two have not talked in a year. Bryan has started to feel very lonely and depressed. As a result, his grades and his performance on the baseball field have begun to suffer. He feels like everyone is watching him and trying to figure out if he is gay. He often wonders if he will be "found out."

Bryan's parents have always been supportive of him and he thinks that they would accept him if he told him about his feelings, but lately his mom has been pressuring him to take her friend Samantha's daughter (Sarah) to prom. His mom has told him that she thinks that he and Sarah would really hit it off. She has expressed concern that he has not dated anyone seriously since his freshman year. She has noticed that he has begun keeping more and more to himself and has accused Bryan of being ashamed of his family because he has never brought a girl home to meet them. Bryan's dad works late hours and although the two have a good relationship, they rarely have heart-to-heart talks about anything. Bryan still remembers when his dad tried to talk to him about sex (at his mom's insistence). Both found the conversation tense, awkward, and embarrassing. Bryan also knew that his dad got many of his facts about the birds and the bees incorrect so he feels like there is no way he can talk to either parent about his confusion. Bryan has started reading coming-out blogs on the Internet, communicating anonymously with other individuals who are questioning their sexual orientation through several chat rooms. He has found this somewhat helpful.

ANALYSIS

Bryan is struggling to understand his own sexual identity and sexuality. It appears that he does not yet know if he is fully attracted to girls, boys, or both. Questioning one's sexual identity can be a painful experience, especially because society frequently socializes individuals into an assumed "heterosexual identity" in early childhood and individuals who do not fit this mold are often thrust into a painful period of sexual questioning because they are not considered the "norm." Sexual questioning can be a very healthy thing, because, as you may remember from Chapters 1 and 4, sexual orientation can be conveyed on a continuum where heterosexuality is at one end, homosexuality is at the other, and bisexuality is in the middle. Sexual researcher Alfred Kinsey has indicated that most people are probably somewhere nearer to the middle, especially women, whose sexuality tends not to be as rigidly defined as men's. Because the socialization into a heterosexual identity is so strong, this may actually force individuals onto one end of the continuum or the other, even if their natural tendency might be somewhere closer to the middle. Bryan could be gay, straight, or bisexual. Each of these is a legitimate and healthy sexual orientation. Remember from Chapters 1 and 4 that sexual orientation has both biological and environmental influences. Bryan should not feel shame because he is questioning his sexual orientation. As we remember from our earlier learning about sexual orientation, it is not simply about sexual behavior but also has to do with identity, who we are sexually and affectionately attracted to, and other cultural and social influences that are impacted by our sexual orientation identification. Sexually questioning individuals may face social stigma as they struggle to define their sexual identities, especially if they find that they are bisexual or gay; however, they should still consider being honest with themselves and others regarding their questions unless they find that doing so would be emotionally, psychologically, or physically dangerous. Kids thought to be gay are frequently bullied (especially boys) and are often the subject of social ridicule. Sexually questioning kids should strongly consider seeking social support from affirming individuals such as parents (if they are affirming), peers, and Internet information sites and support groups (especially as this format allows individuals to remain anonymous). Bryan could really benefit from talking to others who are also questioning their sexual identities as well as those who can support him through his exploration and this difficult time in his life. Those who support him should not push him to "choose" a particular sexual orientation, nor should they judge him.

They should just allow Bryan time to discover his sexual identity in his own time. Counseling would also be an excellent option for Bryan.

 ### Scenario 4

Lesley is 68 years old. Her husband, David, of 44 years died 4 years ago and she has recently started dating again. Lesley thought that her sex life and even her sexual feelings died with her husband and was surprised to find that this was not the case. In some ways she is struggling with guilty feelings because she wants to have sex with another person, who is not her husband. She finds herself attracted to one man in particular, Stephen, and believes that she would like to have sex with him.

Lesley met Stephan on a tour group trip to Alaska. She had always wanted to take a cruise to Alaska but her husband was not interested. He developed cancer shortly after he retired, so instead of engaging in their extensive travel plans, they spent much of their time in chemotherapy and radiation treatments for his advanced-stage cancer. Lesley and her husband struggled with his disease for 5 long years. They had a strong relationship and David repeatedly told her when it became clear that his illness was terminal that after his death he wanted her to date again and live her life to the fullest. Lesley felt very glad to have been able to have conversations with David about what her future might look like when he was gone because she knew that she would not have the courage to date again after being married so long without his support.

Though Lesley had several dates with nice men, none of them progressed into a relationship. Stephan, 72, traveled with the same tour group she did. He and his brother were on the trip together while Lesley was by herself. She and Stephan hit it off right away and they ended up spending quite a bit of time together on the trip. They found out that they only live about 4 hours from each other and agreed to start dating when they returned from the trip.

In keeping his promise to Lesley, Stephan contacted Lesley after they returned and they began dating seriously. Much of their relationship has been through Skype and over the phone. They talk several times a week. Stephan has been divorced for 15 years. They have seen each other two times since returning from Alaska 4 months ago. Although they have stayed in each other's houses, they have not yet had sex. Stephan and Lesley have talked about their attraction to one another and their mutual surprise at the depth of their feelings given their ages.

She has not had sex with anyone since her husband's death and does not know how to proceed. She feels both anxious and excited about the possibilities of having a sexual relationship with Stephan. In Lesley's marriage, David had always been the one to initiate sex. Stephan has not initiated sex with Lesley, though the two have shared many sexual jokes and innuendos, so she is sure that he is sexually attracted to her. She wants to have sex with Stephan but she is not sure how to talk to him about it. She is both excited and a bit embarrassed that she has all of these sexual feelings that she has not had in years.

ANALYSIS

Lesley is just beginning her dating life after being in a marriage for 44 years. Lesley probably never saw herself as ever having to date again after she got married. Many widows and widowers find themselves in these situations if their spouse dies and they are still interested in developing romantic relationships with others. Lesley's case is representative of several issues. For example, developmentally, our sexuality is with us from birth to death. Sexual desires and feelings do not abandon us simply because we are not partnered. They are a part of who we are as individuals. After being married for 44 years, Lesley may find it difficult to initiate sexual relationships within dating encounters. Society tends to be uncomfortable accepting that most older adults continue to have sexual feelings and a healthy desire to be sexual. This is especially the case with older women's sexuality. Lesley may struggle with the feeling that she should not have sex without being in a committed relationship, especially if this is within her value system. Sometimes, widows and widowers feel that they are betraying their deceased spouses when they want to or actually have sex with other people. Though this is a normal feeling and part of the grief process, a significant part of accepting that their deceased partners are gone is by moving on with life. That may mean considering having romantic relationships with others. Lesley has expressed a healthy desire to have sex with a man she is dating. Prior to having sex, she should tell him that he would be her first sexual partner since her husband's death. She should also talk about her feelings (happiness, guilt, shame, sadness, excitement, etc.) about engaging in sex with Stephan prior to having sex as well as her expectations for their relationship. Lesley may find it difficult to have these conversations because presumably she did not have to have them with her husband as their relationship expectations were clarified through their marriage, but she should have them now. Finally, Lesley should remember to use condoms and discuss their mutual STI history. Research demonstrates that older adults are less likely to have these conversations than younger adults because they assume that they are at a lesser risk for contracting STIs. This is simply not true. Anyone who engages in unprotected sexual intercourse exposes him or her to an STI risk. Lesley should know that her feelings of excitement and anxiety are both natural and normal.

She could benefit from talking to supportive friends and/or a counselor to help her sort out this exciting new aspect of her life. Lesley is able to identify her feelings and desire to have sex with her partner, which is representative of a healthy attitude and an honesty in acknowledging her feelings. Both of these are beneficial in dealing with the changing relationship dynamics that naturally occur as a result of having sex.

 ### Scenario 5

Kevin and Asha have been dating for 6 months and admit to liking each other a great deal. They are both 20. Kevin is Caucasian (of German American ancestry) and Asha is a first generation Chinese American. The two met in a student organization related to their psychology major. Asha finds Kevin to be sensitive, caring, funny, smart, and handsome. Kevin believes that Asha is special, smart, and beautiful and together they share a quirky sense of humor. Both like science fiction movies and Kevin is especially delighted by this, as two other past girlfriends did not share his love of science fiction.

Asha is bilingual. When she goes home, she and her family speak Cantonese. She regularly takes trips to her grandparent's home in Hong Kong. Her family has met Kevin and they like him but they have expressed concerns that her relationship with Kevin not distract her from her schoolwork. Asha wants to go to graduate school to become a psychologist. Kevin is also interested in becoming a psychologist but says that he wants to take several years off after his undergraduate education to travel. Asha hopes to get into a doctoral program immediately after college.

Kevin and Asha are physically affectionate with one another. They hold hands and kiss often. They spend a significant amount of time with one another but there is one issue that continues to be highly conflictual in their relationship.

Kevin wants to have sex with Asha since they have established that they are in a committed, loving, monogamous relationship with one another. Kevin has had prior sexual relationships and does not understand why Asha is so "hung up" on remaining a virgin. He tries to accept what she has told him about that behavior being unacceptable both in her culture and in her family but he struggles with his feelings of physical attraction to her and feels very rejected because Asha has told him that she cannot have sex with him. He understands that she is not personally rejecting him, but feels rejected nonetheless. Asha states that having sex before marriage would be disrespectful to her family and would bring them shame. She likes Kevin and does not want to disappoint him but she is uncomfortable even thinking about losing her virginity outside of the marital relationship.

Asha feels very torn. She is attracted to Kevin but feels pressure from him to have sex, even when he doesn't say anything about it specifically, because she knows that he wants them to have sex and also knows that he has had sex within his past relationships. Asha is clear that if they have sex, she will feel very negative about herself and feel like she will bring shame upon her family. She feels frustrated that Kevin cannot really understand her perspective and has begun thinking about breaking up with him if they cannot resolve this issue. Both Kevin and Asha are starting to feel hopeless about the situation though they very much care about one another.

ANALYSIS

Kevin and Asha come from different cultural backgrounds. As discussed in Chapters 1 and 6, our cultural backgrounds influence us in myriad ways. This couple is smart to have discussed some of their cultural differences, because these things always impact who we are, our expectations in a relationship, as well as our value systems and behavior. It is clear that this couple care about one another but they have different cultural understandings of what sex means in a relationship and the consequences of having sex. Kevin takes the viewpoint that sex is a way of expressing the love and commitment he and Asha share with one another. His German American ancestry may lend itself to an individualistic value system, which is common in many Euro-American individuals and within a Euro-American cultural framework. An individualistic value orientation presents the individual as the primary decision maker in his or her own life. Asha is a first generation, Chinese American. This means that her parents came over to the United States from China and she is the first generation to be born or raised in America. First generation children often struggle to live within two very different value orientations—those of their current country and those of their parents' country. The more different these two value systems, the more difficult their struggle might be. We might assume that Asha comes from a collectivistic orientation, where her family's needs are considered more important than her own individual needs. In an individualistic orientation, the individual's needs are considered more important than those of one's family or group. Asha perceives having sex outside of marriage as bringing shame upon her family while Kevin sees it as affirming their relationship. This is a clear example of how individualistic and collectivistic value orientations differ. Kevin views himself as the sole decision maker for his behavior, while Asha feels that she must take her family's views, feelings, and the consequences of her behavior on her family into her decisions. There is no right or wrong orientation—they just represent different value systems. Additionally, there is no easy answer for this couple. They should try to find a compromise so that both of their value systems are respected. If Asha goes against her value orientation, she may feel shame for herself and feel that she disrespected her family. This has the potential to damage her relationship with Kevin and bring about negative feelings for herself. She is clear about this. Therefore, she should not go against her own sense of morality. Kevin should respect their cultural differences and understand how culture shapes both of them. On the other hand, Asha should hear and understand Kevin's point of view. He views having sex as solidifying their mutual emotional commitment to one another. He clearly cares about her and sees sex as expressing this caring. The couple should talk about ways of compromising. For example, Asha should consider if she is open to different types of sexual touching that does not include full intercourse. Is oral sex optional for the couple? Mutual masturbation? Massage and other types of nonsexual touching? If the couple can find a way to meet in the middle and Asha is open to some sexual touching (not intercourse), they may be able to find a workable compromise. If neither is willing to compromise (e.g., Kevin must have full sexual intercourse and Asha will not engage in any forms of sexual touching) their relationship may not be able to survive their value differences. Kevin and Asha should remain respectful of each other's respective value systems without pressuring the other person to adopt his or her point of view. This is damaging for several reasons. One, when we go against our own value system we frequently feel shame and blame ourselves. This does not bode well for a healthy sexual and emotional relationship with our partners. Two, pressuring one's partners does not allow the other person to feel emotionally safe. It also does not allow a couple to work together to develop a mutually agreeable compromise, which is a critical relationship skill in most romantic relationships.

Part III

Controversies and Debates

In this section, readers are asked to observe a debate on a controversial topic in human sexuality. Scholars were invited to take different sides of an issue and support their points from their understanding and expertise in human sexuality. Remember as you read the scholars' points of view that they sometimes agree with one another on certain points while disagreeing on others. It is important to explore these issues in depth by looking at multiple points of view. This might help readers make informed decisions about their own points of view on these topics. The first debate explores when parents should consider talking to their children about sex. The second debate examines abstinence-only education versus abstinence-plus education. The final debate reviews homosexuality from biological and environmental standpoints.

 Controversy 1. When Should Children Learn about Sex, and What Should Be Said?

INTRODUCTION

Parents often struggle with what they should tell their children about sex. They may have questions such as, "When should I start talking to my children about sex?" "What is a developmentally appropriate way (i.e., considering the age and stage of the child) to talk to my child?" "How do I answer my child's questions in ways that are in line with my values?" Parents may also struggle with the fact that they may themselves feel uninformed about sex, sexual issues, and sexuality. Experiences of embarrassment and shame are common when it comes to learning and talking about sex. For example, our parents may have never really talked to us about sex, may have discouraged our questions, or may have even reacted awkwardly when discussions about sex came up. Unfortunately, when parents do not critically evaluate their own values about sex, they may inadvertently pass on their discomfort about sexual issues to their children. In surveys of students across human sexuality courses, it is typically found that the large majority of them did not grow up having multiple conversations with their children about sex and sexuality. Most students reported feeling very uncomfortable discussing sexual topics with their parents. Given that most adults have a long history of being sexually active with more than one partner (approximately 90 percent) it should be surprising that so many adults find it such a difficult topic to talk about with their children. This is why it is of critical importance that parents consider a wide range of things prior to having conversations about sex with their children. For example, parents should think about what their own sexual values are and how they wish to communicate this to their children. Parents should also modify their discussions to their children's developmental level, interpersonal readiness, and personality. Instead of parents viewing conversations about sexual issues with their children as a bonding experience, many see it as an anxiety-provoking, embarrassing experience. Clear, honest, and appropriate communication between parents and children is key here and parents often model how this communication, especially regarding sexual issues, will occur. In Chapter 5, we reviewed sex throughout the life cycle. Research exploring what to tell children about sex and when was discussed in earlier chapters of this book. In sum, this research stated that most young children often turn to their parents first, for sexual information. However, by the time children become adolescents, fewer than 10 percent of them are still turning to their parents for sexual information. What has happened? Why do most teens look elsewhere? Some of the reasons teens no longer talk to their parents about sex include the large amount of information on the Internet, teens' internalization of the feelings of shame and embarrassment about sex, and/or the parent directly or indirectly communicating to the teen that discussions about sex and sexual behavior are not welcome or a source of embarrassment for the parent and teen. Those teens who do talk to their parents about sexual issues feel that their parents will hear them and show an attitude of openness and respect for the teen's thoughts and feelings even if the parent does not agree with them. Research does not support the notion that parents' talking to their children about sex encourages them to have sex at earlier ages.

There are a significant number of developmentally appropriate books that can help parents adjust their language and sexual concepts to their child's level. The literature suggests that discussions about sex should occur early and often so that they are not sprung on children in pre-adolescence. For example, a 2-year-old may be able to name all of her body parts (i.e., nose, ear, elbow, vagina, shoulder), at 3–4 she may learn about body privacy, and she may also ask questions about pregnancy. These are good opportunities for parents to have age-appropriate discussions with their children because, typically, their questions do not go away. Unfortunately, when parents discourage the questions or don't answer them, children just stop asking their parents questions. Teaching children about sex is a controversial topic for many reasons. Some scholars believe that children should not be exposed to discussions about sex until early adolescence while others believe that children should learn about sex from a very young age (i.e., toddlers). Below two scholars will explore if, when, and how we should talk to our children about sex. As you will see, they have complementary points of view regarding the timing of talking to children as well as what their parents should tell them but differ in several ways. Which scholar do you agree with? Why? If you have children, when do you think you will talk to them about sex? What will you say to them?

RESPONSE 1: TALKING TO CHILDREN ABOUT SEX

In the United States, sex is commonly depicted in the media; however, openly talking about sex is rare. For those of us who have had some sex education, it most likely a single conversation in junior high. Too common are vague memories of being segregated from the other sex while a teacher speaks awkwardly about sexually transmitted infections and the dangers of unprotected sex. People describe these conversations as confusing and embarrassing. Avoiding open discussions about sexuality reinforces that sex is bad, mysterious, or secretive. In the absence of information, children attempt to satisfy their curiosity through behavioral experimentation. In adopting a proactive stance on sexual education through open and frequent communication, we decrease misinformation and empower children to make healthy decisions.

One of the first dilemmas is deciding when to speak to children about sex. We know that children are aware of their gender by age 2 and are naturally curious about the biological differences between the sexes. It is recommended that parents begin sex education at this stage by talking about the proper names for body parts. Conversations about differences in biology can be easily incorporated during toilet training. This provides children with foundational knowledge of both sexes and fosters the development of a positive self-image. Children should learn to respect their body and the bodies of others and learn proper physical boundaries. Children naturally explore their own bodies by touching their genitals. Mistakenly, parents assume this exploration is sexual in nature. This can be harmful as parents tend to overreact, creating a sense of secrecy regarding sex and causing shame. Instead, parents can use this as a platform for discussing appropriate touch. Parents can inform their children that there is a time and place for touching themselves, such as during bath time. The topic of sexual abuse should also be addressed at this stage. Knowing that their body belongs to themselves and they have a right to say "no" can foster assertiveness and empowerment. Adults should always provide information that is developmentally appropriate and satisfies their children's curiosity but does not overwhelm them. Children at this age are very concrete; therefore, utilizing visual aids such as books containing simple diagrams of genitalia can prove helpful.

Discussions about sex should continue throughout childhood as curiosity expands to include more topics. During kindergarten and early elementary school, it is common for children to have questions about pregnancy. To assist children in understanding pregnancy, parents may wish to utilize analogies. For instance, explaining that a Fallopian tube is similar in size and shape to a strand of cooked spaghetti can provide children with visuals to facilitate communication. Books that contain information on pregnancy and provide simple diagrams of the internal reproductive organs can assist adults in structuring the discussion and controlling how much information is given. When using a book, adults should always read the book first to make sure it is developmentally appropriate and aligns with their family's values regarding sex.

As children are entering puberty at earlier ages, it is important to discuss emerging sexuality and the physical changes for both genders in early elementary school. Discussing only one gender creates confusion later in life, when they become sexually active. Providing information on both genders demystifies and fosters respect for the opposite gender and teaches healthy communication patterns for use in future relationships. The topic of menstruation should be explained prior to menarche in order to normalize and prepare children for this change. A conversation about erections and nocturnal emissions is recommended as this is often a source of embarrassment. Informing children on breast development and penis size provides realistic expectations and creates self-acceptance and respect for peers. Encouraging children to explore their own sexuality through masturbation and providing some guidelines for privacy normalizes sexual development. Masturbation in girls presents additional challenges, as the genitals are not easily observed. Parents can provide some helpful guidelines by recommending that girls use a mirror to locate the various parts of the vagina. In the absence of this information, children rely on peers, who may provide inaccurate information, cause anxiety, or provide pressure to become sexually active. In having open discussions about these changes, adults can assist children in coping by easing shame or embarrassment and advocating for themselves when faced with these challenges. Studies have demonstrated that people who are more educated on sexuality tend to report higher rates of self-acceptance and more satisfying relationships. In taking a proactive role in educating children, we empower them.

Lisa Brown

RESPONSE 2: THE DEVELOPMENTAL COURSE OF SEXUALITY

There are issues regarding development. One such issue is whether nature (i.e., your genes) or nurture (i.e., the environment in which you grow up) affects development. The answer is, It is *always both*. For example, if height were only determined by the genes you receive from your biological mother and father, it would not matter what you were fed growing up. However, we know nutrition impacts height; therefore, both nature and nurture contribute to your height. Nevertheless, nature and nurture do not always impact development equally; for certain aspects of development, nature may play more of a role and for other aspects nurture.

Since we cannot ethically manipulate certain variables or factors in humans (i.e., take out parts of a healthy brain in a living human or have children grow up in an impoverished environment on purpose) we can only conclude that certain things are related to one another, but not whether a change in one factor *causes* a change in another factor. Therefore, we cannot know for sure exactly how much of one's sexuality is due to nature or nurture.

What we do know is, in this day and age, we are bombarded with images of sex and sexuality. With 24/7 television programming, the Internet, and other forms of mass media, it is difficult to avoid it. Often, children and adolescents are exposed to sexual language, images, and behaviors before they are developmentally prepared to handle them. Therefore, it is important to learn the developmental course of children and adolescents in relation to sex and sexuality.

By age 3, children should learn about their own body. It is important that children learn the *proper names* for their body parts. Making up names for them can give children the impression there is something bad about the actual name. Children at this age should also be taught which body parts are private.

Around age 4 or 5 children may begin to show an interest in basic sexuality, both their own and the opposite sex. For example, they may ask where babies come from or may want to know why certain boys' and girls' body parts differ. Children at this age may touch their own genitals and may even show an interest in the genitals of other children. These are not adult sexual activities, but signs of typical interest. However, they need to learn what is appropriate and what is not. Keep in mind that interest in genital organs is healthy and natural. However, children should be taught no other person (including even close friends and relatives) may touch their private parts (with the exception of doctors/nurses during physical exams and their own parents when they are trying to find the cause of any pain in the genital area) (American Academy of Pediatrics, 2013).

Six- to seven-year-olds may become interested in what takes place sexually between adults. Questions tend to become more complex as their brains mature and they try to understand the connection between sexuality and making babies. They may even come up with their own explanations about how certain body parts work or where babies come from (i.e., babies come from hospitals). It is important for children at this age to understand sex and sexuality in a healthy way; what they learn at this age will stay with them well into adulthood and contribute to meaningful adult relationships.

At around 8 or 9, children are able to understand that sex is something that happens between two people who love each other. They may become interested in how their parents met and fell in love and ask questions about romance, marriage, or homosexual relationships. It is important to explain that liking or loving someone does not depend on the person's gender and is different from liking someone sexually (American Academy of Pediatrics, 2013).

Pre-teens and teenagers may have questions about heterosexuality, homosexuality, and bisexuality. Many teens go through a time when they wonder, "Am I gay?" It often happens when a teen is attracted to a same-sex friend or has a crush on a same-sex teacher. This is common and doesn't necessarily mean you are gay, lesbian, or bisexual. Teens should know that sexual identity may not be completely formed until adulthood.

Remember, nature always affects nurture and nurture always affects nature. No one knows what *causes* a person's sexual orientation. There probably are a number of factors. Some may be biological (i.e., nature); others may not. Until we find a non-invasive way to study the brain and physiology of living humans, we will not know for certain how much of our sexuality is determined by nature or nurture.

Valerie Hill

 ## Controversy 2. Sex Education in the United States: Should We Revamp the Model?

INTRODUCTION

Sex education in the United States remains a hotly debated and controversial topic. Currently, there are two prominent models of sex education: abstinence-only and comprehensive-sex education (also known as abstinence plus). Comprehensive-sex education promoted abstinence as the safest and most preferred type of sexual behavior, citing never having to worry about STIs, pregnancy, and any other negative consequence of sex. Abstinence-only sex education emphasizes ways to avoid having sex until marriage and does not provide much information about safer-sex practices (i.e., condom use) or contraception. Both types of sexual education may discuss sexual health issues (i.e., STIs, abortion, pregnancy); however, promoters of each approach may teach these things differently. For example, it is not uncommon for abstinence-only educators to emphasize the negative consequences of sex to students whereas comprehensive-sex educators may include some of the positive consequences of sex. Until 2010, the U.S. federal government only funded abstinence-only sexual education. Schools that chose to teach something different were often not recipients of federal funding. As you can see, even the federal government remains divided on this issue. Research has shown that comprehensive-sex education programs do not increase students' sexual behavior, which is the common worry of abstinence-only educators. If you remember, Chapter 1 reviewed these issues. A startling finding was that adult sexual behavior in the United States has not significantly changed over the last 65 years. Ninety-five percent of all adults have had premarital sex regardless of their receiving abstinence-only or abstinence-plus sexual education. Thus, it might be argued that the more information teens have, the more informed they can be about their decisions regarding sexual behavior and their sexual health. However, most parents and adults understandably want to protect their children from the negative conse-quences of sex (e.g., unwanted pregnancy, STIs, hurt emotions), which can be devastating, especially at a young age, and the only way to ensure this protection is to abstain from sexual intercourse. Abstinence-only approaches have been criticized for not including a discourse on sexual desire and the emotional connectedness that can occur within a sexual relationship. Many believe that abstinence-only approaches overempha-size the negative consequences of sex without giving equal weight to the positive. Comprehensive-sex education approaches have been criticized for overemphasizing the positive aspects of sex and minimizing the negative aspects. Proponents of abstinence-only education often believed that comprehensive-sex education encouraged adolescents to have sex and did not educate them of the many consequences that come with being sexually active. As you can see, this is an interesting issue and a tough debate and there are no easy answers. Two scholars discuss their opinions regarding these two very different types of sexual education. They will share with you their thoughts about why we should educate our children using these two models. After reading their thoughts, perhaps you will be able to make a more informed decision regarding which approach you will support when it comes to educating children about sex, sexuality, and sexual health issues.

RESPONSE 1: EMPOWERMENT VERSUS ISOLATION: WHY ABSTINENCE-ONLY EDUCATION DOESN'T WORK

There is one form of birth control that is always 100 percent effective, and that is abstinence. It successfully prevents the spread of STIs as well as unintended pregnancy. It is cost effective, widely taught, and well funded in the United States. It sounds like a perfect solution—but, there is just one problem.

It does not work without sex education.

Many studies performed by state health departments show that absti-nence, when taught without a comprehensive and diverse sexual educa-tion, consistently fails to result in less premarital sex or intimacy. Even the best birth control in the world is rendered inert if, between user error and choice, it goes unused. People use contraceptives successfully when two criteria are met: they are educated about its use, and the method is made available. The problem with abstinence-only education is that it is only one variable in a much more complex equation. This is the hidden cost in denying individuals a thorough and unbiased sex education—

abstinence rates actually *increase* when we conceal scientific and proven information from individuals so they can make informed decisions.

A lack of comprehensive classes that openly discuss correct anatomical terminology, birth control methods and efficacy, and sexual activity is associated with a drop in abstinence rates. Many will argue this is paradoxical. However, when we accept that sex education is not just about sex, the reasons that this happens become quite clear.

Even I did not always feel this way. One of my mentors, whom I have always held in high esteem, taught my human sexuality course. She said something that lodged in my brain—that I never forgot. I remember it because I always hear her words when working with youth of varied ages and from diverse backgrounds.

Children remember when you lie, omit things, or avoid explaining them. Children grow into adolescents, and both are driven by a potent sense of curiosity and self-discovery. Ordering them to abstain from sexual activity rejects both these ideals—rejects the idea that one day they, too, shall be autonomous adults. A precarious conundrum then occurs, where these individuals begin to explore on their own, and do so without a lack of guidance. They embrace urban legends regarding contraceptives as they experiment: that bathing or washing prevents pregnancy, that you cannot get pregnant when you have sex the first time, that women do not get pregnant on their period, that oral or anal sex is not sexual activity—and these are just a few quasi-truths that are disseminated as fact. Consider how false information in this case can permanently change a young person's life, or even end it. When we choose to deny individuals correct and factual information, especially where their own bodies are concerned, we engage in potentially fatal negligence of the most severe degree.

Children who are uninformed with a substandard education often grow up and become disenfranchised adults who make mistakes in ignorance that have lifelong consequences. If they are lucky then they make it into therapy, where we see more than a lack of sex education. Intimacy issues occur. In many cases, they cannot discuss sex with their partners even when they do enter a committed relationship or with their doctors when something is awry. When frank discussions are avoided, people not only become embarrassed about sexuality but also can feel shameful about their bodies. By not discussing these issues, by denying them the right to know about themselves, we teach shame instead of pride.

Teaching sex education is not just about lecturing children on what to call a penis and a vagina. It does not only tell them how to prevent pregnancy, or avoid STIs. What we are really doing is teaching *trust*: how to trust us as educators, how to trust each other, and how to trust themselves. It is this empowerment that allows children and adolescents to choose abstinence as a viable option, because it teaches them to understand *why* it is so vital to use it. It teaches them that they are worth something, that sex between consenting individuals should be respected and cherished. It teaches them that it is healthy to have feelings, and also healthy to choose what to do with them.

Abstinence-only curricula deny individuals basic information about their nature. It removes their autonomy. It isolates them, and in this pernicious solitude mistakes are made where misunderstanding runs rampant. If we want people to use abstinence as the powerful tool that it is, it is unethical to withhold this knowledge from them.

Education empowers—ignorance isolates and destroys.

Donna Lordi

RESPONSE 2: ABSTINENCE-ONLY EDUCATION

There is great controversy between abstinence-only programs and abstinence-plus sex education. Although there are factors that deem abstinence-only programs ineffective, there are benefits that cannot be denied when the principles of the program are applied. This essay highlights the basic tenants of abstinence-only programs that have been taught in schools across the country and enforced by the U.S. government and address some of the benefits of abstinence-only programs to adolescents. The purpose of abstinence-only programs is to enhance youth from a holistic perspective through sex education. These teachings are designed to prevent negative effects that can occur due to early sexual involvement, affecting individuals' future marriages and relationships, psychological/ emotional well-being, and social and physical health.

The juxtaposed elements of abstinence-only programs and abstinence-plus sex education have been the center of controversy. Abstinence-only programs emphasize no sexual involvement with anyone until marriage, and the abstinence-plus sex education promotes no sexual involvement with anyone except the person you love and share meaning with. The ultimate goal enforced in abstinence-only education is marriage. According to Advocates for Youth (n.d.), youths are taught to abstain from sexual activity and sexual contact until marriage. They teach the following:

- That the expected standard for teenagers and school-age children is wait until after marriage before having sex;

- That a faithful monogamous relationship within marriage is the expected standard of sexual activity;
- That sexual activity before marriage is expected to have harmful physical and psychological effects.

Although very different than what is taught in many agencies and communities, sexual activity does have some effect on our development. Many believe that the way to manage and even control these factors is by promoting no sexual activity or abstinence. The concept of abstinence only goes against mainstream beliefs regarding sexual activity norms. However, individuals from conservative and highly structured backgrounds embrace abstinence-only programs because they very easily fit into their beliefs and practices. Even though abstinence-only programs have been found to not be as effective as other programs, several benefits have been discovered in using their programs. Benefits have been found in psychological, social, and physical areas.

A review of these benefits is warranted when examining abstinence-only programs. Psychologically, abstinence-only education assists in preventing lasting effects of emotional and psychological damage due to premature sexual activity. Adolescents from abstinence-only programs attain higher academic achievement than sexually active teenagers. They also learn how to reject sexual advances and become more self-assertive, understand how alcohol and drug use increases vulnerability to sexual advances, and recognize the importance of attaining self-sufficiency before engaging in sexual activity. Socially, abstinence-only programs enforce the importance of long-lasting and meaningful relationships, teach adolescents to deal with peer pressure, and promote enhanced communication, critical thinking and decision making, which is a necessity for building relationships. Physically, abstinence-only programs teach that abstaining from sexual activity is the only 100 percent effective method in preventing unwanted pregnancies, sexually transmitted infections, sexually transmitted diseases, and health-related issues. It also teaches that bearing children out of wedlock might have harmful consequences for the child, the child's parents, and society. These benefits demonstrate that some areas of abstinence-only programs have been effective and provided adolescents with lifelong qualities that could positively impact other areas of their lives.

Although abstinence-only programs have not produced the outcomes that the U.S. government and other providers have required of them, the programs have demonstrated some benefits to those adolescents who have participated. Some of the tenets and principles of abstinence-only programs continue to spur controversy and resentment, and so to curb some of the negative messages about abstinence-only programs, reviewing some of their benefits could be helpful. To see and recognize that although not perfect, identifying and building on benefits from abstinence-only

programs could lead others to develop more effective and successful programs that could produce more positive outcomes and aid adolescents in making better life affirming decisions. Possibly, abstinence-plus programs could take many of the benefits from abstinence-only programs and integrate them into new sexual education programing. Sometimes, learning from the past could be a benefit for the future.

La Kesia D. Weathersby-Graham

REFERENCE

Advocates for Youth. (n.d.) Abstinence-only-until-marriage programs: 8-point definition of abstinence only education. Retrieved from www.advocatesforyouth.org/topics-issues/abstinenceonly/132-8-point-definition-of-abstinence-only-education.

 Controversy 3. Homosexuality: Biology, Environment, or Both?

INTRODUCTION

In Chapter 1, we defined *sexual orientation* as our sexual, affectional, and emotional attachment to particular sexual partners. Sexual orientation includes biological and social components as well. For example, sexual orientation is a significant part of our individual identity. It informs who we are and strongly shapes our behavior every day. It shapes who we chose as romantic partners. There has long been a debate about the origins of sexual orientation. Many people want to know if sexual orientation is largely determined by biology or if it is mostly shaped by the environment. Though there are strong views and proponents on both sides, most research points to an interaction between biology and the environment. In Chapter 2, we explored historical and current views on homosexuality and in Chapter 6, we looked at homosexuality (its acceptance or opposition) around the world. Clearly, same-sex relationships have existed as long as people have walked the earth. This has historically been depicted in literature, art, and even ancient laws around the world. Freud helped shape the view in Westernized psychology that homosexuality was a mental disorder, which in some circles is still believed today. In 1973, homosexuality was removed from the *Diagnostic and Statistical Manual for Mental Disorders* and is no longer considered a mental illness. It was removed because there was no empirical evidence to suggest that homosexuality was indeed a mental disorder but also because social and cultural norms began changing and same-sex relationships were starting to become more acceptable in society. In 2011 the Obama administration declared DOMA unconstitutional. As stated earlier in the book, in June 2015, the Supreme Court approved marriage equality for all couples, regardless of gender. This is a significant shift in American society, given that 10 short years ago, same-sex marriage was not legal in the United States, though some states allowed gay couples to have civil unions. Within a decade, American attitudes have shifted, where a slight majority of individuals in society support same-sex marriage, though American society remains deeply divided on this issue. The DOMA (Defense of Marriage Act), which was passed in 1996 defining marriage as an exclusively heterosexual institution (i.e., between a man and woman), did not prevent individual states from allowing same-sex couples to wed but imposed constraints on benefits received by legally married same-sex couples. At the time of the Supreme Court ruling, the majority of states in the United States still did not allow same-sex couples to marry, nor did they recognize marriages of same-sex couples from other states; the Supreme Court's decision, however, overrules individual states' rights to make this decision for their citizens and mandates that all states recognize that marriage is legal between consenting adults. Clearly, American society continues to struggle with this issue.

Biological explanations of homosexuality are diverse and include trying to identify specific genes that influence sexual orientation, prental androgen theory (when the developing fetus is exposed to large amounts of opposite-sex hormones—that is, girls being exposed to large amounts of male hormones in vivo and boys exposed to large amounts of feminizing hormones in vivo may lead to a homo- or bisexual orientation), and the impact of birth order (i.e., some gay men have many older brothers, leading to the hypothesis that the mother's womb environment may change due to her immune system, which influences her youngest son's sexual orientation). Social/environmental explanations of same-sex sexual attraction include the following: social learning theory (that the behavior is modeled by others [i.e., one's peer group] and then supported/reinforced), it is more likely to occur in those who are sexually abused in childhood and those who have poor relationships with their opposite-sex parent. Not all of the above explanations—either biological or social—are supported or even accurate; however, these are the many hypotheses that exist for why there are same-sex and bisexual orientations. Ironically, bisexuality continues to be significantly under-researched and misunderstood. The following two scholars offer their thoughts about sexual orientation. They will weigh evidence that supports their point of view. Always remember to evaluate evidence critically, whether it supports your individual point of view or not. How we develop our sexual orientation is a complicated question that is not clearly answered by the current literature and research. The scholars below will provide some critical thinking points for you to evaluate for yourself.

RESPONSE 1: BIOLOGICAL THEORY

Homosexuality has been observed not only in humans, but in many other species. Scientists have established that homosexuality exists in many species from fruit flies to whales. What we do not know is which biological factors cause same-sex attraction.

One of the first biological explanations for homosexuality is the genetic theory, which claims that there must be a specific gene responsible for sexual orientation. In 1993, one study reported finding a *gay gene* located on the X chromosome. These findings were highly debated, as no other study could replicate the findings. It has been established that many human traits, such as handedness, are a result of multiple genes. Taking this into consideration, the current belief is that multiple genes may cause homosexuality, one of which may be located on the X chromosome.

Another way to establish a genetic link to sexual orientation is through concordance rates or the rates of homosexuality in families. Researchers have used twin studies to establish the role of genetics, as identical twins share 100 percent of their genes. It has been found that if one identical twin is gay, his twin brother is 52 percent more likely to be gay. In fraternal twins, who share 50 percent of their genes, 22 percent of brothers were also gay. This demonstrates that the closer the relation between relatives, the more likely they share the same sexual orientation. It has been found that gay men have more gay relatives, such as aunts and uncles. Considering all of the genetic research available, it is thought that 50–60 percent of sexual orientation is determined by genetics.

Hormones have been thought to play a role in sexual orientation. Previously, researchers believed that homosexuality was caused by an imbalance of circulating hormones in adults. Findings did not support this claim, as no difference in adult hormone levels between straight men and gay men has been discovered. In fact, exposing gay men to higher levels of testosterone reinforces same-sex attraction. There is some evidence to support the prenatal androgen theory, which states that fetuses exposed to high levels of androgens during critical periods of fetal development are more likely to exhibit same-sex attraction. Even the fetus's ability to produce hormones such as testosterone can be affected temporarily by the mother's level of stress during pregnancy. There is some evidence that exposure to synthetic estrogen in female fetuses increases the likelihood of same-sex attraction. The extent to which prenatal hormones influence sexual orientation has yet to be established.

Another prenatal factor under consideration is the maternal immune hypothesis, which states that the mother's immune system becomes sensitized to proteins in the Y chromosome, increasing the effects of anti-male antibodies. These anti-male antibodies effect the sexual differentiation of the fetus's brain, playing a role in male sexual orientation. Research has found that with each older brother a man has, the likelihood of him being gay increases by 33 percent. This theory is further demonstrated as it has been found that having older sisters decreases the likelihood that a man will be gay.

Physiology, particularly brain anatomy, has also been studied as a possible causation for sexual orientation. In the 1990s, researchers began studying the hypothalamus, as this structure plays a role in sex drive, hormone production, and sexual differentiation. It was established that the suprachiasmatic nucleus of the hypothalamus is significantly larger in gay men and has been found to have twice as many cells compared to that of straight men. The corpus callosum and the anterior commissure are larger in gay men (and straight women) than in straight men. These structures serve to connect the cerebral hemispheres of the brain. This provides some evidence that the brain structure of people who share an orientation, such as attraction to men, are similar. Conversely, the brain structures of people who share an attraction to women are similar. This difference in brain structure has been found to impact functionality of the brain, specifically, usage of both hemispheres as it is related to memory and spatial learning abilities. It has been demonstrated that gay men use both sides of their brain in a pattern similar to that found in straight women.

Physiological studies have considered many factors to explain the differences in sexual orientation, from hair whorls (cowlicks) to finger lengths. These studies are vast and not without challenges and criticisms. It seems more likely that all of these biological explanations interact

to cause sexual orientation. With so many other species exhibiting homosexuality, it is abundantly clear that the causation lies within biology.

Lisa Brown

RESPONSE 2: THE ENVIRONMENTAL BASIS OF SEXUAL ORIENTATION AND SEXUAL IDENTITY

There have been many questions about sexual orientation and sexual
identity today. One major question has been whether sexual orientation
is a biological or environmental phenomenon. Although both points of
view have had support, neither of them is without limitation. To this complex question, I am going to argue for the environmental basis of sexual
orientation and sexual identity.

It is easy to notice that the zeitgeist has moved toward a biological
theme; however, this notion might motivate us to ignore the environmental evidence supporting homosexuality. available so that It is important
that we become critical thinkers and are not get swept away by the trends
of the day. In examining information, one cannot ignore that a variety of
issues (i.e., developmental, family/sibling, psychosocial experiences, and
sexual options) impacts our impressions of LGBTQQIAAP (sexual minority groups) ideas about sexual orientation. In this essay, we will discuss two
theories and other psychosocial factors that support the environmental
basis of sexual orientation and sexual identity.

There are two primary theories that promote the environmental basis of
sexual orientation and identity: the Halperin and the Foucault theories.
The Halperin theory believes that homosexuality is an error of nature, as supported by Freudian theory. The error is found when the individual is unable
to resolve parent-child issues and sexual orientation and identity become evident. The writings of Freud provide evidence that sexual orientation is
strongly influenced by parents and family dynamics. These parent and family
dynamics include dominating, detached, and unavailable caregivers and the
presence or lack of male and female siblings. The psychoanalytic theory promotes the Oedipal and Electra complexes. These ideas state that a weak or
nonexistent father and a too strong and ever present mother promote the
strong probability of a homosexual son (the Oedipus complex). Conversely,
a too strong and ever present father and an emotionally unavailable and
weak mother (Electra complex) will produce a lesbian daughter. Each of
these individuals will overcompensate for their psychosexual issues.

The second theory that supports an environmental basis of sexual orientation is the Foucault theory. Foucault argues that homosexuality exists

because society made it acceptable. He believes that the category of homosexuality was created as another form of sexuality to support the sexual behaviors of sodomy and androgynous identity. This idea was initially seen in most cultures and societies as an unacceptable sexually behavior. But the introduction of the idea of homosexuality as an acceptable concept makes it permissible and created a new category of sexuality. With this new classification and a concept with more societal acceptance, the concept of homosexuality has been growing and thriving, as Foucault argued. Society's view of sexuality has changed over time.

Another factor that contributes to the environmental basis of sexual orientation and sexual identity is the psychosocial stage of adolescence. Developmentally, young people are asking themselves certain questions: Who am I? How do I fit in the world? These are very challenging and critical questions; however, because of our changing times, they are also developing and asking themselves about who they are attracted to and how to develop their sexual selves. These are significant curiosities for anyone, especially for a young person who is juggling so many issues at the same time. These sexual curiosities can translate into sexual decision making, which can have some negative consequences. Some research shows that homosexuality was positively related to living in an urban environment. When the environment supports the expression of homosexual behavior, and a place to meet others, the presence of homosexuality increases.

In this essay, I have discussed several ideas that support the environmental basis of sexual orientation and sexual identity. The goal of this essay was to promote discussion, provide information to discuss, and influence your ability to be critical in your thinking as you become aware of differing issues and questions. It is important to restate that this is a very complex issue. The understanding of sexual orientation and identity formation will continue to be important concepts as it evolves over time and a comprehensive examination of all factors is imperative to this end.

Byron Waller

REFERENCES

Foucault, M. (1979). *The history of sexuality, Volume 1: An introduction.* London: Allen Lane.

Halperin, D. M. (1990). One *hundred years of homosexuality. And other essays on Greek love.* New York: Routledge.

Directory of Resources

ACADEMIC JOURNALS

Journal of Adolescent Health—Publishes research findings specific to psychology, social work, youth development, medicine, mental health, and other disciplines committed to improving the lives of adolescents and young adults.

Journal of Policy Analysis and Management—A combination of two journals, *Policy Analysis* and *Public Policy*, providing information about child welfare, child policy education, employment and training, health, family policy, and science policy.

Journal of School Health—Communicates information regarding the role of schools, school personnel, or the school environment.

WEB SITES

aids.gov—This site provides information about HIV/AIDS, including news, seminars, prevention, and support.

cdc.gov—The Centers for Disease Control and Prevention provides pertinent scientific information critical to protecting and informing the public about dangerous infectious and noninfectious diseases.

garote.bdmonkeys.net/bsri.html—BEM Sex Role Inventory

gutenberg.org (e-books of Havelock Ellis's work)—Project Gutenberg is a volunteer effort to digitize and archive cultural work in a digital library.

http://www.guttmacher.org/pubs/FB-Teen-Sex-Ed.html—A Web page describing sex facts pertaining to teenagers, including abortion, sex education, and pregnancy.

http://www.webmd.com/parenting/features/abstinence-vs-sex-ed—A Web page discussing the difference between abstinence-only versus sex education approaches to educate children.

kinseyinstitute.org—The Kinsey Institute at Indiana University works toward advancing sexual health and knowledge worldwide by providing information about sex, gender, and reproduction.

myperiodblog.com—An open forum designed to encourage discussion about menstruation and cultural and social attitudes about periods.

plannedparenthood.org—Planned Parenthood provides vital reproductive health care, sex education, and information to millions of women, men, and young people worldwide.

sexetc.org—A site to educate teens and parents about birth control, HIV/AIDS, pregnancy, sexual abuse and violence, relationships, sex, and the LGBT community.

thegenderbook.com—A site compiled of resources, stories, and support pertaining to gender identity.

trojancondoms.com—The main Web site for Trojan condom products.

womenshealth.gov—A site hosted by the Office of Women's Health, part of the U.S. Department of Health and Human Services, which provides information reviewed by subject matter experts and tailored content to the specific needs of women, including pregnancy, menopause, aging, mental health, illnesses and disabilities, and more.

VIDEOS FROM SEXPLANATIONS CHANNEL ON YOUTUBE, AT HTTPS://WWW.YOUTUBE.COM/USER/SEXPLANATIONS/VIDEOS

HIV FAQ
HIV Test
What Is Herpes?
Protecting against Herpes
The Gender Map
Interthoughts Part 1and Part 2—An interview with Eden Atwood who shares her thoughts about what it means to be intersex
Female Anatomy—The Vulva

MORE VIDEOS

Babycenter.com—Pregnancy and development videos

Business of Being Born (https://www.youtube.com/watch?v=KvljyvU _ZGE)—An in-depth exploration of the modern maternity care system

Gender Roles: Interviews with children, https://www.youtube.com/ watch?v=-VqsbvG40Ww

Kotex Commercial, https://www.youtube.com/watch?v=lpypeLL1dAs

Masters of Sex—Clips on gathering research on monitoring sexual response cycle and interviews

No Dumb Questions—A documentary about the events surrounding a man's sex change operation

The Pill—A PBS documentary about birth control

Red Moon trailer on YouTube—Attitudes about menstruation

sexetc.com—Video on gender spectrum

Tampax Commercials, https://www.youtube.com/watch?v=3OeDttza9iU

Glossary

Abstinence: Avoidance of any type of sexual intercourse.

Acquaintance rape: Rape by a friend, acquaintance, or a date; also known as *date rape*.

Adrenarche: The maturation of the adrenal glands, usually between the ages of 6 and 8.

Afterbirth: The expulsion of the placenta from the uterus after a baby is born.

Amnion: A thick-skinned sac filled with water that surrounds the fetus.

Anal stage: The second stage of psychosexual development, in which the anus is the primary erogenous zone and pleasure is derived from controlling bladder and bowel movement.

Anxious-avoidant attachment: A form of parent-child bonding in which parents tend to be emotionally unavailable or unresponsive a great deal of time. As a result, children learn to suppress natural desires to seek out a parent for comfort when frightened, distress, or in pain.

Anxious-resistant attachment: A type of childhood insecure attachment style in which a parent typically will not tend to the child's needs, which generates great distress in the child even when the parent is present, the result being the child fails to develop feelings of security and exhibits clingy or dependent behavior, but will reject the attachment figure when engaged in interaction. Also called *ambivalent attachment*.

Artificial insemination: Introduction of semen into the uterus by non-coital means.

Attachment: Two meanings: (a) a drab, mundane form of companionship where one's partner gives few positive rewards, other than predictability, for remaining in the relationship; (b) the emotional tie between parent and child, or between two adults.

Attitudes: The manner in which a person evaluates someone or something, usually positively or negatively.

Bacteria: Small, single-celled organisms that lack a nuclear membrane, but have all the genetic material (RNA and DNA) to reproduce themselves.

Berdache: In North American Indian tribes of past centuries, a person, usually a man, who assumed the dress, occupations, and behavior of the other sex in order to effect a change in gender status.

Bisexual: An individual with a sexual orientation toward men and women.

Braxton-Hicks contractions: Uterine contractions experienced during the last trimester of pregnancy that are often incorrectly interpreted as the beginning of labor. Also called *false labor*.

Bridge maneuver: A variation of sexual intercourse in which the man lies on his back while the woman is on top of him and inserts his penis into her vagina. The female masturbates herself to orgasm while simultaneously using her vagina to stroke the man's penis.

Bypassing: When misunderstandings result from missed meanings.

Candida albicans: A fungus that is normally present on the skin and in mucous membranes such as the vagina, mouth, or rectum.

Capacitation: A process that sperm undergo while traveling through the woman's reproductive tract in which their membranes become thin enough so that an enzyme necessary for softening the ovum's membrane can be released.

Castration anxiety: The conscious or unconscious fear of losing all or part of the sex organ or their respective functions.

Catfish: An individual who uses false identities via social media to pursue deceptive online romances.

Catfishing: The act of fabricating an online identity to deceptively attract people into emotional and romantic relationships. Common motivators are revenge, loneliness, curiosity, boredom, or financial gain.

Cesarean section, C-section: A surgical method of childbirth in which delivery occurs through an incision in the abdominal wall and uterus.

Cognitive susceptibility: State of mind, identified by psychological and situational factors, that suggests a readiness for or predisposition toward initiating sexual activity.

Cohabitation: Living together and sharing sex without marrying.

Coming out: Acknowledging to oneself and others that one is lesbian, gay, or bisexual.

Companionate love: A type of emotion that combines feelings of deep attachment, commitment, and intimacy.

Compatibility theory: The premise that women specialize in activities that do not interfere with infant care and enable them to work a job that fits around the demands of child care.

Contact comfort: The physical and emotional comfort that an infant receives from being in physical contact with its primary caretaker.

Couvade, couvade syndrome: The experiencing of pregnancy symptoms by male partners; sometimes called *sympathy pains*.

Crowning: The appearance of the fetus's head at the vaginal opening during birth.

Culture: Shared patterns of behaviors and interactions, cognitive constructs, and affective understanding that are learned through the process of socialization that is distinct from other groups.

Dating scripts: An idealistic manner in which males and females are expected to interact with each other in romantic situations. For example, it is expected for the male to pay for dinner on the first date.

Diaphragm: A latex rubber cup, filled with spermicide, that is fitted to the cervix by a clinician; the woman must learn to insert it properly for full contraceptive effectiveness.

Dilation: The gradual widening of the cervical opening of the uterus prior to and during labor.

Disorganized attachment: An insecure attachment style in which the caretaker inflicts both fear and reassurance to a child. As a result, children become confused and apprehensive of parents.

Drag: A style of dress used to symbolically represent the clothing associated with one gender role, usually worn by the opposite sex.

Drag queen: A person, traditionally male, who dresses in drag and emulates exaggerated femininity and female gender roles.

Dualism: The belief that body and soul are separate and antagonistic.

Dyspareunia: Recurrent or persistent genital pain during intercourse, usually resulting from organic factors (e.g., vaginal, prostate, or bladder infections).

E. coli: Bacteria naturally living in the human colon that often cause urinary tract infection.

Ectopic pregnancy: The implantation of a blastocyst somewhere other than in the uterus, usually in the Fallopian tube.

Ego: A part of the psyche that mediates the primitive drives of the id with the demands of the social and physical environment.

Ejaculatory incompetence: A condition in which a male is unable to ejaculate in the vagina; sometimes referred to as *retarded ejaculation*.

Electra complex: Freud's theory that 3- to 5-year-old girls want to take their father away from their mother.

Endocrine system: A network of ductless glands that secrete their chemical substances, called *hormones*, directly into the bloodstream, where they are carried to other parts of the body to exert their effects.

Endometrium: The inner mucous membrane of the uterus where a fertilized egg implants. Its thickness varies with the phase of the menstrual cycle.

Erectile disorder: A sexual problem in which a man has persistent or recurrent difficulty getting and maintaining an erection.

Erikson's theory of psychosocial development: A stage theory that assumes a crisis occurs at each stage of development that is psychosocial in nature. These crises involve psychological needs conflicting with the need of society.

Essure: A nonsurgical (transcervical) female sterilization technique in which the Fallopian tubes are blocked by micro-inserts.

Ethnicity: The degree of identification an individual feels with a particular ethnic group.

Excitement phase: The second stage of Kaplan's model of sexual response, which consists of physiological arousal and changes and, possibly, orgasm.

Familiarity: To have a reasonable knowledge or acquaintance with a subject, object, or place.

Female orgasmic disorder: A persistent or recurrent delay in, or absence of, orgasm following a normal sexual excitement phase and which causes personal distress.

Female sexual arousal disorder: Difficulty for a woman in achieving sexual arousal.

Fidelity: Sexual loyalty and faithfulness to a spouse or partner.

Fixation: A Freudian concept that describes a state in which an individual becomes obsessed with an attachment to another person, being, or object. Theoretically, this occurs when an individual develops a lack of proper gratification during one of the psychosexual stages of development.

Flirting: A social activity in which a person implies sexual or deep interest in another person through use of verbal and written communication or body language.

Foreplay: Sexual activities shared in early stages of sexual arousal, leading to a more intense, orgasm-oriented form of activity such as intercourse.

Frame of reference: A complex set of assumptions and attitudes people use to filter perceptions to create meaning.

Gender: The social construction of femininity and masculinity.

Gender constancy: The knowledge that one's sex is constant and will not change. This knowledge is usually acquired by age 6 or 7.

Gender dysphoria: The feeling of being trapped in a body of the opposite sex.

Gender identity: One's subjective sense of being a man (or boy) or a woman (or girl). This sense is usually acquired by the age of 3.

Gender identity disorder: A disorder with the following criteria: (a) behaviors that indicate identification with the opposite gender and (b) behaviors that indicate discomfort with one's own anatomy and gender roles.

Gender role: Complex groups of ways males and females are expected to behave in a given culture.

Gender role socialization: Guiding a child or individual into socially acceptable behaviors depending upon one's gender through the use of rewards, punishment, and education.

Gender role stereotyping: Expectation that individuals will behave in certain ways because they are male or female.

Gender schema: A grouping of mental representations about male and female physical qualities, behaviors, and personality traits.

Gender schema theory: A theory that describes how individuals become gendered in society through social learning and cognitive learning. This theory also illustrates how gender roles are transmitted and maintained.

Genital stage: The final stage of psychosexual development, which begins in puberty. During this stage, the teenager seeks out sexual gratification through sexual contact with others.

Gonadarche: The maturation of the ovaries and testicles.

Gynecomastia: Excessive development of the male breasts.

Heterosexual: Refers to attractions or activities between males and females.

Heterosexual privilege: Benefits automatically granted by society to individuals who are perceived as being heterosexual. The same benefits are denied to non-heterosexual individuals.

Homogamy: Marriage between individuals who share similarities on the basis of socioeconomic status, class, gender, ethnicity, or religion.

Homosexual: An individual with a sexual orientation primarily toward members of the same sex.

Hooking up: Sexual relations with a nonromantic partner (usually a friend).

Hormone replacement therapy: Treatment of the physical changes of menopause by administering dosages of the hormones estrogen and progesterone.

Hormones: Chemical substances that are secreted by ductless glands into the bloodstream. They are carried in the blood to other parts of the body, where they exert their effects on other glands or target organs.

Hot flashes: A warm feeling over the upper body experienced by menopausal women as a result of increased levels of the follicle-stimulating hormone and the luteinizing hormone.

Human sexuality: A part of your total personality. It involves the interrelationship of biological, psychological, and sociocultural dimensions.

Hypoactive sexual desire: A sexual problem characterized by a persistent and pervasive absence of sexual fantasies and desire.

Hypothalamus: A part of the brain that regulates the release of hormones from the pituitary gland.

Hysteria: Exaggerated or uncontrollable emotion or excitement among a group of people.

Id: The pleasure principle of the human psyche. It responds impulsively to instincts to fulfill primitive drives such as sex and aggression.

Incest: Sexual behavior between relatives who are too closely related to be married.

Incompetent suitors: A type of stalker who targets strangers or acquaintances. These types of stalkers are indifferent to the distress exhibited by their victims, which suggests that they have cognitive limitations and poor social skills.

Indeterminent gender: Sometimes referred to as *third gender*. A term used to describe an individual who shares both male and female sex characteristics and does not identify as either male or female.

Infanticide: The act of killing a child within a year of birth. This term typically describes a person who kills his or her own child.

Infertility: The inability to produce offspring.

Interpersonal attraction: The desire to approach someone, which is the fundamental basis of attraction.

Intersexual: Individuals with a combination of male and female anatomical features, or in which chromosomal sex is inconsistent with anatomical sex.

Intimacy: Those feelings in a relationship that promote closeness or bondedness and the experience of warmth.

Intimacy seekers: A type of stalkers who exhibit severe mental illness involving delusional beliefs about their victims. The stalking is maintained through the belief that they share an intimate connection with the victim.

In vitro fertilization: A process in which a mature ovum is surgically removed from a woman's ovary, placed in a medium with sperm until fertilization occurs, and then placed in the woman's uterus. This is usually done in women who cannot conceive because of blocked Fallopian tubes.

Kwido: A person (of either sex) who belongs to a third gender or is transgender (historically regarded as having special spiritual power).

Latency stage: Outdated Freudian theory that children aged 6–12 years old have no sexual feelings or interests.

Libido: Sexual desire, or drive.

Limbic system: The part of the brain referred to as the "seat of emotions," which produces emotions in response to physical and psychological signals.

Mahu: A slang term in modern day Hawai'i referring to a transvestite or transgendered person.

Male orgasmic disorder: A condition in which a man has difficulty reaching orgasm and ejaculating into a woman's vagina.

Male privilege: The social, economic, and political advantages automatically granted to men exclusively on the basis of their sex.

Marriage: A form of interpersonal bond or union that is recognized legally, religiously, or socially, granting the uniting partners mutual conjugal rights and responsibilities.

Maturity: Erikson's final stage of psychosocial development, in which the individual achieves a sense of integrity, meaning they fully accept and take responsibility for their situation and have come to terms with death. The inability to achieve this feeling results in despair.

Menopause: The term for a woman's last menstrual period.

Mere exposure effect: A phenomenon in which people gravitate toward and have a preference for things merely because they are recognizable and familiar. The more familiar something appears to be the more likely we are to feel positive about it.

Missionary position: A face-to-face position of sexual intercourse in which the woman lies on her back and the man lies on top with his legs between hers. It was called this because Christian missionaries instructed people that other positions were unnatural.

Moral: What is judged to be right according to a system of ethics.

Nocturnal emission: An ejaculation that occurs during sleep in teenaged boys and men; a *wet dream.*

Objectify: The act of treating a person as an instrument of sexual pleasure without regard to personality or civil liberties. Sometimes referred to as *sexual objectification.*

Oedipus complex: A developmental stage in which the boy wants to possess his mother sexually and sees the father as a rival (similar to the female *Electra complex*).

Oral stage: The first stage of psychosexual development wherein the infant's mouth becomes the focus of libidinal gratification.

Orgasm: Pleasurable sensations and series of contractions that release sexual tension, usually accompanied by ejaculation by men.

Ovarian failure: The loss of ovarian function before the age of 40.

Ovulation: The expulsion of an egg from one of the ovaries.

Oxytocin: A pituitary hormone associated with milk release, labor and orgasmic contractions, and erotic attraction and touch.

Paraphilia: General term for a group of sexual disorders in which a person's sexual arousal and gratification depend almost exclusively on unusual behaviors.

Pedophilia: A condition in which sexual arousal is achieved primarily and repeatedly through sexual activity with children who have not reached puberty.

Penis envy: A Freudian concept that posits that female adolescents experience anxiety upon realizing that they do not have a penis.

Perfect use: The ability of a method of contraception to prevent pregnancy as measured by consistent and correct use.

Performance anxiety: A fear of failure during sexual relations that can lead to erectile disorder in men and inhibited orgasm in women.

Phallic stage: The third stage of psychosexual development, in which the infant's libido centers upon his or her genitalia as the erogenous zone. In this stage, the Electra complex in girls and Oedipus complex in boys begins to manifest.

Phimosis: Condition resulting when penile erection causes pain because the foreskin is too tight.

Pituitary gland: A gland located at the base of the brain that secretes eight hormones, including follicle-stimulating hormone and luteinizing hormone.

Plateau phase: The second phase of the sexual response cycle proposed by Masters and Johnson. Physiologically, it represents a high state of arousal.

Pleasure principle: The instinctual seeking of pleasure to avoid pain in order to satisfy biological and psychological needs.

Polygamy: A practice, in some cultures, of being married to more than one spouse, usually referring to a man having more than one wife.

Postpartum depression: A period of low energy and discouragement that is common for mothers following childbearing. Longer-lasting or severe symptoms should receive medical treatment.

Predatory stalker: The motivation for this type of stalking is rooted in sexual deviance and interest. The goal is to obtain sexual gratification or to obtain information about the victim prior to committing a sexual crime.

Preference molester: An individual with a primary sexual orientation to children and having no interest in adult sexual partners.

Premature ejaculation: The inability of a man to control ejaculation for a sufficient length of time during coitus.

Prenatal androgen theory: This theory asserts that sexual orientation is devised in the womb during fetal development. Homosexuality in human males is due to the absence of androgenizing effects (under-masculinization) and homosexuality in women is due to an excess of androgenizing effects (over-masculinization) during early brain development.

Priapism: Continual, undesired, and painful erection of the penis that lasts longer than 4 hours.

Progesterone: Ovarian hormone that causes the uterine lining to thicken.

Prostatitis: Inflammation of the prostate gland.

Prostitution: Participating in sexual activity for pay or profit.

Psychoanalysis: A system of psychological theory and treatment designed to investigate the connections and interactions of the conscious and unconscious elements of the mind as well as to bring repressed fears and conflicts into the conscious mind (e.g., dream interpretation, free association).

Psychosexual development: The blending of sexual aspects of one's development with other psychological factors.

Psychosocial development: The cultural and social influences that help shape human sexual identity.

Rape: Engaging in a sexual act without the other individual's consent or against the individual's will.

Reality principle: A Freudian concept that describes the mind's ability to assess the reality of the external world and to act upon it accordingly.

Rejected stalker: Stalking that typically takes place at the termination of a relationship, although friends, coworkers, and family members can become targets of the stalking. The initial attempt is to reconcile the relationship or to exact revenge for the broken relationship.

Resentful stalkers: This type of stalkers feel that they have been mistreated or that they are victims of some type of injustice or humiliation. The motivation for this stalker is to seek revenge and is maintained by the need for power and control over the victim to induce fear.

Resolution phase: The term for the return of a body to its unexcited state following orgasm.

Retroviruses: A class of viruses that integrate their genetic code into that of the host cell, establishing permanent infection.

Rh factor: The presence of Rh agglutinogens (antigens) in the blood, which indicates that a person is Rh positive, whereas its absence designates the person as Rh negative.

RhoGAM: Medication administered to a mother to prevent formation of antibodies when the baby is Rh positive and its mother is Rh negative.

Roe v. Wade: A landmark court decision by the U.S. Supreme Court in 1973 that ruled Texas state law unconstitutionally violated a woman's right to have an abortion.

Schemas: *See* gender schema.

Secondary sexual characteristics: The physical characteristics of mature women and men that begin to develop at puberty.

Secured attachment: A style of attachment in which individuals do not fear abandonment and find it easy to get close to others.

Sensate focusing: Exercises designed to reduce anxiety and teach mutual pleasuring through nongenital touching in nondemanding situations.

Serial monogamy: The practice of having a series of monogamous sexual relationships.

Sex: Any mutually voluntary activity with another person that involves genital contact and sexual excitement even if intercourse or orgasm did not occur.

Sexism: The prejudgment that because of gender a person will possess negative traits.

Sexual aversion disorder: An irrational fear of sexual activity.

Sexual coercion: The act of forcing another person into unwanted sexual activity by physical or verbal coercion (restraint or constraint).

Sexual harassment: Unwanted sexual advances or coercion that can occur in the workplace or in academic settings.

Sexual orientation: The set of physical and emotional qualities that attracts human beings to one another sexually and romantically.

Sexual pain disorder: *See* dyspareunia.

Sexual script: A guideline for engaging in appropriate sexual behavior and sexual encounters that are learned through culture and other interactions.

Situational molester: A child molester who typically takes on the persona of a model of authority (e.g., football coach, teacher, scout leader) and sexually abuses children if the conditions are favorable. These types of molesters commit sexually deviant acts against minors for various reasons and do not have a preference for pre-pubescent children.

Socialization: The process of internalizing society's beliefs; the manner in which a society shapes individual behaviors and expectations of behaviors.

Socializing agents: The social influences (e.g., parents, peers, the media) that shape behaviors.

Social learning theory: A concept formulated by Albert Bandura that posits that people learn from one another through observation, imitation, and modeling.

Social scripts: A complex set of learned responses to a particular situation that is formed by social influences.

Sodomy: A term that specifically refers to anal intercourse, but is often used to refer to almost any sexual behavior someone might not consider normal.

Spermicides: Chemicals that kill sperm. In most products, the chemical is nonoxynol.

Stonewall riots: A series of violent and spontaneous demonstrations by members of the gay community against a police raid that preceded the gay liberation movement in the 1960s and 1970s.

Stranger rape: Rape of a person by an unknown person.

Strange situation: A procedure devised by Mary Ainsworth to observe attachment relationships between a caregiver and a child. The child is placed in a room to engage in play for a period of time while caregivers and strangers enter and leave the room to create a response in a child that determines the type of attachment the child has to the caregiver.

Superego: The ethical component of our personality that provides the moral standards by which the ego operates.

Swinging: A type of open marriage relationship in which a couple has extramarital relations together with other couples.

Systematic desensitization: A therapy technique used to reduce anxiety by slowly introducing elements of the anxiety-producing theme.

Transgender: An individual whose gender roles are the opposite of those that society expects based on his or her anatomy.

Transition phase: The last part of the startup stage of labor, during which the cervix dilates to 10 centimeters in order for the baby to be able to enter the birth canal.

Transsexual: An adult whose gender identity does not match his or her biological sex.

Transvestic fetishism: Same as *transvestism*.

Transvestism: A condition in which sexual arousal is achieved primarily by dressing as a member of the opposite sex.

Transvestite: A person who achieves sexual satisfaction from wearing clothes usually worn by the other gender.

Typical use: The ability of a method of contraception to prevent pregnancy as actually used at home by people not being monitored.

Umbilical cord: The lifeline between mother and fetus, which contains two arteries and one vein. Food, oxygen, and chemicals are transported to the child through the vein.

Unconscious: The part of the human mind that contains our biologically based instincts for the primitive urges of sex and aggression.

Vaginismus: The involuntary contraction of the muscles surrounding the vaginal entrance so that entry of the penis is prevented.

Values: Those beliefs to which we attach the most worth.

Viral: Refers to a virus that is quickly and widely spread.

Virus: A protein shell around a nucleic acid core. Viruses have either RNA or DNA, but not both, and thus cannot reproduce themselves. They invade host cells that provide material to manufacture new virus particles.

Waist-to-hip ratio: The circumference of the waist divided by the circumference of the hips. It is believed that this measurement plays a role in physical attractiveness.

Worldview: The way in which a person thinks about and interprets the world.

Bibliography

Advocates for Youth. (n.d.). *Abstinence-only-until-marriage programs: 8-Point definition of abstinence only education.* Retrieved from www .advocatesforyouth.org/topics-issues/abstinenceonly/132-8-point -definition-of-abstinence-only-education.

Alexander, E., & Hickner, J. (1997). First coitus for adolescents: Understanding why and when. *Journal of the American Board of Family Practice, 10,* 96–103.

American Psychiatric Association. (2013). *Gender dysphoria.* Retrieved from http://www.dsm5.org/Documents/Gender%20Dysphoria%20Fact %20Sheet.pdf.

The ancient roots of our Judeo-Christian sexual prohibitions (2012). Retrieved from http://www.cybercollege.com/history.htm.

Apfelbaum, B. (1989). Retarded ejaculation: A much misunderstood syndrome. In S.R. Leiblum & R.C. Rosen (Eds.), *Principles and practice of sex therapy: Update for the 1990s* (pp. 168–206). New York: Guilford Press.

Bailey, J.M., & Pillard, R.C. (1991). A genetic study of male sexual orientation. *Archives of General Psychiatry, 48,* 1089–1096.

Bailey, J.M., et al. (1993). Heritable factors influence sexual orientation in women. *Archives of General Psychiatry, 50,* 217–223.

Belsky, J. (1999). Modern evolutionary theory and patterns of attachment. In J. Cassidy & P.R. Shaver (Eds.), *Handbook of attachment* (pp. 141–161). New York: Guilford Press.

Benoit, D., & Parker, K.C.H. (1994). Stability and transmission of attachment across three generations. *Child Development, 65*(5), 1444–1456.

Bernstein, N. (2005). *Sex and peer pressure.* Retrieved from http://www.nbcnews.com/id/6867362/t/sex-peer-pressure/#.UxeSn02YZdg.

Biro, F.M., & Dorn, L.D. (2005). Puberty and adolescent sexuality. *Pediatric Annals, 34*, 777–783.

Blackwood, B. (1935). *Both sides of Buka passage: An ethnographic study of social, sexual and economic questions in North-Western Solomon Islands.* Oxford: Clarendon-Oxford University.

Blanchard, R. (2001). Fraternal birth order and the maternal immune hypothesis of male homosexuality. *Hormones and Behavior, 40*, 105–114.

Blanchard, R., & Bogaert, A.F. (1996). Homosexuality in men and number of older brothers. *American Journal of Psychiatry, 153*, 27–31.

Blumberg, R.L., & Pilar Garcia, M. (1977). The political economy of the mother-child family: A cross-societal view. In L. Lenero-Otero (Ed.), *Beyond the nuclear family model* (pp. 99–163). London: Sage.

Bogoras, W. (1909). *The Chukchee.* Jessup North Pacific Expedition, Memoirs of the American Museum of Natural History. Leiden: E.J. Brill.

Boswell, J. (1980). *Christianity, social tolerance, and homosexuality: Gay people in Western Europe from the beginning of the Christian era to the fourteenth century.* Chicago, IL: University of Chicago Press.

Brewer, G., & Archer, J. (2007). What do people infer from facial attractiveness? *Journal of Evolutionary Psychology, 5*, 39–49.

Broude, G.J. (2005). Sexual attitudes and practices. In *Encyclopedia of sex and gender: Men and women in the world's cultures* (Vol. 1, pp. 177–186). New York: Kluwer Academic/Plenum Publishers.

Broude, G.J., & Greene, S.J. (1976). Cross-cultural codes on twenty sexual attitudes and practices. *Ethnology, 15*, 409–429.

Broude, G.J., & Greene, S.J. (1983). Cross-cultural codes for husband-wife relationships. *Ethnology, 22*, 263–280.

Brown, D.E. (1991). *Human universals.* Philadelphia, PA: Temple University Press.

Brown, J.D., L'Engle, K.L., Pardun, C.J., Guo, G., Kenneavy, K., & Jackson, C. (2006). Sexy media matter: Exposure to sexual content in music, movies, television and magazines predicts Black and White adolescents' sexual behavior. *Pediatrics, 117*, 1018–1027.

Brown, M.F. (2003). *Who owns native culture?* Cambridge, MA: Harvard University Press.

Bullough, V.L. (2003). Magnus Hirschfield, an often overlooked pioneer. *Sexuality and Culture, 7*(1), 62–72.

Buss, D.M. (1988). Love acts: The evolutionary biology of love. In R.J. Sternberg & M.L. Barnes (Eds.), *The psychology of love* (pp. 100–118). New Haven, CT: Yale University Press.

Buss, D.M. (1988). The evolution of human intrasexual competition: Tactics of mate attraction. *Journal of Personality and Social Psychology, 54*, 616–628.

Buss, D.M. (1989). Sex differences in human mate preferences: Evolutionary hypotheses tested in 37 cultures. *Behavioral and Brain Sciences, 12*, 1–49.

Calderone, M.S. (1983). Fetal erection and its message to us. *SIECUS Report, 11*(5/6), 9–10.

Campaign Free Tibet. (1994). We have no rights, not even our bodies. In M. Davies (Ed.), *Women and violence: Realities and responses worldwide* (pp. 133–136). London: Zed Books. (Adapted and reprinted from a report compiled for Campaign Free Tibet.)

Campbell, T. (2014, March 6). Touching men's sexy boxer shorts activates brain's reward system in women, study suggest. *The Huffington Post.* Retrieved from http://www.huffingtonpost.com/2014/03/06/touching-boxer-women-think-differently_n_4906315.html.

Cantor, J.M., et al. (2002). How many gay men owe their sexual orientation to fraternal birth order? *Archives of Sexual Behavior, 31*, 67–71.

Cardoso, F.L., & Werner, D. (2005). Homosexuality. In *Encyclopedia of sex and gender: Men and women in the world's cultures* (Vol. 1, pp. 204–215). New York: Kluwer Academic/Plenum Publishers.

Cass, V.C. (1979). Homosexual identity formation: A theoretical model. *Journal of Homosexuality, 4*, 219–235.

Centers for Disease Control and Prevention. (2007). *Diseases and conditions.* www.cdc.gov/diseasesconditions/.

Centers for Disease Control and Prevention. (2010). *National intimate partner and sexual violence survey.* Retrieved from http://www.cdc.gov/violenceprevention/pdf/nisvs_executive_summary-a.pdf.

Centers for Disease Control and Prevention. (2011). *Youth risk behavior survey.* Retrieved from http://www.cdc.gov/mmwr/pdf/ss/ss6104.pdf.

Chana, G. (Writer) & Steward, D. (Director). (2003, February 17). The pill [Television series episode]. In A. Brown (Producer), *The American experience.* USA: Public Broadcasting Service (PBS).

Chisholm, J.S. (1996). The evolutionary ecology of attachment organization. *Human Nature, 7*, 1–38.

Cobb, N. (2001). *The child: Infants and children*. Mountain View, CA: Mayfield Publishing Company.

Cochran, S.D., & Mays, V.M. (2000). Relation between psychiatric syndromes and behaviorally defined sexual orientation in a sample of the U.S. population. *American Journal of Epidemiology, 151*, 516–523.

Collins, R.L., Elliott, M.N., Berry, S.H., Kanouse, D.E., Kunkel, D., & Hunter, S.B. (2004). Watching sex on television predicts adolescent initiation of sexual behavior. *Pediatrics, 114*, e280–e289.

Derne, S. (1994). Structural realities, persistent dilemmas, and the construction of emotional paradigms: Love in three cultures. *Social Perspectives on Emotion, 2*, 281–308.

Diamond, L.M. (2005). A new view of lesbian subtypes: Stable versus fluid identity trajectories over an 8-year period. *Psychology of Women Quarterly, 29*, 119–128.

Diamond, L.M. (2008). Female bisexuality from adolescence to adulthood: Results from a 10-year longitudinal study. *Developmental Psychology, 44*, 5–14.

Dietz-Uhler, B., & Murrell, A. (1992). College students perceptions of sexual harassment: Are gender differences decreasing? *Journal of College Student Development, 33*, 540–546.

Drakulic, S. (1994). The rape of women in Bosnia. In M. Davies (Ed.), *Women and violence: Realities and responses worldwide* (pp. 176–181). London: Zed Books.

Drescher, J., & Throckmorton, W. (2014, February). Letter to the president of Uganda. Message posted to cesnet-1@listserv.kent.edu [List serve for Counselor Education and Supervision].

Duerr, H.P. (1993). *Obszünitüt und Gewalt: Der Mythos vom Zivilisations proze*. Frankurt am Main, Germany: Suhrkamp Verlag.

Dunn, K.M., et al. (2002). Systematic review of sexual problems: Epidemiology and methodology. *Journal of Sex & Marital Therapy, 28*, 399–422.

Eaton, D.K., et al. (2006). Youth risk behavior surveillance – United States, 2005. *Journal of School Health, 76*, 353–392.

Ellis, L. (1989). *Theories of rape: Inquiries into the causes of sexual aggression*. New York: Hemisphere.

Ember, C.R., & Ember, M. (2003). *Encyclopedia of sex and gender: Men and women in the world's cultures*. New York: Kluwer Academic/Plenum Publishers.

Ember, M. (1975). On the origin and extension of the incest taboo. *Behavior Science Research, 10,* 249–281.

Erikson, E. (1968). *Identity: Youth and crisis.* New York: Norton.

Fierstein, H. (2013, July 21). Russia's anti-gay crackdown. *The New York Times.* Retrieved from http://www.nytimes.com/2013/07/22/opinion/russias-anti-gay-crackdown.html?_r=0.

Finer, L.B. (2007, January/February). Trends in premarital sex in the United States, 1954–2003. *Public Health Reports,* 73–78. Retrieved from http://www.guttmacher.org/media/nr/2006/12/19/index.html.

Finkelhor, D., & Yllo, K. (1985). *License to rape: Sexual abuse of wives.* New York: Holt, Rinehart, & Winston.

Foucault, M. (1979). *The history of sexuality, Volume 1: An introduction.* London: Allen Lane.

Frederick, D.A., et al. (2007). Desiring the muscular ideal: Men's body satisfaction in the United States, Ukraine, and Ghana. *Psychology of Men & Masculinity, 8,* 103–117.

Freud, S. (1964). New introductory lectures on psycho-analysis. In J. Strachey (Ed. and Trans.), *The standard edition of the complete psychological works of Sigmund Freud* (Vol. 22, pp. 1–182). London: Hogarth Press. Original work published in 1933.

Friedrich, W.N., et al. (1991). Normative sexual behavior in children. *Pediatrics, 88,* 456–464.

Furnham, A., Swami, V., & Shah, K. (2006). Body weight, waist-to-hop ratio and breast size correlates of ratings of attractiveness and traits. *Personality and Individual Differences, 41,* 443–454.

Gagnon, J. (1990). The explicit and implicit use of the scripting perspective. *Annual Review of Sex Research, 1,* 1–44.

Gagnon, J., & Simon, W. (1999). Sexual scripts. In R. Parker & P. Aggleton (Eds.), *Culture, society and sexuality: A reader* (pp. 31–40). New York: Routledge.

Gangestad, S.W., & Simpson, J.A. (2000). Toward an evolutionary history of female sociosexual variation. Special Issue: Biological foundations of personality: Evolution, behavioral genetics, and psychophysiology. *Journal of Personality, 58,* 69–96.

Garnets, L.D., & Peplau, L.A. (2001). A new paradigm for women's sexual orientation: Implications for therapy. *Women and Therapy, 24,* 111–121.

Goode, W.J. (1967). *World revolution and family patterns.* New York: Free Press.

Goodman, B. (Writer), & Maggio, J. (Director). (2005, February 14). Kinsey [Television series episode]. In C. Allan (Producer), *The American experience*. USA: Public Broadcasting Service (PBS).

Gorer, G. (1938). *Himalayan village: An account of the Lepchas of Sikkim*. London: Joseph.

Greenberg, J.S., Bruess, C.E., & Conklin, S.C. (2011). *Exploring the dimensions of human sexuality* (4th ed.). Sudbury, MA: Jones and Bartlett Publishers.

Gregor, T. (1985). *Anxious pleasures: The sexual lives of an Amazonian people*. Chicago, IL: University of Chicago Press.

Grunseit, A., et al. (1997). Sexuality education and young people's sexual behavior: A review of studies. *Journal of Adolescent Research, 12*, 421–453.

Guffey, M.E. (1999). *Business communication: Process and product* (3rd ed.). Belmont, CA: Wadsworth.

Halperin, D.M. (1990). *One hundred years of homosexuality: And other essays on Greek love*. New York: Routledge.

Hatfield, E., & Rapson, R.L. (1993). *Love, sex, and intimacy: Their psychology, biology, and history*. New York: HarperCollins.

Hatfield, E., & Rapson, R.L. (2005). *Love and sex: Cross-cultural perspectives*. Lanham, Maryland: University Press of America.

Hendrix, L. (2003). Courtship and marriage. In *Encyclopedia of sex and gender: Men and women in the world's cultures*. (Vol. 1, pp. 71–76). New York: Kluwer Academic/Plenum Publishers.

Herdt, G.H. (1984). *Ritualized homosexuality in Melanesia*. Berkeley: University of California Press.

Homans, G.C., & Schneider, D.M. (1955). Kinship terminology and the American kinship system. *American Anthropologist, 57*(6), 1194–1208.

Hyde, J., & DeLamater, J. (2003). *Understanding human sexuality* (8th ed.). Boston, MA: McGraw-Hill.

Hysteria. (n.d.). In *Bing Encyclopedia online*. Retrieved from http://www.bing.com/search?q=hysteria+definition&qs=AS&pq=hysteria+de&sc=8-11&sp=1&cvid=dbacc25b27f14c47a8e35820b742e3d4&FORM=QBLH.

Hysteria. (n.d.). In *The Free Dictionary*. Retrieved from http://medical-dictionary.thefreedictionary.com/hysteria.

Jacobs, S.E., & Cromwell, J. (1992). Visions and revisions of reality: Reflections on sex, sexuality, gender and gender variance. *Journal of Homosexuality, 23*(4), 43–69.

Jacoby, S. (2005, July/August). Sex in America. *AARP The Magazine*, pp. 62–68, 98–99.

Janus, S.S., & Janus, C.L. (1993). *The Janus report on sexual behavior*. New York: John Wiley & Sons.

Johnson Lewis, J. (n.d.). *Comstock law*. Retrieved from http://womens history.about.com/od/laws/a/comstock_law.htm.

Kaiser Family Foundation. (2000). *Sex education in America: A view from inside the nation's classrooms*. Menlo Park, CA: Author.

Kalafut, M. (2008). *Oxytocin: 'The cuddle & love hormone'*. [Web log comment]. Retrieved from http://molly.kalafut.org/misc/oxytocin .html.

Kelly, G.F. (2011). *Sexuality today* (10th ed.). New York: McGraw-Hill Higher Education.

Kendal, L. (1998). When a woman loves a woman in Lesotho: Love, sex and the (western) construction of homophobia. In S.O. Murray & W. Roscoe (Eds.), *Boy-wives and female husbands: Studies in African homosexualities* (pp. 223–242). New York: Palgrave.

King, B.R. (2009). *Human sexuality today* (6th ed.). Upper Saddle River, NJ: Pearson Education.

Kinnish, K.K., Strassberg, D.S., & Turner, C.W. (2005). Sex differences in the flexibility of sexual orientation: A multidimensional retrospective assessment. *Archives of Sexual Behavior, 34*, 173–183.

Kinsey, A.C. (1948). *Sexual behavior in the human male*. Philadelphia, PA: W.B. Saunders.

Kinsey, A.C., et al. (1953). *Sexual behavior in the human female*. Philadelphia, PA: Saunders.

Kirby, D. (2001). *Emerging answers: Research findings on programs to reduce teen pregnancy*. Washington, DC: The National Campaign to Prevent Teen Pregnancy.

Koss, M.P., Gidycz, C.A., & Wisniewski, N. (1987). The scope of rape: Incidence and prevalence of sexual aggression and victimization in a national sample of higher education students. *Journal of Consulting and Clinical Psychology, 55*(2), 162–170.

L'Engle, K.L., Brown, J.D., & Kenneavy, K. (2006). The mass media are an important context for adolescents' sexual behavior. *Journal of Adolescent Health, 38*, 186–192.

L'Engle, K.L., & Jackson, C. (2008). Socialization influences on early adolescents' cognitive susceptibility and transition into sexual intercourse. *Journal of Research on Adolescence, 18*(2), 353–378

Lacey Jr., J.V., et al. (2002). Menopausal hormone replacement therapy and risk of ovarian cancer. *Journal of the American Medical Association, 288*, 334–341.

Langfeldt, T. (1981). Sexual development in children. In M. Cook & K. Howells (Eds.), *Adult sexual interest in children* (pp. 99–120). London: Academic Press.

Laumann, E.O., Gagnon, J.H., Michael, R.T., & Michaels, S. (1994). *The social organization of sexuality: Sexual practices in the United States.* Chicago, IL: University of Chicago Press.

Lee, G.R. (1982). *Family structure and interaction* (2nd ed.). Minneapolis: University of Minnesota Press.

Levine, S.B. (2003). The nature of sexual desire: A clinician's perspective. *Archives of Sexual Behavior, 32,* 279–285.

Longmore, M.A. (1998). Symbolic interactionism and the study of sexuality. *Journal of Sex Research, 35,* 44–57.

MacLean, P. (1962). New findings relevant to the evolution of psychosexual functions of the brain. *Journal of Nervous and Mental Disorders, 134* (4), 280–301.

Mahoney, P., & Williams, L.M. (1998). Sexual assault in marriage: Prevalence, consequences, and treatment of wife. In J.L. Jasinski & L.M. Williams (Eds.), *Partner violence: A comprehensive review of 20 years of research* (pp. 113–162). Thousand Oaks, CA: Sage.

Manson, J.E., et al. (2003). Estrogen plus progestin and the risk of coronary heart disease. *New England Journal of Medicine, 349,* 523–534.

Martin, B., & Lyons, C.A. (2011). *Abnormal psychology* (4th ed.). Redding, CA: BVT Publishing.

Masters, W.H., & Johnson, V.E. (1970). *Human sexuality inadequacy.* Boston, MA: Little, Brown.

Mayo Clinic Staff. (2015). *Postpartum depression.* Retrieved from http://www.mayoclinic.org/diseases-conditions/postpartum-depression/basics/definition/con-20029130.

McLeod, S. (2008). *Psychosexual stages.* Retrieved from http://www.simplypsychology.org/psychosexual.html.

Mead, M. (2004). A case history in cross-national communication. In W.O. Beeman (Ed), *Studying contemporary Western society: Method and theory* (pp. 144–161). New York: Berghahn Books.

Meigs, A. (1976). Male pregnancy and the reduction of sexual opposition in the New Guinea Highlands. *Ethnology, 15,* 393–407.

Miller, R. (2012). *Intimate relationships* (6th ed.). New York: McGraw-Hill.

Mongan-Rallis, H. (2005). Understanding GLBT issues. Retrieved from http://www.d.umn.edu/~hrallis/professional/presentations/ally_training/het_privilege.htm.

Mullen, P.E., Pathé, M., & Purcell, R. (2000). *Stalkers and their victims.* Cambridge, UK: Cambridge University Press.

Murdock, G.P. (1949). *Social structure*. New York: Macmillan.

Murdock, N.L. (2009). *Theories of counseling and psychotherapy: A case approach*. Upper Saddle River, NJ: Prentice Hall.

Murray, S.O. (2000). *Homosexualities*. Chicago, IL: University of Chicago Press.

Nonoyama, M., et al. (2005). Influences of sex-related information for STD prevention. *Journal of Adolescent Health, 36*, 442–445.

North Dakota State University (2010). *Safe Zone Training* [PDF document]. Retrieved from http://www.fs.fed.us/cr/Safe_Zone_Training _PacketUpdated.pdf.

O'Brian, R. (2003). Economic activities and gender roles. In *Encyclopedia of sex and gender: Men and women in the world's cultures*. (Vol. 1, pp. 91–96). New York: Kluwer Academic/Plenum Publishers.

O'Donnell, B.L., O'Donnell, C.R., & Stueve, A. (2001). Early sexual initiation and subsequent sex-related risks among urban minority youth: The reach for health study. *Family Planning Perspectives, 33*, 268–275.

Olds, J., & Milner, P. (1954). Positive reinforcement produced by electrical stimulation of septal area and other regions of rat brain. *Journal of Comparative and Physiological Psychology, 47*(6), 419–427.

Parsons, T. (1951). *The social system*. New York: Free Press.

Perpinan, M.S., Sr. (1994). Militarism and the sex industry in the Philippines. In M. Davies (Ed.), *Women and violence: Realities and responses worldwide* (pp. 149–152). London: Zed Books.

Pew Research Center. (2013, June 4). The global divide on homosexuality: Greater acceptance in more secular and affluent countries.*Global Attitudes & Trends*. Retrieved from http://www.pewglobal.org/2013/06/ 04/the-global-divide-on-homosexuality/.

Queen, S., & Habenstein, R.W. (1974). *The family in various cultures* (4th ed.). New York: Lippincott.

Radcliffe-Brown, A.R. (1950). *African systems of kinship and marriage*. London: Oxford University Press.

Roan, S. (1993, July 12). Are we teaching too little, too late? *Los Angeles Times*, pp. E1, E4.

Russell, D.E.H. (1998). *Dangerous relationships: Pornography, misogyny, and rape*. Thousand Oaks, CA: Sage.

Ryan, G. (2000). Childhood sexuality: A decade of study. Pt. I. Research and curriculum development. *Child Abuse & Neglect, 24*, 33–48.

Schmitt, D.P., et al. (2003). Universal sex differences in the desire for sexual variety: Tests from 52 nations, 6 continents, and 13 islands. *Journal of Personality and Social Psychology, 85*, 85–104.

Segal, E.S. (2003). Cultural constructions of gender. In *Encyclopedia of sex and gender: Men and women in the world's cultures*. (Vol. 1, pp. 3–10). New York: Kluwer Academic/Plenum Publishers.

Serpenti, I.M. (1965). *Cultivators in the swamps*. Assen, The Netherlands: Van Gorcum.

Shibley Hyde, J., & DeLamater, J. (2003). *Understanding human sexuality* (8th ed.). New York: McGraw-Hill.

Shtarkshall, R.A., Santelli, J.S., & Hirsch, J.S. (2007, June 11). Sex education and sexual socialization: Roles for educators and parents. *Perspectives on Sexual and Reproductive Health*, 39(2), 116–119.

Simons, J.S., & Carey, M.P. (2001). Prevalence of sexual dysfunctions: Results from a decade of research. *Archives of Sexual Behavior*, 30, 177–219.

Soble, A. (2008). *The philosophy of sex and love: An introduction* (2nd ed.). St. Paul, MN: Paragon House. Original from the University of Michigan.

Sternberg, R.J. (1986). A triangular theory of love. *Psychological Review*, 93, 119–135.

Stodghill II, R. (1998, June 15). Where'd you learn that? *Time*, pp. 52–59.

Tran, A. (2013, November). *Slips-of-the-tongue errors* [Cartoon]. Retrieved from http://mercercognitivepsychology.pbworks.com/w/page/330156 83/Slip-of-the-Tounge%20Errors.

Turner, C.F., et al. (2005). Same-gender sex among U.S. adults: Trends across the twentieth century and during the 1990s. *Public Opinion Quarterly*, 69, 439–462.

Van Dis, H., & Larsson, K. (1971). Induction of sexual arousal in the castrated male rat by intracranial stimulation. *Physiological Behavior*, 6, 85–86.

Vannoy, R. (1980). *Sex without love: A philosophical exploration*. Buffalo, NY: Prometheus Books.

Walker, L. (1979). *The battered woman*. New York: Harper & Row.

Wallechinsky, D., & Wallace, I. (1981). History of sex surveys: A thousand marriages part 1. In *Trivia Library*. Retrieved from http://www.trivia-library.com/a/history-of-sex-survey-a-thousand-marriages-part-1.htm.

Ward, L.M., & Friedman, K. (2006). Using TV as a guide: Associations between television viewing and adolescents' sexual attitudes and behavior. *Journal of Research on Adolescence*, 16, 133–156.

West, C.M. (1998). Lifting the "political gag order": Breaking the silence around partner violence in ethnic minority families. In J.L. Jasinski &

L.M. Williams (Eds.), *Partner violence: A comprehensive review of 20 years of research* (pp. 184–209). Thousand Oaks, CA: Sage.

West, R. (2012). *The ancient roots [CE1] of our Judeo-Christian sexual prohibitions*. Retrieved from http://www.cybercollege.com/history.htm.

White, D.R. (1988). Rethinking polygyny. *Current Anthropology, 29,* 529–572.

Williams, W.L. (1992). *The spirit and the flesh: Sexual diversity in American Indian culture*. Boston, MA: Beacon Press.

Wilson, G., & Rahman, Q. (2005). *Born gay: The psychobiology of sex orientation*. London: Peter Owen.

Wright, H. (1938). *The sex factor in marriage: A book for those who are or are about to be married*. New York: Vanguard Press.

Zajonc, R.B. (2001). Mere exposure: A gateway to the subliminal. *Current Directions in Psychological Science, 10,* 224–228.

Zimmer-Tamakoshi, L. (2005). Rape and other sexual aggression. In *Encyclopedia of sex and gender: Men and women in the world's cultures.* (Vol. 1, pp. 230–246). New York: Kluwer Academic/Plenum Publishers.

About the Author and Contributors

Katherine M. Helm, PhD, is a professor of psychology and director of Graduate Programs in Psychology at Lewis University, where she teaches a wide range of graduate and undergraduate counseling and psychology courses. Dr. Helm is also a licensed psychologist. She regularly sees individual clients and couples and supervises a clinical training program for master's and doctoral practicum students. Dr. Helm's scholarly contributions and interests are in the areas of individual and couples counseling, sexuality issues and education, training and supervision, multicultural issues in counseling, the treatment of trauma for sexual abuse, pedagogy of multicultural courses, and cultural sensitivity training. Dr. Helm has counseling and consultative experience in psychiatric hospitals, community mental health, college counseling centers, and agency settings.

Lisa Brown, LCPC, CDVP, specializes in counseling children and adolescents, the LGBT population, and survivors of domestic violence. In addition to her work as a counselor, she works as a clinical coordinator and teaches graduate clinical mental health counseling and undergraduate psychology courses at Lewis University.

Valerie Hill, PhD, is an associate professor and the undergraduate program director in the Department of Psychology at Lewis University. Her doctorate is in developmental psychology from Northern Illinois

University. Her research interests include social cognition, student learning, and effective teaching practices.

Donna Lordi is completing her master's degree in clinical mental health. She has extensively studied issues of human sexuality, gender and transgender issues, and sexual orientation. She has presented at several local and regional conferences on these issues and is contemplating doctoral study in human sexuality.

Byron Waller, PhD, is an associate professor of counseling at Governors State University. He also has a practice in counseling in the Chicago area.

La Kesia D. Weathersby-Graham has a master's in psychology from Governors State University and practices in the south suburban area of Chicago, Illinois.

Index